LIVING ABROAD AUSTRALIA

ULRIKE LEMMIN-WOOLFREY

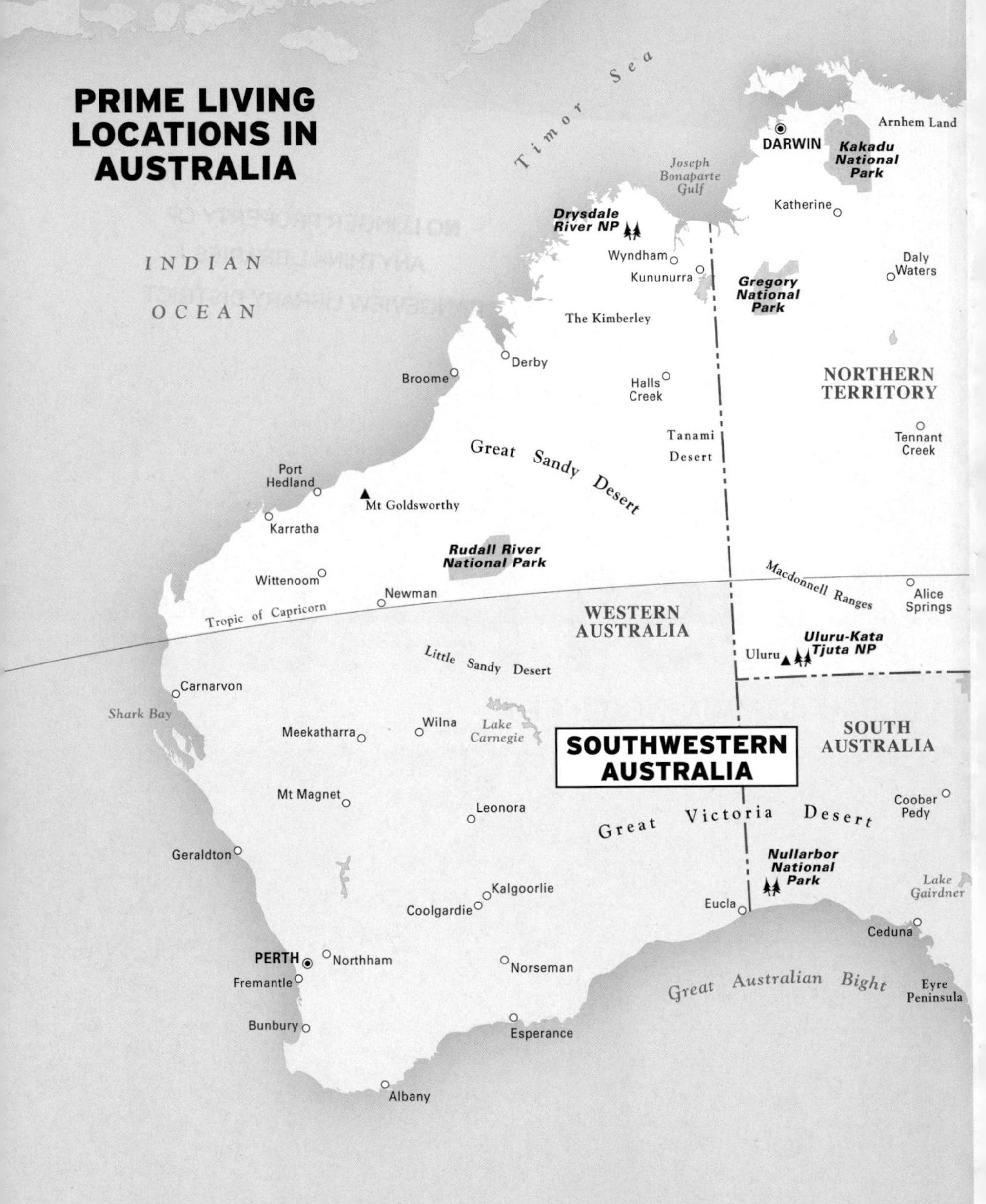

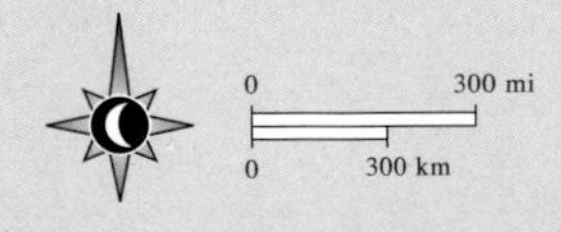

SOUTHERN

OCEAN

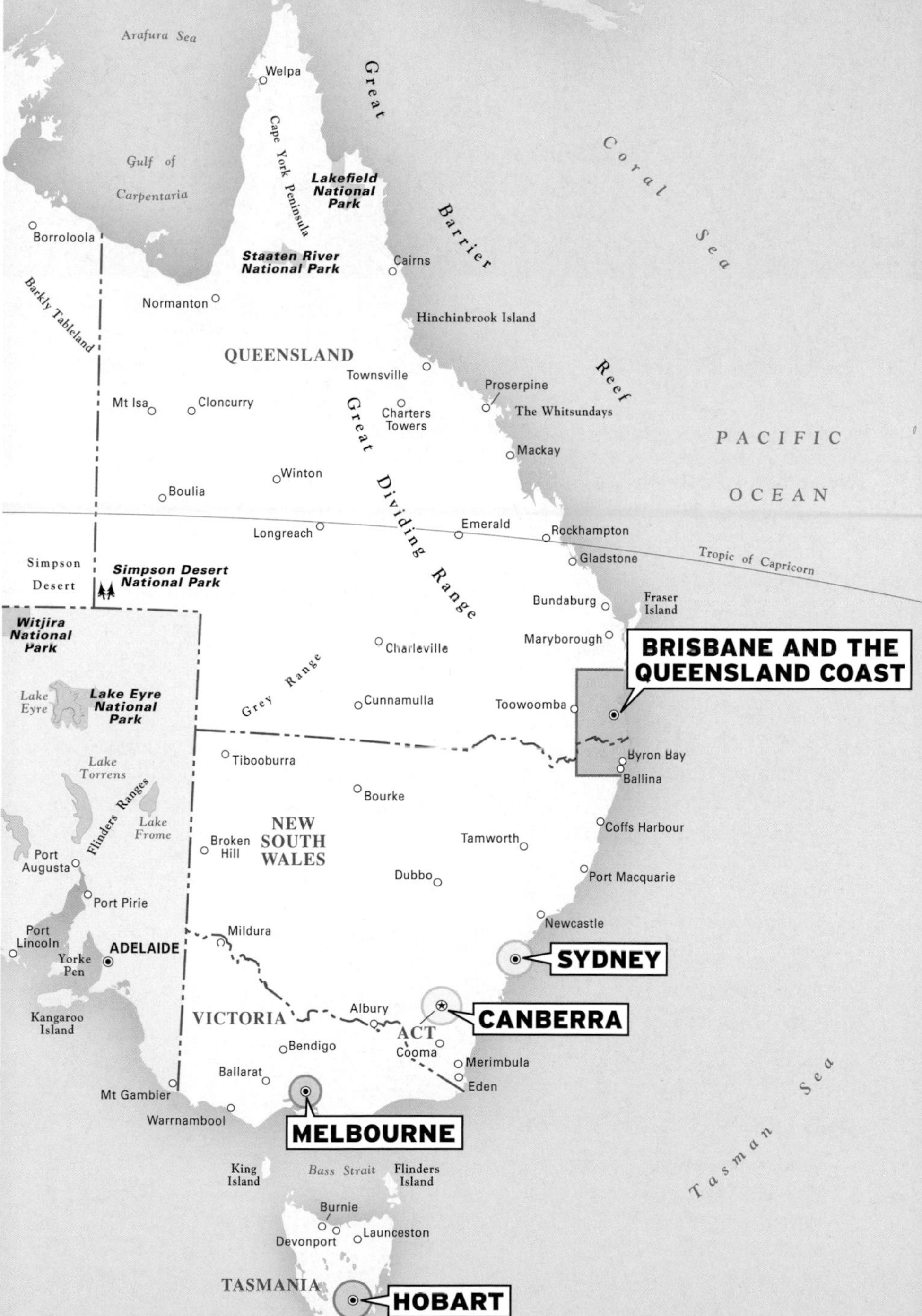
PAPUA NEW GUINEA
Arafura Sea
Gulf of Carpentaria
Welpa
Cape York Peninsula
Great Barrier Reef
Coral Sea
Lakefield National Park
Borroloola
Staaten River National Park
Cairns
Barkly Tableland
Normanton
Hinchinbrook Island
QUEENSLAND
Townsville
Proserpine
The Whitsundays
Mt Isa
Cloncurry
Charters Towers
Great Dividing Range
PACIFIC OCEAN
Mackay
Winton
Boulia
Emerald
Longreach
Rockhampton
Gladstone
Tropic of Capricorn
Simpson Desert
Simpson Desert National Park
Bundaburg
Fraser Island
Witjira National Park
Maryborough
BRISBANE AND THE QUEENSLAND COAST
Charleville
Grey Range
Lake Eyre
Lake Eyre National Park
Cunnamulla
Toowoomba
Byron Bay
Ballina
Tibooburra
Lake Torrens
Flinders Ranges
Bourke
Lake Frome
NEW SOUTH WALES
Coffs Harbour
Broken Hill
Tamworth
Port Augusta
Dubbo
Port Macquarie
Port Pirie
Newcastle
Mildura
Port Lincoln
Yorke Pen
ADELAIDE
SYDNEY
Albury
CANBERRA
VICTORIA
ACT
Kangaroo Island
Bendigo
Cooma
Merimbula
Ballarat
Eden
Mt Gambier
MELBOURNE
Tasman Sea
Warrnambool
King Island
Bass Strait
Flinders Island
Burnie
Devonport
Launceston
TASMANIA
HOBART

Contents

AT HOME IN

Australia

Australia. A land so vast that it encompasses deserts, snowy mountaintops, virgin rainforests, and two oceans lapping at its shores. A country with animals strange enough for a fairy tale, with people who live everywhere from artificial caves to shining skyscrapers, and with a musical culture that stretches from someone playing the didgeridoo in the Outback to a symphony orchestra performing in one of the most iconic buildings on earth.

Although my knowledge about anything Australian was pretty limited before moving here, I found many of the preconceived notions I did have about the continent to be true. The entire nation is obsessed with the great outdoors. The parks and beaches are teeming with people as soon as there is one ray of sunshine. A house is not a house unless it has a barbecue and entertainment deck out back. The cities are bursting with culture and modern shops and coffeehouses. And life is good.

Here, people really do work to live, rather than live to work. Work-life balance is important, and the weekend is king. This low-stress lifestyle and healthier attitude toward work is exactly why migrating to Australia has been popular for generations.

The challenge of adjusting to a different lifestyle in a new country can be an adventure. As an expat, I've truly been able to get to know this amazing country, its people, its history and culture, and its off-the-beaten-path treasures. Australia is still very much a land of wonder, full of remote and undiscovered places. You may even discover something new about yourself.

Clockwise from top left: bathing boxes in Brighton, the National Gallery of Victoria, jars of Vegemite in a grocery store, Qantas airplane, Australian banknotes, Flinders Street Station in Melbourne.

What I Love About Australia

- The heady mix of imposing eucalyptus trees, tall palms, and majestic evergreens, such as the Moreton Bay fig. Australia is opulently green.
- Koalas, platypuses, kangaroos, and wild cockatoos—for an animal lover this is like a trip to the zoo, only without the fences.
- Even a single ray of sunshine is excuse enough for Aussies to sit outside at cafés and linger over breakfast and the daily newspaper.
- The atmosphere in the Melbourne Cricket Ground—where up to 70,000 people cheer on their Australian Rules football teams—is simply electric.
- Even if you live in the center of a large, bustling city, a decent beach is never far away.
- The continent is so varied that weekend trips will never get boring.
- Whether you are a scuba diver or a snorkeler, the world's greatest marinelife is on your doorstep.
- When someone starts shouting "Aussie, Aussie, Aussie," the reflexive response is to shout "oi, oi, oi."
- There are nearly 2,000 vineyards—and they deliver.
- School uniforms eliminate at least some of the peer pressure on kids and ensure a quicker turnaround time in the morning.
- Arriving at the Sydney Opera House for a performance makes you feel like you are treading a red carpet, simply because the setting is so stunning.
- Cherry blossoms in September.
- In even the prettiest of parks, you won't find a sign telling you to keep off the grass.
- Did I mention the koalas?

WELCOME TO AUSTRALIA

INTRODUCTION

When you ask expats about their reasons for coming to Australia, the answers are as individual as the people who make up this varied country. To some it is the big cities: Sydney for its iconic buildings and nightlife, Melbourne for its art and literature vibe, Perth for its beaches, Brisbane for the outdoor sunshine life, Hobart for its seclusion and closeness to the wilderness, and Canberra for its community and great education system. And then there are excellent restaurants and the coffeehouse culture, constant festivals and events, and fun and unique spectator sports.

For others, the only way to really appreciate Australia is to get out of the cities. Beyond their borders lies a country that is so diverse, so different, so vast that it really needs to be seen to be believed.

Even "just" driving from Melbourne to Adelaide, taking in the scenic Great Ocean Road along the way, gives newcomers a whole different perspective on what Australia is all about. I say "just" because even this seemingly short distance on the map takes some 10 hours of solid driving along the main roads without detours—and this is a short hop in Australian distances.

Leaving the city behind, the scenery starts to change immediately: pretty farmland with fenced partitions full of healthy cattle, flocks of sheep both fluffy and shorn naked; the corn belt,

through which the main roads are punctuated by giant silos filled with the recent harvest; and picturesque settings all lush and green. Explore a little farther and you'll find massive rocky outcrops and sheer mountains. Cliffs hem an ocean that is wild and known for its excellent surfing. The forests are full of wonderfully amazing animals: koalas sitting in nooks high up in eucalyptus trees and kangaroos nibbling on the bushes in any clearing.

Go farther yet and the land is no longer quite so ordered and severe. Large stretches of countryside are given over to the natural flora: the scraggly bush, with shrubs and trees which together with the open blue sky paint a picture of typical Australia—solitary, vast, and simply stunning. Explore farther and you'll find wetlands dotted with emus and pelicans, and lone roads that stretch seemingly endlessly through the countryside before finally finding a small hub of civilization again. Head out even farther and the green turns to red, the bush into desert, the small towns and villages cease, and you can go for thousands of kilometers without seeing a single soul. Consider that large parts of Australia haven't even been mapped as yet, and you get the idea.

All that, and more, is Australia. A healthy standard of living is important here in the land Down Under. Making time for friends and family is key to having a good work-life balance. There is still a reasonably healthy economy and an extensive health care system. And people from varied backgrounds continue to shape its diverse population.

People fly for days to visit these shores, to explore the land at the other end of the world, and they try and do it justice in a few short weeks. But it is the expatriates, those who are lucky enough to live at least for a while in this so-called Lucky Country, who have the advantage: a short-haul flight, a ride on the train, or a well-planned road trip gives us access to a land of wonders. So go out there and explore, and make the most of your time Down Under.

The Lay of the Land

Australia is the world's only island continent, seemingly at the other end of the world from whichever way you look at it. From Sydney, the nearest country is New Zealand, some four hours' flight away, and besides the small island nations of the South Pacific, it is eight hours flying time to Southeast Asia and 13 hours to the United States. This splendid isolation has given Australia unique flora and fauna, culture, outlook, and economics. In a famous essay on Australia's early history, Geoffrey Blainey referred to the isolation from the West as "the tyranny of distance," but even more memorably and optimistically, Donald Horne called it "the Lucky Country."

In addition to its isolation, Australia is totally dry, except for the Mediterranean climate around the extensive coastline. Seventy-five percent of the population lives within 80 kilometers of the Pacific or Indian Ocean. Although the interior is dry, it is loaded with mineral wealth and a growing agriculture industry, based on irrigation, primarily in wheat, sheep, and cattle.

Overwhelmingly, the most important coastline is the southeast. The coast from Brisbane in the north to Adelaide in the

Facts and Figures about Australia

the Australian Coat of Arms

- Australia is the world's sixth largest country and its largest island.
- Until 1967, Aborigines were not counted in the annual census, but classed under "flora and fauna."
- In 1859 Thomas Austin brought 24 rabbits, 5 hares, and 72 partridges into Australia and released them on his property to take potshots at. The rest is history.
- The then-prime minister of Australia, Harold Holt, went for a swim near his home at Portsea in Victoria on December 17, 1967, disappeared beneath the waves, and was never seen again.
- Australia was the first country in the world to have a complete system of banknotes made from polymer plastic.
- The country has three different time zones: Australian Eastern Standard Time (AEST), covering Queensland, New South Wales except the town of Broken Hill, the Australian Capital Territory, Victoria, and Tasmania; Australian Central Standard Time (ACST), covering the town of Broken Hill, South Australia, and the Northern Territory; and Australian Western Standard Time (AWST) for Western Australia. Perth has a two-hour time difference to Sydney during the winter and a three-hour time difference during daylight saving time.
- Vegemite, Australia's favorite toast-topping, is a yeast extract made with leftovers from brewer's yeast. A German chemist discovered that the waste of yeast used in brewing beer could be made into a concentrate, resulting in a protein-rich paste.
- Australia is the only continent without an active volcano.
- The Sydney Opera House was designed by Danish architect Jørn Utzon, who left Australia after a disagreement with the government and never returned to see the finished product.
- The largest cattle ranch in the world is Anna Creek Station in South Australia, the size of Belgium and nearly the size of Massachusetts.
- The kangaroo and the emu were chosen for the Australian Coat of Arms because they are incapable of walking backward and therefore symbolize a nation moving forward.

central south is well-populated and was the first area to be settled by nonnatives. This part of Australia remains the financial and population hub of the country, and Sydney, Melbourne, and the national capital of Canberra, are the most important centers.

The country as a whole is roughly the size of the United States without Alaska. It consists of plateaus in the west tapering off to the Indian Ocean, a series of massive interior deserts second only to the Sahara in size, and on the east coast a fringe of mountains, called the Great Dividing Range, that shelter the humid subtropical coast from the desert winds. Amid the Great Dividing Range are pockets of temperate rainforest that contain the most extensive variety of unique Australian birds and plants. But Australia's famed and unique wildlife, especially the kangaroos, are found throughout the country in areas away from population centers.

COUNTRY DIVISIONS

One continent, one country, six states—New South Wales, Victoria, Tasmania, South Australia, Western Australia, and Queensland—along with two main territories—the Northern Territory and the Australian Capital Territory—plus a few so-called external territories, such as the Australian Antarctic Territory, and numerous islands and countless smaller divisions all make up Australia. Size-wise, Western Australia and Queensland are the largest states, followed by the Northern Territory, South Australia, New South Wales, Victoria, and Tasmania. The national capital, Canberra, is situated in the smallest territory, the Australian Capital Territory, which is self-governing but not independent from Australia as a whole.

While there is one federal government and some national administrative organizations, such as the Australian Federal Police, most decisions are made at the state or municipal level. Officially each state is subdivided into counties, municipalities, and shires, although you rarely hear mention of those. Typically each city has integrated smaller "cities" or parishes that were formerly independent little towns and now suburbs, each with an often splendid town hall. For example, people say they live in Richmond or St. Kilda instead of simply saying they live in Melbourne. On the surface these seem like mere suburbs, but they still wield plenty of political power and run

Most Australians live in cities along the coast.

A Topsy-Turvy Land

a warm Christmas in Melbourne

It's easy to forget that a different hemisphere means that everything is upside down.

Here, the driving is on the left. The academic year starts in February and ends in December. And the lay of the land is the opposite of what we're used to in the Northern Hemisphere: it gets hotter the farther north you go, because you're inching closer to the equator. When looking for a house, you need to make sure you have north-facing windows, rather than south-facing.

And the seasons are even more confusing. Spring is in October, fall is in April, winter is in July, and summer is in December. Christmas, which comes at the height of summer, is probably the biggest shock. The shop windows are decorated with both bikinis and fake snow. But Christmas is still Christmas, complete with a big ham or turkey with all the trimmings—even though it will probably be cooked at night (because it is simply too hot to have the oven on in the daytime) and served in the garden.

But even Australians who are used to it know that there is something off about celebrating Christmas in the summer. The atmosphere is just more authentic and cozy when it is cold and preferably snowing outside. So, what do they do? They also celebrate Christmas in July. There even are decorations up in some places.

Everything is simply topsy-turvy.

their divisions sometimes completely differently from their neighbors, even if the outward evidence of that is only the color and size of the trash cans.

POPULATION DENSITY

Australia is the sixth largest country in the world and has some 23.15 million inhabitants. The population averages two people per square kilometer, making it also the least densely populated country in the world. Considering that Australia is also the driest inhabited country in the world, it is hardly surprising that some 90 percent of people live within 120 kilometers of the coast, and in Tasmania 99 percent live within 50 kilometers of the coast. More than 70 percent of the overall population lives in cities, but conversely, some 70 percent of the Aboriginal or Torres Strait people live outside urban areas.

According to the Australian Bureau of Statistics, the 2014-2015 census showed that 28.2 percent of Australians were born overseas, 46 percent have at least one parent who was born overseas, and nearly 20 percent speak a language other than English at home. Add to that some 670,000 citizens of Aboriginal or Torres Strait Islander origin and you have a pretty diverse bunch living here, with plenty of short-term and long-term expatriates from all over the world thrown into the mix.

WEATHER

Australia is split in half by the Tropic of Capricorn, and generally speaking, anything north of it is part of the tropics, and below it is temperate. This doesn't quite work out perfectly in the real world, but the farther north you go, the warmer it gets, and farther south you experience four seasons with hot and cold spells.

Central Australia is pretty much all desert, with some grassland surrounding it. The southeast is temperate, with the mountains in Victoria and New South Wales even getting enough snow to produce some good ski resorts. The southwest and northeast are subtropical, and the north is tropical and equatorial.

That means that Australia has something for everyone. The continuous warm weather you may see on television is typical of Brisbane; in the south you will need to dress warmly in winter. And while Australia is the driest inhabited country in the world, its various regions get their fair share of rain. The temperate regions, including Melbourne and Sydney, have some rain every month and a pretty steady flow throughout the year, but subtropical Perth and Brisbane are subjected to annual rainy seasons.

In general, Canberra and Hobart are the coldest places to live, surrounded by mountains in the south, and except for absolutely scorching Alice Springs and Darwin, Brisbane and Perth are the hotter cities. Sydney is generally said to have perfect weather, and Melbourne is famous for its "four seasons in one day" experience with the weather, when you have to learn to dress in layers.

FLORA

When the Australian landmass broke away from the southern supercontinent Gondwana some 100 million years ago, it took with it some unique flora and fauna and the conditions to evolve and nurture some more. Eighty percent of plant and animal species found in Australia are seen nowhere else in the world. Due to its range of climates, you can find a wide variety of life: mangroves and palm trees, dense million-year-old rainforest and impressively tall eucalyptus trees, unique flowers and gigantic evergreens.

You will notice in Australian gardens that all those plants you may have carefully nurtured in pots around the house back home grow like weeds here. The variety of plants is simply mind-blowing, and although most people will cite the tall eucalyptus and the bottlebrush as the most iconic plants in Australia, the cheerful yellow daisies growing in abundance by the side of the road, the cherry blossoms in September, and the imposing Moreton Bay fig trees are also striking. The wide range and variety of greenery make Australia a dream for gardeners and those who simply enjoy gardens.

FAUNA

Utterly unique and enchanting, many of Australia's animals could be from a fairy tale. Apart from the scientific marvels such as the monotremes, or egg-laying mammals, which include the platypus and the prickly echidna, there are the marsupials, mammals that carry their underdeveloped young around in a cozy pouch until they are ready for the world, along with vast colorful birdlife and a few creepy-crawlies thrown in for good measure.

You know you have settled in Australia when at sunset flocks of cockatoos perch near you, making an incredible noise; red, green, and pink parrots regularly come into your garden looking for seeds and nuts; possums clamber around the electric wires outside your house at night; and maybe, if you are very lucky on a country drive on the weekend, you spot an elusive koala nestling in the fork of a tree or see a kangaroo powerfully propelling itself through the bush. Yes, there are nasty spiders and dangerous snakes in

Australia's best-known marsupial

this country, but generally they stay out of your way and are not really interested, unlike the possums. These actively come down from the trees to have a good look at you. And while it is illegal to hug a koala in most states, you can—if you can't find one in the wild—get a close look at these eucalyptus-munching cuties in any nearby wildlife center and appreciate that you are truly living in Australia.

INTRODUCED FAUNA

The rabbits by the side of the road, the camels ruminating in the desert, those poisonous toads that scare everybody—none are native to Australia, but they

Camels were introduced to the country's large desert areas.

are very common and are usually a pest. Those cute button-nosed bunnies were imported by a farmer from Britain because he wanted to have something to shoot at in the back garden. Not many years later those 20 or so rabbits had produced uncountable new generations that literally changed Australia's landscape from shrubby undergrowth to desert. The introduction of the myxomatosis virus decreased their numbers, but only for a while until new generations had become immune to it. The camels were imported because they suited the large desert regions in Australia, and now they have gone native and are so prolific that they are exported to the Middle East. The cane toads were introduced to combat an epidemic of beetles munching on the sugarcane harvests, and while they managed to get rid of the beetles, they are now a pest themselves without any natural predators. Even the iconic dingo didn't initially belong here, but was introduced thousands of years ago by the Aborigines. Since then, the dingoes have thrived; they thieve from farmers to such a degree that a 5,400-kilometer-long dingo fence, reportedly the world's longest fence and one of the world's longest structures, was built between South Australia up to Queensland, trying to keep the dingoes and farm animals apart. Probably the best-known nonnative species is sheep, brought from South Africa by some of the first British settlers to establish the wool industry. And where would we be today without the famous Australian sheepskin boots and Australian lamb?

Social Climate

Just like the United States of America, Australia is a proud nation and fiercely patriotic. If you want to become part of this society, even if just for a limited period of time, you will have to understand and agree to its values. Migrants applying for residency will have to agree to the "Australian Values Statement," which pretty much lists everything Australians so fiercely believe in. It states that Australian society values respect for the freedom and dignity of the individual, freedom of religion, commitment to the rule of law, parliamentary democracy, equality of men and women, and a spirit of egalitarianism that embraces mutual respect, tolerance, fair play, and compassion for those in need and pursuit of the public good.

With such a diverse cultural and religious population, these are not just values but staples that bind Australian society and make it work. Without mutual respect and the freedom to be themselves, this multicultural nation could simply not function. Equality of opportunity for individuals, regardless of their race, religion, or ethnic background is a given.

GENERALIZATIONS AND STEREOTYPES

If you are of a certain age, you may remember Crocodile Dundee, that leathery-skinned, loud, and enthusiastic bighearted Aussie who wore the hat with corks dangling off the rim and, of course, chased crocodiles for a living. Yes, you will probably find one or two of those types around somewhere in the north (minus the hat), but just like the beer-swigging German or the overweight ill-informed American, they are rarer than you might think.

Australians come in just as many variations as people from any country. When you say that all Australians are sports-mad, you are partly right, but look around and you'll find plenty of arts, literature, and culture festivals with strong support. In 2010, Australia elected its first female prime minister, Julia Gillard, who has now been replaced, but ask some red-blooded Aussie males and they'll still tell you a woman's place is in the kitchen. Australians are proud of not having a class system, yet the gap between the haves and have-nots is wide and frequently complained about, and people often work three jobs to put their kids through upmarket private schools. Aussies love the outdoors, camping and roughing it in the fresh air, yet 80 percent of the people live in the cities, and five-star luxury lodges are springing up everywhere in the Outback.

More reasonable generalizations are that Aussies are a friendly, outgoing, boisterous, and welcoming bunch. Like anywhere else, acting aloof as an expat won't get good results. Be open and approachable, maybe join in something like Aussie Rules football, and you'll make friends easily enough.

AUSTRALIA AND FOREIGNERS

Like the United States, Australia is a country populated by immigrants, even if many families go back many generations as Australian-born. In the 1950s and 1960s immigration was encouraged to populate the land, but today, immigration, and especially illegal immigration, is seen as a problem, and negative attitudes toward immigrants can be found in a not insubstantial number of Australians. With rising levels of education and awareness, younger generations are much more accepting of foreigners of any color, but like everywhere in the world there is a section of the population that is openly racist. Asians seem to bear the brunt of the dislike of the xenophobic minority, but foreigner-bashing becomes lighthearted when there is a "Pom" involved: The British, even though they were the unwilling European settlers of the land, are the foreigners everybody loves to hate. Americans may hear the odd snide comment about "Yanks," but poking fun and not tolerating any arrogance or condescension are very much part of Australian culture and the Aussie sense of humor, and it shouldn't be taken too seriously. After all, according to the Australian Human Rights Commission, 84 percent of Australians believe that multiculturalism has been good for Australia.

HISTORY, GOVERNMENT, AND ECONOMY

Australia's post-European settlement history is documented extremely well. The cities are replete with many grand old historical buildings, and residents can go to the bronze plates at Darling Harbour in Sydney and find their ancestor's name and ship they came over on. Older historical information, especially Aboriginal history, is harder to find, because a lot of it has been lost over the years.

Looking farther back, Australia's indigenous population is one of the oldest on the planet. The Aborigines have always been seminomadic and connected to the land, rather than builders of great pyramids or temples. The lack of structures led early European visitors to believe Australia was mostly uninhabited, but the indigenous people have roamed this continent for at least 50,000 years. And even in the brief 200 years that Europeans have been here, Australia has grown from a penal colony through peaceful independence from Great Britain into a continent-size federation, a land with a high quality of life and one of the highest standards of living in the world.

The ancient as well as the more recent history of this continent has shaped its people, their attitude, and their choices

in life. Just like everywhere else on this planet, history is what we build on, and in Australia, there are plenty of building blocks to choose from.

History

BEFORE THE EUROPEANS

When the Australian landmass broke off from the supercontinent Gondwana and became a continent some 15 million years ago, it was indeed the *terra nullius* or empty land the Europeans thought they had found only a few hundred years ago. But despite the vastness and the seemingly uninhabitable landscapes, people eventually came to populate the island continent. The original inhabitants of Australia are called Aborigines, from the Latin *ab origen,* meaning "from the beginning." They arrived some 50,000 years ago either by boat via the shallow northern seas or perhaps via land that was then still connected to New Guinea, today submerged under the Torres Strait.

In splendid isolation, the many different ethnic groups lived in a seminomadic style. They brought their dogs, today's dingoes, and hunted three-meter-tall kangaroos, marsupial lions, tigers, and the hippopotamus-size Diprotodon. They remained hunter-gatherers, never turning to farming, and were often hostile toward other indigenous ethnic groups. By the time of European contact, there were between 350 and 750 distinct indigenous languages in Australia, of which only around 100 survive today. The Aborigines never developed a writing system, passing along their history and stories orally and via dance and song. Like the languages, songs varied widely, although similar themes and styles can be seen in their visual art, which is generally acknowledged as the longest continuous art form still in use and still understood anywhere in the world.

Sadly, after European settlement, the indigenous people were dispersed, killed,

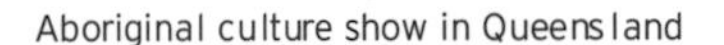
Aboriginal culture show in Queensland

and put on reservations designed to contain the "wild tribes" of Australia. They lost much of their sense of tradition, their skill at telling about the "dreamtime"—meaning the time of the great ancestors when all life-forms, human and animal, were connected—and their sense of identity; along with this went any opportunity to trace their history and ancient culture. While traditional storytelling skills are once again increasingly being nurtured and encouraged, most descriptions of ancient history have already been lost.

Among the original inhabitants' innumerable contributions to modern Australian life were their names for animals, plants, and places, which are in wide use today, plus their unique hunting and musical tools, such as the boomerang and the didgeridoo, and beautiful art that is revered the world over.

FIRST EUROPEAN SETTLEMENTS (1788-1850)

While Malay fishing vessels regularly visited the northern shores of Australia, it wasn't until Dutch sailors first began making contact on voyages from Cape Town to Indonesia via the west coast of Australia in the early 1600s that the Europeans took notice. More and more expeditions were sent "down under" to discover and chart the great land, of which nothing was known. Australia and its surroundings were gradually explored.

Portuguese explorer Luís Vaz de Torres proved that he was either a very lucky navigator or already knew about the Torres Strait between New Guinea and Cape York in the north of Australia when he sailed past the main continent. The Dutch navigators Anthony van Diemen and Abel Tasman discovered Van Diemen's Land, now Tasmania, in 1642 and charted the western Australian coast, which they named New Holland. The French came, explored, took some kangaroos and other specimens, and left again, but Australians generally date the first proper European contact to April 29, 1770, when Captain James Cook, commanding the HMS *Endeavour* on a mission of exploration, landed at Botany Bay, adjacent to modern-day Sydney.

Cook's meticulous charts of the eastern

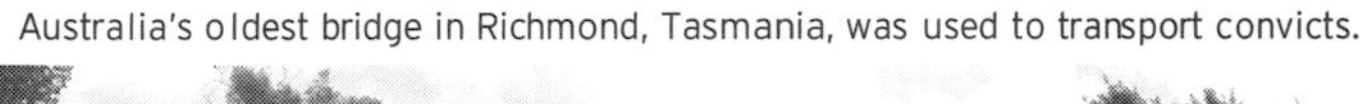
Australia's oldest bridge in Richmond, Tasmania, was used to transport convicts.

Australian coast were highly valued by the Royal Navy and the British government, but it was the 800 specimens of Australian flora collected by ship's botanist Joseph Banks and tales of the fantastic Australian animals that caused a sensation in London. The discovery of the region also soon provided Britain with much needed relief for a domestic problem.

Prior to 1776, convicts were transported to America for 7-year, 14-year, or life terms to relieve overcrowded prisons and provide low-cost labor to colonial businesses. With the outbreak of the Revolutionary War in 1776, English prisoners sentenced to "transportation" had nowhere to go and were held in rotting ships in English harbors, a situation that had reached crisis proportions by 1786. Prime Minister William Pitt's government ordered a fleet of shipborne convicts sent to the new land under the command of Captain Arthur Phillip. The convict fleet arrived in Botany Bay on January 26, 1788, and although the colony was called New South Wales and the continent itself was not named Australia until 1824, today this date is celebrated as Australia Day.

After realizing that Botany Bay did not offer sufficiently good land for farming and lacked fresh water, Captain Phillip moved north to what is now Port Jackson or Sydney Harbour, globally recognized as one of the great natural harbors of the world. This move is seen as the best thing Captain Phillip ever did. He landed at Sydney Cove, today's busy Circular Quay ferry port, and named the settlement for Britain's home secretary, Lord Sydney. Convict transportation continued until 1850, peaking after 1800 when a second penal colony was established at Hobart in Van Diemen's Land in 1803.

The cities of Melbourne, Brisbane, Adelaide, and Perth were successively settled. The colony of New South Wales passed briefly from the command of Captain Phillip to Captain Bligh, of *Mutiny on the Bounty* fame, who found himself the object of a coup d'état staged by disgruntled army officers. A governor named Lachlan Macquarie was sent to straighten out the situation, and he cleaned up the administration, brought the military into line, improved agriculture, and sponsored exploration. *Macquarie* continues to be a byword for "quality" in Australian life, and institutions, streets, towns, and enterprises routinely take the Macquarie name as a branding strategy.

The cities themselves continued to be named for British officials and members of the royal family. Thomas Brisbane (a colonial secretary), the Duke of Newcastle (a prime minister), Lord Melbourne (also a prime minister), and Queen Adelaide all were honored. The colonies of Queensland and Victoria acquired their names during the long reign of Queen Victoria in the

a replica of the first ships that arrived in Australia

19th century. A good working knowledge of the history of the British cabinet and royalty is invaluable in roughly calculating the age of a given neighborhood or street in Australia.

The period of convict history was marked by a considerable social divide between the military and gentry and the descendants of the convicts, many of whom stayed on after completing their sentences, were granted land, got married, and had children. These class distinctions have ebbed through the generations since the end of transportation in 1850, but there are two distinctive Australian dialects to this day, and there continue to be subtle yet broad divisions in Australian society between the gentry and the laboring class. The gentry tends to speak with a light Australian accent, using mostly standard English, while the laboring class has traditionally had a much thicker accent that draws heavily on slang (often rhyming slang) and the dialect known as Strine, which is how "Australian" is pronounced in Strine.

ESTABLISHING COMMONWEALTH AND CULTURE (1850-1901)

With the end of transportation, Australians began to lobby Great Britain for a stronger role in determining their own affairs. The British, learning from their mistakes in the American Revolution, wisely devised the so-called dominions, nations that retained allegiance to the British crown and had common defense and foreign policy but were internally self-governing. New South Wales, Victoria, Tasmania, Queensland, South Australia, Western Australia, and New Zealand began a decades-long evolution toward self-government at the colonial level and ultimately federated in 1900, with the notable defection of New Zealand. The transition happened in stages that echo in Australia's current political system: An appointed royal governor with full powers eventually gave way to a strong governor advised by an appointed legislative council. Eventually that appointed council became the upper house, with the election of a legislative assembly, from which a colonial premier and cabinet were elected. Ultimately, the royal governor was limited to a largely ceremonial role.

This period was remarkable also for the commercial development of Australia. Massive gold strikes at Ballarat, near Melbourne, made Melbourne one of the richest and fastest-growing cities in the world in the 1850s. This coincided with the era of the great clipper ships that would ride the hard-blowing westerlies from Cape Town to Melbourne before crossing the Pacific to the United States. During this period, Melbourne eclipsed Sydney, and a good-natured rivalry between the two cities has been a central point of Australian life ever since. The presence of large amounts of money in the colonies resulted in a massive increase in "bushranging." The traditional English highway robber transformed into the Australian bushranger with distinct overtones of Robin Hood, and several bushrangers, including Ned Kelly and Mad Dog Morgan, became folk heroes.

In this period of the nation's growing economic importance, the Australian Outback was opened for sheep and cattle ranching on a massive scale, and a mythology grew up around the hard life of the drovers managing the sheep. Jackeroos (trainees, typically sons of "connected" families) worked as cowboys on the gigantic stations (ranches) that could be more than 200,000 hectares in size, and wandering shearers would travel the Outback from station to station and engage in famous shearing contests that were the subject of significant betting at the time.

ANZAC Day

a detail of Sydney's ANZAC Memorial

ANZAC Day, April 25, is the anniversary of the Australian and New Zealand Army Corps' landing on the Gallipoli Peninsula on Turkey's Aegean coast on April 25, 1915, during World War I. It was the first battle Australia participated in as an independent nation. While the Germans were fought in the trenches across Europe, Russia was under attack from the Turks in the Caucasus, and in order to aid the battle, the Allies intended to divert Turkey by attacking the Gallipoli Peninsula. The idea was that once the peninsula was taken, the Allies would be able to take control of the Dardanelles strait, open a trade route to Russia, and besiege Istanbul, then called Constantinople.

After a hard-fought but losing battle, the last ANZAC forces eventually withdrew from the Gallipoli Peninsula on December 20, 1915. Overall many lives were lost, but what is celebrated is dubbed the ANZAC spirit—a sense of identity, camaraderie, and bravery.

One song that is often associated with Australia is "Waltzing Matilda," a traditional folk song about a kind of rucksack that Australian farmworkers carried on their backs. To waltz Matilda basically means walking around the bush or farmland with a backpack on. The song was incorporated by songwriter Eric Bogle in 1971 in an antiwar song called "The Band Played 'Waltzing Matilda'." There is some controversy as to whether he wrote the song about Gallipoli or Vietnam, but either way, it has since been played at remembrance ceremonies on ANZAC Day.

As dawn was the time of the original landing, each year on ANZAC Day dawn services are held all over Australia, New Zealand, and other countries connected with the battle. The dawn service is often followed by a so-called gunfire breakfast, featuring tea with a shot of rum in it, and during the day parades are held, speeches given, bugle calls made, and wreaths laid.

There are also traditional ANZAC Day biscuits made from oats and coconut, which trace their origins to women at home sending the men in battle food to keep them going. You can get them at shops, but many families bake their own traditional version in the spirit of remembrance.

Then there is the football. This is an Australian holiday, after all. Every year in the afternoon of ANZAC Day the famous ANZAC Clash between Australian Football League teams is held at the Melbourne Cricket Ground. All in all it's a worthwhile day of events to add to the calendar.

EARLY 20TH CENTURY (1901-1945)

The great issues of the 1890s for Australia had been labor-capital challenges caused by a worldwide collapse in commodities prices and the fight over the terms of federation into a single commonwealth. New Zealand opted out of the federation altogether; several of the states and sections of society were uneasy about the concept of federation and the constitution that had been hammered out. With the return to prosperity and the debut of the commonwealth, these issues mostly faded, and Australia enjoyed a golden period that was shattered by the onset of World War I.

Although formation of the commonwealth had given Australia control over its own foreign policy, broadly speaking the public and the government were pro-British Empire, and Australia dutifully followed Great Britain into the war in 1914. They were in for a shock. Respect for the Australian military was low among the British, and initially Australian units were used only as replacements in existing British divisions. Australia was at first denied any role in charting the direction of the war in the strategy rooms or on the battlefield. Public uproar led to the combining of the Australian and New Zealand forces, the Australia New Zealand Army Corps (ANZAC), but not to autonomous command. The initial major force was sent to the Gallipoli Peninsula, in modern Turkey, to fight under British generals in a combined army-naval attack on Constantinople (now Istanbul), the capital of the Ottoman Empire.

The invasion of Gallipoli on April 25, 1915, is celebrated today in Australia as ANZAC Day, and most Australians believe the nation was forged in that battle. The attack itself was a bloodbath and resulted in defeat, massive casualties, and eventual withdrawal. The defeat profoundly shocked the nation; Australians would never again participate in large-scale operations under direct British field command, although they served loyally under the overall command.

For most Aussies, the British disregard for essential preparations at Gallipoli was due to a general British disregard for the Australians and their country, and although Australia had the second highest volunteer rate among the nations of the Empire, a split emerged in Australian society over loyalty to Great Britain. This debate is still ongoing today, with a small but highly organized pro-monarchy faction still fighting to keep the British monarch as Australia's monarch, while republican forces have been gathering strength since 1915; in 1999 they almost ousted the monarchy in a national referendum.

Aussies owe a sense of national identity to World War I, for at Gallipoli they served for the first time not as members of the colonies but as a united national army. Gallipoli also fostered the cultural value of the "fair go"—the idea that people need to be given a fair chance. In the popular perception, a fair go was exactly what the slaughtered ANZACs were denied at Gallipoli. It was an idea that had existed in the society long before Gallipoli, but was seared into the fabric of the culture thereafter. Even today, governments have fallen with more than a little credit given to the idea that the other party deserves a fair go at running the country. Corporate, academic, and diplomatic culture is suffused with the fair go concept, which, blended with the general egalitarianism of Australia, makes people somewhat suspicious of certain aspects of economic competition and free enterprise.

Following the war, Australia assumed a role in administering a number of former German colonies in the South Pacific and had its first taste of colonial governance. The postwar period was significant not for international events but rather for the great rise in popularity of Australian sports. Rugby, cricket, and Australian Rules football began to be played in large stadia before massive crowds. The general prosperity of the times sparked an already profound Australian love of sports to reach epic proportions, where it remains today. Emblematic of the rivalry between Sydney and Melbourne, which reached a peak during this period, Sydney embraced rugby, and Melbourne, Aussie Rules football. In politics, the two cities could not agree on which would serve as the national capital, so the city of Canberra was established between the two to serve as neutral ground.

The heady prosperity of the 1920s gave way to the devastating Great Depression, in which the effects of the worldwide economic collapse were greatly magnified by another collapse in worldwide commodities prices. With the slump came searing and widespread poverty, and political radicalism soared. Tensions reached a peak in 1932 when a pro-fascist military officer interrupted the opening of the Sydney Harbour Bridge by riding up on a horse and slashing the bridge-opening ribbon so that the radical New South Wales premier Jack Lang would not have the honor.

Most ordinary Australians were profoundly shocked by radicalism, the massive poverty and economic dislocation that caused it, and by a growing sense that the British Empire would be unable to provide for Australia's defense owing to its own economic woes. But nevertheless, Australia again loyally followed Britain into World War II in 1939.

The war went very badly for the British in the first 18 months, and there were few resources that could be diverted to the defense of Southeast Asia. Further, the European colonial system had long sunk into a polite form of despotism that led to the Japanese being initially hailed as deliverers when they successfully invaded Malaysia, the Philippines, Indonesia, and South Pacific islands in 1941 to 1942. Great Britain attempted to mount a defense of Malaysia and Singapore but was rapidly and comprehensively defeated, and in early 1942 the Australians found themselves on the retreat and in the clear path of the Japanese advance.

The American-British war strategy placed a priority on defeating Germany. Accordingly, Australia, though still a small nation of 10 million in population, played a leading role in the South Pacific War. Supported by the American fleet, the Australians led the counteroffensive in New Guinea that stopped the Japanese advance. The sacrifices were heavy, but after the end of the war, Australia had earned the international credibility to play an important role in the formation of the United Nations and organizations such as the Southeast Asia Treaty Organization (SEATO) and the Australia, New Zealand, United States Security Treaty (ANZUS).

Australia had faced its darkest economic times before and during the war, but it returned to prosperity in 1945 and achieved a new level of international prominence and total independence from Britain. Australians continue to acknowledge a debt of gratitude to Americans for their support in the war (especially the older generations), and Australian-American trade cooperation and investment rapidly intensified during the postwar period.

MODERN AUSTRALIA (1945-PRESENT)

Since 1945, in many ways Australia has brought its individual historic threads together into a new and exciting culture and economy that preserves the national concepts of mateship and the fair go, along with a new sense of multiculturalism that reflects significant postwar immigration as well as the country's belated but genuine attempts to address the gulf between mainstream and indigenous Australians.

Although Australia has generally followed the United States' lead in international affairs, supporting the United States with troops and logistics in the wars in Vietnam and Iraq, the country engaged with China earlier, and in many ways more successfully, than the United States and has also participated positively in the postcolonial transition of Africa. After the great resource boom in the 1950s and 1960s that led writer Donald Horne to dub Australia "The Lucky Country," Australia found itself in a tougher economic state in the 1970s and early 1980s, and has substantially diversified and globalized its economy since that time, generally reducing governmental controls and regulations to enable the free market to operate with less friction.

The 1940s and 1950s were a period of tremendous investment in infrastructure projects, much of it aimed at irrigation to expand the range of land under cultivation. Significant diamond, iron, oil, and uranium discoveries in the postwar period have continued to fuel Australia's economic dependence on resource exports. To provide a labor force for the resources boom, Australia had to alter its traditional emphasis on allowing only "white" immigrants, and the "White Australia" policy was substantially reformed with a resulting huge influx of southern European immigrants. The policy was abolished altogether in the 1970s, resulting in substantial Asian immigration. The end result today is a highly multicultural society with decidedly British roots but an increasingly internationalized urban population.

In cultural terms, Australian literature and cinema went through a renaissance in the 1970s and 1980s, with filmmakers such as Peter Weir (*Gallipoli, Picnic at Hanging Rock, Witness*), Bruce Beresford (*Breaker Morant, Driving Miss Daisy*), George Miller (*Mad Max, Babe, Happy Feet*) and outstanding Australian films such as *Priscilla, Queen of the Desert, Muriel's Wedding,* and Baz Luhrmann's *Strictly Ballroom,* which achieved near cult status. Australian musicians and actors such as the Bee Gees, Mel Gibson, Olivia Newton-John, Keith Urban, Russell Crowe, Toni Collette, Rachel Griffiths, Nicole Kidman, and many more have also become internationally known in their fields.

In the 1980s, with the ascendancy of the Labor Party after a long period of domination by the center-right Liberal-Country Party coalition, there was a new level of commitment to opening doors for women and indigenous Australians, in the latter case culminating with National Sorry Day in 1998. On this day the nation observed a national apology to the indigenous Australian people to acknowledge, in particular, that 100,000 indigenous Australian children were forcibly removed from their homes between 1915 and 1969 and raised in orphanages and camps.

Since a steep but brief period of recession in the early 1990s, Australia has experienced nearly continuous economic expansion. In particular, Sydney has reached world-class status among global cities, although Melbourne continues to present itself as a compelling alternative to Sydney's brashness. Regional cities such as Brisbane, Perth, and Adelaide have developed highly attractive economies and are quickly growing in population.

The 2000 Olympic Games gave Sydney in particular and Australia in general a lift in prestige, and Australia's continued remarkable success in Olympic competition provides the nation a quadrennial focal point as well as a surging sense of national pride and confidence. Yet Australian confidence, tempered by its own "tall poppy" dislike of cockiness, is appealing rather than annoying. Australia has entered the 21st century with some issues in the environmental arena as a leading resources nation, but in all other respects as a remarkably integrated country where the lessons of the past have paid dividends in the present.

Government

FEDERAL GOVERNMENT

The Commonwealth of Australia is of relatively recent vintage, founded in 1901, and the framers of the Australian Constitution had the opportunity to integrate aspects from the American, British, and Canadian constitutions that they admired, plus a few inventions of their own. Consequently, the Australian system of government is primarily British in character but has significant features borrowed from North America. In addition, there are features that are historical remnants of the development of the country from its colonial roots.

Australia is a constitutional monarchy, which means that Queen Elizabeth II reigns as monarch of Australia with Prince Charles as heir apparent. In the constitution, her royal powers are nearly absolute, but in practice they are "reserve powers" to be exercised only in a national emergency; those powers are vested in the governor-general appointed by the queen based on the recommendation of the prime minister. In 1975 Governor-General John Kerr sacked the elected Labor government when it could not pass its money-supply bills in the Senate, so it's not without precedent that the governor-general takes political action. But by and large the "GG" is a ceremonial figure, usually popular and more seen than heard.

The federal government is composed of a Senate and a House of Representatives. An equal number of senators are elected from each of the six states, and House members are elected in proportion to the population: In this way, the Australian legislature is like that of the United States.

Unlike in Britain, it is common to have members of the cabinet from the Senate, although by convention they rarely serve in the most senior posts. Only one senator, John Gorton, has served as prime minister, and in his case he resigned his Senate seat to obtain a House of Representatives seat as soon as he became prime minister. In addition to the cabinet, the prime minister appoints junior (noncabinet) ministers to run minor departments.

Supporting the government is a permanent bureaucracy of departments, each department headed by a

Parliament House in Canberra

nonpolitical permanent secretary. In addition, Australia has a High Court headed by a chief justice. They are life appointees, and the High Court closely resembles the U.S. Supreme Court.

The most famous omission from the Australian Constitution is a Bill of Rights. Australia simply doesn't have one, and many controls over private property and private conduct are just as perfectly constitutional in Australia as they are perfectly unconstitutional in the United States. For example, in Australia it is legal to have randomized breath tests and to use cameras to photograph speeding vehicles, with the result of fewer road casualties.

Australian governments are voted on at least every four years, in which elections for half the Senate and all the House seats are contested. The government can seek an earlier election date, but not a later one. Also, under special circumstances, the government of the day may be granted a double dissolution, in which all the Senate seats in addition to the House are contested: This is intended to be used in cases when the government's program has been defeated in the Senate, but in practical terms it's used to maximize electoral opportunities.

In Australia, voting is compulsory for citizens age 18 and over, with fines levied against those who fail to vote. Australia uses a preferential voting system. In this system, voters rank candidates in order of preference. If one candidate does not receive a majority of the votes, then the lowest vote-getter is eliminated and his or her votes distributed to the voter's second preference. In this way, candidates add to their vote tallies until one candidate reaches a majority. Voters cast one vote in their House race, but in the Senate race cast as many votes as there are seats up for election in that state.

The federal government collects all state and national taxes and shares the revenues with the states in a negotiated split. Another difference between the United States and Australia is that sales tax is collected federally instead of by the states, and there is one consistent nationwide rate for the Goods and Services Tax (GST).

The federal government operates a national health scheme, Medicare, and also owns several important national industries, such as stakes in the airline Qantas and Telstra, a phone company. The federal government also oversees the Australian Capital Territory, which is the area surrounding Canberra and a small coastal enclave at Jervis Bay.

STATE GOVERNMENT

The state governments are structured in essentially the same format as the federal government; the governor-general of a state is a governor, the prime minister is a state premier, and the upper house is known as the Legislative Council. Queensland does not have an upper house.

State governments obtain their funds from the national income tax via revenue sharing. A key role of the state government is responsibility for schools, police, zoning, roads, and the extensive public transportation in major cities.

MUNICIPAL AND SHIRE GOVERNMENT

Municipal governments obtain funding from local property taxes and other local fees on businesses and residents for services. In some locations, shire (county) government replaces the municipality as the local government. In Australia, local government provides garbage collection, local police, local development and zoning, child services, elder care services, and beach and sports facilities.

In Australia, cities are often exceedingly small geographic areas with limited populations. The Lord Mayor of Sydney, for example, presides over only the Sydney Central Business District, which has approximately 100,000 residents.

LEGAL SYSTEM

In Australia, there are four types of federal courts and three types of state courts (although Tasmania has two levels of local courts, and Western Australia has four).

The federal courts include the High Court, which has final right of appeal and hears constitutional cases; the Federal Court, which oversees most corporate, copyright, industrial, customs, immigration, and bankruptcy aspects of federal law; the Family Court, which oversees divorce, custody, and child support cases; and Federal Magistrates Courts, which hear less complex cases that otherwise would be heard by the Federal Court or the Family Court.

The state courts include the State Supreme Court, which oversees appeals, and in the case of Tasmania, oversees the work handled by District Courts elsewhere; the District Court, which oversees most criminal trials and major civil suits; and the Magistrates Court, which oversees smaller civil suits and petty matters such as driving offenses.

POLITICAL PARTIES

The major political parties are the Australian Labor Party (ALP), Liberal Party, National Party, the Greens, and the Australian Democrats. The ALP is the oldest party, founded in the 1890s. In addition to representing the interests of organized labor, it represents the center-left of Australian politics. The Labor Party is typically either in government or leading the opposition. In recent years it has had conspicuous success at the state level, but less so federally, where it has been in opposition more than 65 percent of the time since World War II.

The Liberal Party was founded in the 1940s to replace the United Australia Party as the leader of the center-right. It has formed a coalition with the National Party during its entire existence, including arrangements regarding contesting seats.

The National Party was founded as the Country Party in the 1910s and has been the junior partner in coalition with the Liberal Party since the 1940s. The National Party represents the interests of rural Australia and is generally more conservative than the Liberal Party.

The Greens are the newest party of significance, gaining Senate seats in the federal legislature in the last decade or so. It represents environmental causes and in general is the most left-wing party.

The Australian Democrats were formed in 1977 to provide a middle road between the Liberal-National coalition and the ALP. The Democrats have held the balance of power in the Senate on many occasions and have used their power as a brake on the most extreme left- or right-wing ambitions of the governments of the day.

Economy

The Australian economy is primary-resource intensive and goes through boom-and-bust cycles because of this. In recent decades the economy has diversified, and the effects of boom-and-bust are less now than in the past, but the economy still booms when its resource prices are high, and since 2000 this has generally been the case. Despite a high degree of dependence on primary resources, 75 percent of Australia's workforce is employed in the service sector, roughly equivalent to the United States. Inflation is generally low, less than 3 percent for most of the 2000s.

The gross domestic product in 2014 was US$1,454.68 billion or US$37,828.24 per capita, equivalent to 300 percent of the world average. This makes Australia one of the 20 largest economies in the world, and its per capita income is in the top 10 worldwide. The Australian dollar is the fifth most widely traded currency in the world, valued for its stability and for the hands-off nature of the Australian government toward currency manipulations. Major trading partners include the United States, China, Japan, Singapore, Germany, South Korea, India, and New Zealand.

Australia is becoming friendlier to entrepreneurs, but it remains a country where big business and multinationals have been the rule rather than the exception, primarily resulting from the capital-intensive nature of Australian industry. Accordingly, relationships are very important to the conduct of business, and the "old school tie" still opens many doors in Sydney and Melbourne. Dominant multigenerational family enterprises run by the Murdochs, Packers, Holmes à Courts, and others are common in Australia. Media ownership, in particular, has been concentrated in the hands of a few families.

Australia is known for high wages and for a strong trade union movement, which is the mainstay of the Australian Labor Party in political terms and, through the Australian Council of Trade Unions, a powerful negotiator of rights and benefits for workers.

The country has a strong commitment

the Australian Securities Exchange in Sydney

Australian Made, Australian Grown

There is no doubt that Australians are fiercely proud of their country, its people, its achievements, and everything it has to offer—cheering for their compatriots in international sports events, praising the country's natural wonders, or claiming that because something is Aussie it is naturally better than anything that isn't.

A detailed consumer survey found that 65 percent of Australians buy Australian-made products whenever possible. Since 1986 domestic products have been labeled "Australian Made, Australian Grown" (AMAG) by the not-for-profit organization Australian Made Campaign Limited (AMCL). The AMAG logo provides consumers with a recognized symbol for genuine Aussie products and produce and supports domestic growers, processors, and manufacturers by helping them clearly identify their products as Australian. AMCL also runs a campaign encouraging consumers to look for the logo when shopping.

The logo, a sleek gold kangaroo hopping in a smooth green triangle, is attached to products ranging from strawberries to industrial machinery and validates the product as being produced to extremely high standards or being environmentally friendly, fresh, seasonal, and trustworthy.

The nationalist drive started as early as the 1930s, when multiple advertising campaigns nudged people into preferring Australian-made products. Today, the AMAG logo can only be used on products that are registered with AMCL, and it's used with one of only five descriptors: "Australian made," "Australian grown," "Product of Australia," "Australian seafood," or, for export use only, "Australian." To use the logo, goods must meet the criteria set out in the Australian Consumer Law as well the more stringent AMCL Code of Practice. More than 1,700 businesses are registered to use the AMAG logo, found on more than 10,000 products sold here and around the world.

Pride in their products, pride in their jobs and workforce, and indeed, trying to keep jobs in the country all drive the AMAG movement. For the average expatriate, unless you are buying machinery or household goods, on a day-to-day basis the logo means fresh, seasonal, local products that have been delivered to the shops without massive carbon footprints and have been vetted under strict regulation. That is certainly worth looking out for.

to building and maintaining infrastructure and strong historical support for electricity, telecommunications, and transportation projects. Internet access is widespread. A national highway system has been in place for many years, and the national ring road around Australia is being upgraded to include more divided, limited-access, high-speed corridors.

The country is less regulated than comparable countries in Europe but has strong regulatory oversight compared to the United States.

MAJOR INDUSTRIES

The major natural resource industries are uranium, bauxite, iron, diamonds, coal, and oil. Key agricultural industries are

Wool is one of Australia's most important products.

wool, beef, and wheat. Australia is a major food exporter and nearly energy self-sufficient. Sydney is home to world-class banking, legal, and finance industries. Sydney and Melbourne are the centers of the communications industries.

Melbourne is home to primary industries. The automotive and wine industries are based in Adelaide. Mining is based in Perth and to a lesser extent in Brisbane, while Brisbane is home to the tourism industry. Canberra, as the capital, is home to the government.

In terms of pace and reputation, Sydney is often described as the New York or Los Angeles of Australia, while Melbourne is described as more similar to Chicago. Perth is a mining city, Brisbane a tourism and agriculture town, and Adelaide has a heavy-industry focus, including much defense-related contracting. Two regional industrial cities in New South Wales, Wollongong and Newcastle, focus on heavy industry, including paper, oil, gas, and coal; Tasmania is mostly agricultural, with some mining and primary industries and a small specialized industry serving Antarctic activities.

PEOPLE AND CULTURE

Winston Churchill once described England and the United States as "two countries divided by a common language," and the idea holds true for Australia and the United States as well. The United States and Australia share a language and both have British colonial history, sophisticated Western economies, a large pool of immigrants, and an extensive and important Pacific coastline. But Aussies and Yanks don't always speak the same language or talk about their values in the same way.

Culturally, Americans and Australians are divided by a different approach to pioneer survival. In the American West, self-reliance was a primary means of survival and advancement, and Americans have learned as individuals and as a society to be independent and enjoy the wide-open spaces beyond the city, where they appreciate noninterference, low taxes, and the opportunity to pursue happiness in their own way. In Australia, conditions were so harsh beyond the sheltering coastal ranges that cooperation was as essential to survival as self-reliance was in the States.

Looking out for your mate is a major Australian cultural value that cannot be underestimated and permeates every aspect of city and country life. Also, Australia's history as a penal colony, during which time thousands were brought here for extended prison terms for offenses

as minor as stealing food to feed families impoverished by the industrial revolution, has made for a society that values the "fair go" more than others might. That history has also fostered a general suspicion of sophistication and power.

Australia's 20 million people have inherited one of the richest combinations of mineral and agricultural resources in the world. Australians enjoy a fabulous lifestyle compared to the grinding poverty of nearby Indonesia, and a sense of guilt and obligation has made Australia progressive in terms of evolving new means of engagement with minorities. As a wealthy and diverse nation with many immigrant minorities, Australia has a mostly tolerant culture that generally embraces diversity and shuns direct confrontation.

Australia is also a land born of the 19th century, when grog (alcohol) was the safest thing to drink in crowded cities before the advent of proper sewage treatment. Australia retains distinct vestiges of its drinking past. Add to that a sometimes worrying love of gambling and an at times overtly "adult" lifestyle, and you have a culture that may come across as rough and ready. But all of these elements underpin Australian culture, and it is essential to understand them to make sense of Australians and Australia.

Ethnicity and Class

Australians are ethnically highly diverse, with the roots of the "true" Australians in the small surviving number of indigenous Australians who arrived some 50,000 years ago. Centuries later came an influx of English, Scottish, Welsh, and Irish settlers who emigrated 1780-1850 as convicts, soldiers, bureaucrats, or land grantees. The gold rush period of the 1850s through the 1870s brought a further inflow of Asians, Americans, and other Europeans, including the first sizable German immigration, and the railroad-building era brought some southern Europeans and more Chinese to the country. A major expansion in immigration started after World War II, when a wave of immigrants arrived from southern and eastern Europe to help with major public works projects such as the Snowy River hydroelectric scheme, and for a period Melbourne had the third largest Greek-born population in the world. Asians began arriving in great numbers after the Vietnam War in the 1970s along with many Middle Easterners. Today, the vast majority of Australians have at least one ancestor who arrived after 1900, making Australia truly a land of new arrivals.

The countryside and the cities produce quite different characteristics and accents. Rural Australians love their pioneer culture, and the archetypal characters in famous Australian ballads and stories are bush-based, often from the 19th century, and exhibit a blend of tolerance, a streak of mischief known as larrikinism, and a healthy disrespect for authority. Outlaw figures such as bushranger Ned Kelly are openly admired by many, despite their nefarious careers, and sporting figures are widely idolized. On the other hand you have more educated urban Australians who pride themselves on their cosmopolitan outlook, interest in art, and sniff at the old Australian ways.

TOLERANCE AND DISCRIMINATION

The habit of judging people and assigning status based on how they look, sound, dress, and act is a global phenomenon, but it impacts immigrant-laden countries such as Australia and the United States more than others. On the whole, Australians are remarkably tolerant of different cultures, but the high percentage of immigrants can create more tension than in countries that have fewer expatriates and migrants.

In the law, discrimination on the basis of gender, race, age, or religion is illegal in Australia; in practical terms, the concentration of immigrants, especially those lacking English-language skills, in so-called immigrant neighborhoods shows that Australia still has work to do to blend newcomers smoothly into the general culture.

Tolerance is generally better among those who are more affluent and educated, where there is less competition for jobs with immigrants and more exposure to different cultures through work, study, or travel. Ethnic divisions and clashes have tended to be in lower-income inner-city areas, and ethnic tensions tend to focus on cultures that are considerably different from the Australian mainstream, especially among those who show a disinclination to fully integrate into the Aussie way of life. Native English-speaking immigrants generally face some kidding and are sometimes invited into arguments over foreign policy, but Americans and Canadians, for example, face very little trouble on a day-to-day level.

Conversely, Australia has gone to considerable lengths to promote tolerance, even establishing government-funded national television broadcasts in foreign languages that bring in programming from other countries.

Australia does face lingering class divisions that go back to the days of the convicts versus the free settlers. There is a lingering establishment in Australia, primarily comprising Anglo-Saxon Protestants who continue to dominate high-earning or high-visibility professions such as medicine, law, politics, and finance, and who live in highly affluent circumstances and socialize within a tight circle of the right people. The influence of the establishment dwindles on a daily basis, but it remains a fact of life. Expatriates on senior corporate assignments will often gain temporary admission to these groups; at their best, they offer a terrific network to introduce or circulate new ideas and acquaintances. In recent years, an encouraging trend has been that people from a much wider range of cultural and ethnic backgrounds have been gaining access into the so-called Australian elite.

Historically, Australia has been beset not only by issues of tolerance of foreign cultures but of its own indigenous population, which has been the victim of rampant discrimination in past generations. The indigenous Australians, nearly wiped out in the 19th century not only by European diseases but the Europeans themselves, have made a modest comeback in numbers, but their lack of access to education, employment opportunities, and medical care has restricted their presence in the cities, except in lower-income areas. It wasn't long ago that the Australian government issued an apology to the indigenous people for their treatment, and events that recognize the treatment of indigenous people, such as National Sorry Day, have encouraged a growing rapprochement between the cultures. However, this is tough ground for newcomers, and it's best to spend some time here before engaging with this issue in conversation or activity, as it is a sensitive matter that can provoke hostility.

Social Values

Australians are famous for being friendly and outgoing, and generally are not known for their driven work style but rather for their love of family, sports, travel, and time off. While they are often shy around new arrivals, especially those who speak a foreign language, which relatively few native-born Australians do, they are generally happy suburbanites whose great passions in life revolve around sports on Saturday and the Sunday barbecue, and occasionally begrudgingly showing up for work.

Australians have a mild penchant for socialism and a strong interest in social justice and, oddly for such an isolated country, foreign affairs. Aussies are fairly well-read, though academics are respected but rarely beloved as they are not sporty. Trade union membership is three times the level it is in the States, which has been decried as hampering Australia by impeding progress rather than promoting it.

Although everything British is usually belittled and ridiculed, Australian magazines and tabloids are full of stories about the monarchy, and every bit of news on the royal family is quickly spread through gossip. And despite their suspicion of authority, Australians are generally good rule-followers and respectful of conservative social institutions. They are highly secular, with religious participation very low among the general population, and conservative Christian-oriented parties have not gained much traction in national elections. Nationalist anti-immigrant politicians occasionally attract attention, but generally Australians support immigration and new Australians, especially those who exhibit a desire to assimilate into Australian culture.

TALL POPPIES AND A FAIR GO

One of the most important social values bears reiterating: the concept of the fair go. The fair go, or giving someone a chance, is extremely important in Australian culture, and Australians and newcomers who ignore this do so at their peril, whether it applies to family, friends,

Family time in the park is usually on the weekend agenda.

On the Barbie

Australian lamb being barbecued

Along with a beer at the pub with mates and backyard cricket, there probably isn't anything as quintessentially Aussie as the ubiquitous barbecue. Invitation to one of these occasions is akin to being accepted into Aussie culture. If invited, by all means, go, and make sure you dress casually, don't take anything too seriously, and have some fun.

Beef is the traditional Aussie barbecue: sausages, burgers, or steaks; but chicken, lamb, and fish are just as frequently served. The saying "put a shrimp on the barbie" is deemed stereotypically Australian by many foreigners, but its origins are obscure because Australians call them "prawns," not shrimp.

Barbecues typically take place in the late afternoon on Saturday and Sunday, but can be at almost any time on the weekend after 11am. Also barbecued are veggies, often kebab style, including tomatoes, onions, and mushrooms. Typically the beer flows, and a salad is also prepared.

Humorist Eric Bogle put it best in *Aussie Barbecue:*

When the steaks are burning fiercely
When the smoke gets in your eyes
When the snags all taste like fried toothpaste
And your mouth is full of flies
It's a national institution
It's Australian through and through
So come on mate and grab your plate
Let's have a barbecue.

colleagues, or public figures. This concept is connected to the "tall poppy" syndrome, meaning that touting your own accomplishments or not being modest is frowned on. According to gardening wisdom, a poppy that grows too tall needs to be cut down. Public figures have experienced this in the public forum; an actor who recently claimed to have outgrown Australia found herself cut down in the media for weeks.

MATESHIP

Mateship means many things but originates in the era when people had to rely on each other when settling in a hostile land. The term is also discussed in connection to the devastating Gallipoli campaign during World War I that galvanized Australia's national psyche. Today it may involve having a few beers at a barbecue with your mates or leaving the family behind on Saturday to concentrate on sports and fun instead of on obligations. Mateship is fundamental to the Australian way of life, and a basic understanding of it will take you a long way in understanding Australians.

SOCIAL ATTITUDES

A corollary of the tall poppy syndrome is the generally accepted idea that in Australia there are no class distinctions. Although Australia has no traditional aristocracy or a caste system, there are still at least two distinct classes: those who have a solid education and money, lack of thick accent, and tend to succeed in life, attending the "right" schools; and those of the working class, less educated, less fortunate, and a lot more vocal when it comes to cutting down those tall poppies. There are people who work hard to leave their working-class roots behind and send their kids to the "right" schools to get closer to the "better" class. In the media and popular culture, it is clear that there is a distinct disdain for those of the wealthier class; these people get cut down regardless of whether they were born into it or got there through personal achievement. So elements of the tall poppy syndrome reflect the sincere desire of the working class that there really were no class distinctions.

GENDER ROLES

Although Australia was the first Western nation where women could vote and stand for election, in 1902, women are still not quite on an equal footing with men. One of the more recent prime ministers, Julia Gillard, is a woman, as is one of the country's richest people, Gina Rinehart, but as of September 2015, only 40 out of the 150 members of the House of Representatives are women, and of the 76 senators, 29 are female. Recent statistics have shown that although women are just as well educated as men, only 59.5 percent of women participate in the workforce, compared to 71 percent of men. Australia ranks 36th in the World Economic Forum's 2015 Global Gender Gap index, eight ranks behind the United States, out of 145 countries.

Women lead men in university enrollment in Australia at a ratio of 60:40 and are fast approaching parity in professions such as law and medicine. Scientific research is still predominantly male, but the gap is closing fast. As a general rule, professions dominated by women are paid less than professions dominated by men, and there is also a gender gap within professions that reflects the enduring double standard. But things improve each year, and generally women have the same kind of status equality in Australia as in the United States.

In home life many old stereotypes remain, with women primarily looking after health care, children, education, cooking, and cleaning. Progressive homes with better labor sharing are common in the cities, particularly among the younger generation.

LGBTQ+ CULTURE

The attitude toward gay, lesbian, bisexual, transsexual, and queer individuals in Australia is in many ways similar to the attitude in the United States, where there is general acceptance in educated urban

Australia Day

Dressing up for Australia Day is a must.

On January 26 each year, Australians display pride on the day when the first fleet landed in Sydney Harbour bringing the first European settlers to this country. Weeks before, shops go crazy with flags and all sorts of dress-up paraphernalia, including simple hats, facial tattoos of the flag, "thongs" (flip-flops), T-shirts, house decorations, and car stickers. Everything and everyone is decorated in green and gold or draped in the flag, and then there is the party to organize; this is a day to be shared with "mates" (friends). Backyard cricket, a decent barbecue, and plenty of "tinnies" (beer) are a must, along with a good supply of Aussie music: Men at Work's "Land Down Under," John Farnham's "True Blue," INXS, and even Kylie Minogue are on the playlist, together with a group rendition of "Waltzing Matilda" and the chant "Aussie, Aussie, Aussie," answered with "oi, oi, oi."

Each city holds a parade where anyone in the spirit can march, but mostly there are clubs of the countries whose emigrants make up Australia as it is today: Everybody dresses up in their country's traditional garb but carry the Australian flag to show their new allegiance. There are sheepshearing contests, exhibitions of anything from classic cars to indigenous animals, and everybody is out and about in the morning before heading home to party. The evening sees fireworks lighting up the skies, and the cheering, singing, and drinking continue through the night before hangovers are treated with big breakfasts over the long holiday weekend.

areas and diminishing but still common cultural hostility in other regions and demographic groups.

At the time of writing, same-sex marriage is still illegal at the federal level, but all states and territories have a system of same-sex civil unions. Gay and lesbian couples are permitted to adopt children in Western Australia, Tasmania, and the Australian Capital Territory, and allowed to adopt stepchildren in Victoria. Lesbians may legally use assistive reproductive technologies, while gay men can legally use "altruistic surrogacy" in New South Wales, Victoria, Western Australia, and the ACT. Gays and lesbians are allowed to serve in the military. Gender reassignment has been legal nationwide since 2006. In 2013, an Australian community activist who is neither male nor female won an appeals verdict in the Supreme Court of New South Wales that recognized a third sex status for the first time in Australia.

While legal discrimination is fading, gay and lesbian newcomers will face a range of social discrimination similar to the United States. Antigay humor is not acceptable in the mainstream media but lives on at the conversational level, and Aussie tolerance should not be mistaken for active acceptance. In general, Australia tends to be more tolerant than the United States, but some of the political parties oppose the expansion of rights for gays and lesbians and the path to full equality is not yet mapped out.

Australian LGBTQ+ individuals are socially and politically organized and especially visible in Sydney and Melbourne. In Sydney, the heart of the gay scene is Darlinghurst and Paddington on the eastern edge of the CBD, along with the inner west suburbs of Newtown, Erskineville, and Glebe. In Melbourne the primary gay scene is in South Yarra and Windsor, while an alternative gay community thrives in Collingwood and Richmond.

Religion

From the number of churches and faith-affiliated schools around Australia, you would think that Australians are a religious bunch, but that's not necessarily the case. Only 10 percent of the population attends weekly religious services, and about 20 percent say they go monthly. In the United States the number attending weekly religious services is more like 40 percent.

St. Paul's Anglican Cathedral in Melbourne

The main churches in Australia are the Anglican Church (Episcopalian), the Roman Catholic Church, and the Uniting Church (a fusion of Presbyterians, Methodists, and Congregationalists). There are small Jewish, Islamic, and Buddhist communities in the cities, with a large Jewish community in and around Balaclava in Melbourne, where there are Jewish schools, synagogues, and supermarkets selling kosher food. A strong Pentecostal movement is the fastest-growing segment in Australian religious life.

Faith-affiliated schools, however, remain popular in Australia, with roughly 20 percent of schoolchildren attending a private religious school, primarily Roman Catholic. The Presbyterian, Anglican, Lutheran, and Pentecostal churches all operate day schools and some boarding schools.

The Arts

Australia is known around the world as a rugged, outdoorsy, sports-mad country, but there is also a thriving arts scene with literature festivals, people who spend weekends visiting the good selection of art galleries, and film festivals, although they may not have the power or notoriety of some American or European ones. If you are more artsy than inclined to hiking, you will feel at home and have plenty to get interested in.

LITERATURE

Most people will be hard-pressed to name an Australian author, but you may be surprised to hear which well-known authors actually are Australian, including Markus Zusak (*The Book Thief*) and Peter Carey (*Oscar and Lucinda*). Patrick White is the only Australian to have been awarded the Nobel Prize in Literature, but other authors worth reading include Tim Winton (*Cloudstreet*), Steve Toltz (*A Fraction of the Whole*), Kate Grenville (*The Secret River*), Geraldine Brooks (*Years of Wonder*), and, of course, well-known best-selling authors such as Liane Moriarty, Monica McInerney, James Clavell, Thomas Keneally, and Nevil Shute. Both Sydney and Melbourne hold annual Festivals of Literature, when acclaimed writers visit and talk about their work, events that usually sell out. There is the Council of the Arts' Literature Board, encouraging young and new writers, and in Melbourne, for example, the Wheeler Centre is a Victoria government initiative and the centerpiece of Melbourne's designation as an UNESCO City of Literature.

MUSIC

If you are of a certain age, you will know bands such as Midnight Oil, the Bee Gees, the Seekers, Crowded House, Split Enz, AC/DC, and INXS. Then there are Kylie Minogue, Olivia Newton-John, Savage Garden, Delta Godrem, Keith Urban, and plenty more. The variety and spread of musicians reflect the diversity to be found in Australia. New bands are constantly springing up, and programs such as *Australian Idol* and *The Voice,* offshoots of the overseas original versions, are ever popular. Most bands on a world tour schedule a few concerts in Australia, although these tend to concentrate on the larger cities, such as Sydney and Melbourne, but often Perth and Brisbane as well.

FILM

Australia was "discovered" in the 1970s when influential film directors such as Peter Weir, Bruce Beresford, and George Miller arrived on the scene. Weir's *Picnic at Hanging Rock* (1975) started an art-house revolution that brought wide attention to the national film industry, which was receiving government support. Bruce Beresford's *Breaker Morant* was the first Australian film to win widespread acclaim as well as an award at Cannes. The postapocalyptic *Mad Max* introduced Mel Gibson to international audiences, and *Crocodile Dundee* was an international comic hit for actor Paul Hogan. Excellent films such as *Priscilla, Queen of the Desert, Strictly Ballroom,* and *Muriel's Wedding* made people sit up and take note of Australian movies.

Owing to the absence of government financial support for film, budgets are low and work is scarce, and talented actors and producers generally make the move to the United States. Guy Pearce, Cate Blanchett, Toni Collette, Nicole Kidman,

Judy Davis, Geoffrey Rush, Hugh Jackman, and Heath Ledger are among the best-known emigrant Australians, and several of them have won Oscars. Baz Luhrmann (*Moulin Rouge, The Great Gatsby*) and Gillian Armstrong (*My Brilliant Career*) have had notable success in Hollywood.

Sports and Games

There is hardly anything more important in Australia than sports. Whether it is the Olympics, "the footy," the tennis, the Melbourne Cup, a host of other exciting professional events, or just a game of professional or backyard cricket, nothing unites and rivets Australians like sports.

The biggest crowds come out for football, which comes in four flavors—soccer, Rugby Union, Rugby League, and Australian Rules football—to divide the focus. Australian Rules football is the most different from games played in other countries and is the most popular. Aussie Rules is the sport of choice in Melbourne, Perth, and Adelaide; rugby is more popular in Sydney and Brisbane.

The truly unifying national game is cricket, and the 11 members of Australia's national team are household names. It doesn't hurt that Australia has been the dominant force in world cricket for more than a decade, winning four World Cups in 1999, 2003, 2007, and 2015.

Cricket is a relative of baseball and the main summer sport. Innumerable families and kids play backyard cricket, which supplies a stream of players to local clubs, who in turn supply the state teams and the national team. The national team plays five-day matches, called tests, against the top nine other cricketing nations. These events grip the nation on television, radio, or live at legendary cricket grounds such as the MCG (Melbourne), Sydney Cricket Ground, the Gabba (Brisbane), the Wakka (Perth), and the Adelaide Cricket Oval. Cricket and football memoirs are routinely best sellers in Australia.

In addition to the main spectator sports, golf, tennis, surfing, and the Olympics are highly popular, and Australia wins a completely disproportionate number of medals for its population. In 2000 Australia won 58 medals at the Summer Games in Sydney, fourth among all nations and one behind China, which has 60 times Australia's population. Australia has racked up large numbers of medals in almost every Olympics in men's and women's swimming. In 2004 in Athens, Australia again finished fourth; in 2008 the team won 46 medals, coming sixth; but alas in 2012 Australia won 35 medals, coming in 10th place. In Rio in 2016, the Australian team achieved 30 medals, the 8 golds however ranking them once more 10th in the world.

There is a National Sports Academy, and promising young athletes are whisked away for training at an early age. In golf, legends such as Greg Norman, Stuart Appleby, Ian Baker-Finch, and Steve Elkington have been noted winners of major championships, while numerous Australians have achieved tennis fame at Wimbledon and other grand-slam events, including John Newcombe, Margaret Court, Evonne Goolagong, Pat Cash, Patrick Rafter, and Lleyton Hewitt. In Melbourne, the Melbourne Cup horse race is a public holiday, and for years the country has shut down for a few minutes during the running of the race.

To many Australians, personal sports

Sports are an important part of Australian life.

are of far more importance: surfing, skiing, running, windsurfing, sailing, climbing, tennis, golf, and backyard cricket. There is hardly an Aussie who is not involved in some sort of sporting experience, at least in their younger days, and sports are a regular outdoor feature of Australian school life. Many private boys and girls schools make two sports compulsory through year 10 or 11, and Australians are generally relentlessly fit and eager to participate in a wide variety of sporting activities. It is often the glue that holds families and neighborhoods together, if not in participation then at least in cheering for a team. If you are moving to Melbourne, try to pick an AFL team, preferably before you arrive, because you will be asked about it from the moment you touch the ground.

PLANNING YOUR TRIP

A lot of would-be expatriates coming to Australia never get the chance to explore this vast country before they move here. If you get the chance to have a look around and maybe even decide where it is you would like to settle, seize that opportunity and let Australia draw you into its charm, adventure, and beauty. A fact-finding trip, besides providing new impressions, will also make your subsequent move a lot easier and smoother. A few strategies will help you accomplish both.

Virtually all trips to Australia start in Sydney, although a few flights overfly Australia's capital of flash and land in Melbourne, and there are an increasing number of direct flights to Brisbane. Immigrants from Europe to Perth come directly to the west. But 90 percent start in Sydney, where the majority of them stay. Getting to know Sydney is a lot of fun and an excellent introduction to the country no matter where you end up. In most cases, a fact-finding trip should include a stop in Sydney for acclimation purposes before you continue to a second city, if that will be your ultimate destination. For prospective retirees, business investors, or those who are lucky enough to swing it, a month is in order for a full Aussie fact-finding trip, to take in all the potential delights of the cities and countryside.

Preparing to Leave

WHAT TO BRING

Australia is a country so like the United States that first-time arrivals have to make some effort to understand the differences between the two countries.

Electric Converters

Australia runs on 240 volts, which means that appliances made for 110-volt countries such as the United States may not work when plugged into electrical outlets. The shape of the standard plugs is tantalizingly similar but crucially different. Devices that can handle variable voltage, meaning laptops, iPads, or cell phones, need a simple plug adapter, which you can buy at airports or in the travel section of major retailers. For other appliances, check the instruction manual or contact the manufacturer; they may advise you to get a small transformer that steps the voltage down.

Clothing

Outside hotels and major businesses, Australian buildings have fairly rudimentary heating and cooling systems because of the mild climate, and in the extremes of winter or summer there can be episodes of humid heat or cold that can be a bit of a shock for those accustomed to modulated temperature. If you are planning a visit to Australia July-August or January-February, plan to dress in layers. Heavy jackets or parkas are advised if you are coming in the winter months (July-September) and are planning to visit Tasmania or mountain areas, but a leather jacket, a light rain shell, and a cardigan also come in handy. Think "layers" and you can't go too wrong.

Generally, Australian society is highly informal and tolerant when it comes to clothing, so light and casual travel attire is always acceptable as day wear. For restaurants, smart casual is typical. Suits are commonly worn in business settings, although jackets are optional during the summer months.

If you are attending a formal event such as a theater opening night or dining at a very upscale restaurant, suits and cocktail dresses are typical, but casual dress is the norm for most nightlife that caters to travelers.

Sun Protection

When traveling in Australia, be very aware of the sun. There is less ozone in the Southern Hemisphere, and you will burn much faster here. Australia has the highest rate of skin cancer in the world, with more than half the population developing skin cancer by the age of 70; the

a typical electrical outlet in Australia

ATMs are easy to find.

risk is higher for men (2 in 3) than women (3 in 5). When you will be exposed to the midday sun for more than 30 minutes, apply sunscreen, and step up the screening factor above what you are used to. If you typically wear SPF 15, wear SPF 30 in Australia. Also, a good pair of "sunnies" (sunglasses) is a must, and a good hat is strongly recommended. If you feel like assimilating into the Australian look, buy and wear an Aussie Akubra hat, the iconic slouch hat available from Akubra (www.akubra.com)—just leave the Crocodile Dundee corks behind.

Money

The good news for travelers to Australia is that the country is highly adapted to electronic payment systems—more so than just about any country on earth—and establishments of any size will accept credit cards, such as Visa and MasterCard, although less so Amex. ATMs are available in every suburb within a two-block radius of the main train or bus stop, and most shops that cater to travelers accept debit cards.

However, it's always a good idea to carry Australian cash, and you would be well advised to invest in a money holder, because Australian coins are large and heavy compared to those of most other countries. Because there are no $1 or $2 bills, only coins, you can accumulate a lot of change in your pocket. The size of Australian paper money differs depending on the denomination, and the $100 bill is significantly larger than the $5 bill; it will not fit in a standard wallet. If you don't mind a bit of heavy jingle in your pocket, a standard money clip will do just fine for the bills.

If you want to minimize the risk of losing your cards and your cash, try using an international debit card, which you can load with money before your trip. It can also help you stick to a budget.

WHEN TO GO

There are about 300 good days each year to visit Australia; the only times to generally avoid are holiday periods. These include the period between December 25 and around January 20, the heavy summer holiday season: Airfares are high and seats hard to find. The same goes for the Easter holiday, from the Wednesday before Easter through the following Tuesday. The end of January has no airfare bargains, but the excitement of Sydney in late January, when the month-long Festival of Sydney culminates in the Australia Day weekend around January 26, tempts a lot of travelers.

For pure enjoyment of the great weather and minimal crowds, try the period immediately after the Easter holiday or any time in October-November; both are magnificent. The ANZAC Day national holiday on April 25 is a time when a lot of people travel, so tickets are expensive then as well. School holiday schedules differ at public and private schools, and this tends to disperse holiday travel demand during the school holiday months, such as May and September.

Arriving in Australia

VISAS AND PASSPORTS

From a tourist's perspective, obtaining an Australian entry visa is not much trouble, but you do have to remember to obtain a visitor's visa in advance. Travelers from most countries can obtain an Electronic Travel Authority (ETA), which takes about five minutes to get online and costs $20, payable by credit card only (Visa, MasterCard, or Amex). An ETA is equivalent to a visa, but it doesn't appear in your passport. Airline staff will be able to access your record at check-in time. You can apply at www.eta.immi.gov.au if you live in the United States, Canada, or most Western European countries. A full list of eligible nationalities can be found here as well.

If you do not live in an ETA-eligible country, you can find the right office to contact at www.border.gov.au/about/contact/offices-locations, and you will make a traditional visa application through a visa office or an authorized third party. Allow up to one month to process a visa application via the traditional channels.

This will permit you to stay in Australia for up to three months at a time; it is valid for 12 months for multiple stays of up to three months per visit, although you are not allowed to work. If you are planning to combine some business meetings with your fact-finding trip, make sure you apply for the short-validity business ETA, which has the same time frame.

TRANSPORTATION

Taxis

Most first-time visitors arrive in Sydney or Melbourne and take a taxi to their first-night hotel. Taxis are widely available, especially at airports. The cost will be about double what you are used to if you are living in a U.S. city, except perhaps New York, but the trip is short from Sydney's international airport to most hotels in the Central Business District (CBD) or the airport area. In general, taxis are an acceptable and common option to get to and from the airport, costing around $40 for a trip into the city center, but they are less reliable for getting around the city and not as cost effective. It's better to use public transportation if you are not renting a car.

Driving and Renting a Car

Car rental pickups are usually done at the airport, as with most major cities. It's best to book a car through your travel agent, although major global brands such as Avis and Hertz are in most locations. Cars, by

State License Plate Slogans

Old license plates decorate a wall.

You will marvel at all the different license plates you'll see on cars from all over the vast continent, most of them with some slogan promoting the state they are from. There are very old, old, and new slogans, some that only made a brief appearance, and others that even tell you to drive safely. Here is a sample of what you can find on Australia's roads.

- **New South Wales:** First State, The Premier State, Towards 2000, Share the Spirit, Centenary of Federation
- **Victoria:** Garden State, The Place to Be, On the Move, Drive Safely, Nuclear Free State, Vic—Stay Alert Stay Alive
- **Queensland:** Sunshine State, Smart State, Beautiful One Day Perfect the Next
- **Western Australia:** The Real Thing, The Golden State, State of Excitement, Wildflower State, Home of the America's Cup
- **South Australia:** Festival State, Better by Bike, The Wine State, The Defence State, The Creative State, Gateway to the Outback, The Electronics State
- **Tasmania:** Apple Isle, Holiday Isle, Natural State, Your Natural State, Explore the Possibilities
- **Australian Capital Territory:** Nation's Capital, Heart of the Nation, Feel the Power
- **Northern Territory:** Outback Australia, The Never Never, The Difference Is Opportunity

the way, tend to be much smaller outside the United States. You don't need a special driver's license while you are in Australia, but you should familiarize yourself with a few basics for the road.

First of all, Australians drive on the left, and the driver is on the right-hand side of the car, so you have to shift gears with your left hand. It takes a little getting used to, but it sounds harder than it actually is. The pedals are configured the same as in the United States, but the gears are typically reversed, so shift differently when putting the car into reverse in a manual. Save yourself some trouble by getting an automatic transmission, so all you have to focus on is driving on the left. You will find that it is quite easy to follow the flow of traffic while driving, or even changing lanes. The biggest danger is in turning, when you may habitually drift toward the right side of the road, which will put you up against oncoming traffic. It's easy to learn; just make sure you concentrate fully on your turns rather than thinking about directions or the kids in the backseat.

Australia is expressway-challenged, and you will find yourself more often than not on crowded urban arterial roads. It's not too tough, but allow extra time for urban transit.

The other complication is that speed limits and distances are expressed in kilometers per hour (km/h) and kilometers. Generally speaking, you will be driving at 50-60 km/h on city roads, 80 km/h on highways, and up to 130 km/h on expressways. For a quick conversion, halve the miles and multiply by three. But then, your car's speedometer will be in km/h, so just keep an eye on your speed; you'll quickly get used to it.

Private Transportation

Chauffeured private cars are widely available, especially to and from airports, but it is an expensive and unusual way for egalitarian Aussies to get around, and using private cars is not recommended. If you are traveling for a corporate relocation, you may want to use a private car instead of a taxi if you are headed for an outlying suburban corporate headquarters. Stretch limos are very rare; private cars tend to be less conspicuous sedans.

Public Transportation

Statistics show that Australians, at least the city-dwelling ones, use public transportation more than people in most countries, especially those that have a highly decentralized population. Typical options in most cities are buses and light-rail systems, although the coastal cities have ferry systems; Sydney's is an important part of getting around the inner harbor area. In each city, there are multiday transit passes available from ticket offices, usually at main rail and bus stations, and

Driving (and parking!) is on the left.

Public transportation is very efficient in Australia.

these cannot be recommended strongly enough for reducing the cost and aggravation of using public transportation. In Melbourne, for example, you will need to buy a Myki card before you step on any bus or tram (streetcar), as you can no longer buy tickets onboard. Major rail stations and ferry and bus hubs have ticket, route, schedule, and fare information available, but the best way to get information is via each state's transportation authority page, as transit is controlled at the state rather than the metropolitan level.

CUSTOMS

When entering Australia, the old sayings "know before you go" and "if in doubt, throw it out" apply. Don't bring any food, pet products, furs, hazardous materials, cash over $10,000, farm products, or pharmaceuticals you do not have a prescription for or are not clearly over-the-counter. Since Australia has not been exposed to many common Western agricultural pests and diseases, the government is extremely vigilant; it should be taken seriously. A full list of prohibited items is available from **Australian Customs** (www.customs.gov.au). If you are unsure, it is generally a good idea to declare whatever you have on you; you may be allowed to take your item with you.

Your duty-free exemption is $900 worth of goods ($450 for people under age 18), excluding alcohol and tobacco products; 2.25 liters of alcoholic beverages; and a newly reduced limit of up to 50 cigarettes or 50 grams of other tobacco products for travelers age 18 or older.

Sample Itineraries

The vast majority of North American travelers to Australia arrive here from Los Angeles and head to Sydney as their ultimate destination. The best way to explore Australia is to base yourself in a city and explore outlying areas as day trips. If you have two weeks or a month to explore, there are multicity sample itineraries below. For the sake of simplicity, Sydney is used as the base city, but you can substitute any of the other cities fairly easily in the one-week and two-week itineraries. In the one-month itinerary, the complete schedule will take you all around this country-continent that you will soon call home; it provides some unforgettable tourist sights as well as the opportunity to see the prime living locations in some depth and get a feel for the country, its people, its sights, and what it might be like to live here.

Getting There

The flight to Australia is a long one from almost anywhere, and your first day will consist of simply getting here, particularly if you are arriving from Western Europe or the U.S. East Coast. Typical itineraries involve a connection in Los Angeles. Qantas is a good airline to fly on this trip, but Air New Zealand, Air Tahiti Nui, and United also fly this route; Air New Zealand connects via Auckland, and Air Tahiti Nui connects via Papeete. Qantas connects with American Airlines from many major cities nonstop from Los Angeles, so you may not have to face two connections, which take time and drain energy levels. Qantas is also a good way to start acclimating to Australian accents, vocabulary, and etiquette.

If you can fly business or first class, and this is a good time to use those frequent flyer miles you've been saving up, you can use the Admirals Club Lounge at LAX to freshen up, get Internet access, or even take a shower or get a meal, which will help ensure you arrive a little fresher and more enthusiastic than you might otherwise.

Communications

On a fact-finding trip, the first thing to do on landing is to obtain a communications setup, important for keeping in contact with friends and family and for communicating while you are on the go in Australia.

At most airports and in every city center you will find either a **Telstra** or an **Optus** shop where you can pick up a local SIM card that may be compatible with your current cell phone; if your phone is locked, as almost all U.S. cell phones are, they can sell you a phone as well as a SIM card. The SIM card starter set will cost $70-100 and includes a certain amount of free talk time.

There is always **Skype** (www.skype.com) when you have access to the Internet; the connection is generally good from here, although sometimes with a slight time delay. With Skype you can pay for a voice mail account and to receive calls via your PC as well.

ONE WEEK

Days 1-2

On the day of travel, as soon as you are on the plane, set your watch to Sydney time and try and eat and nap accordingly. It may only be a few hours on the plane, but every little bit helps to ensure you arrive without wasting too much time coping with jet lag. However tempting it is to celebrate, try to minimize alcohol intake, unless you think a stiff whiskey might help you go to sleep when your body is not quite ready. Hydrate with plenty of water, and walk up and down the aisles a few times during the flight to keep the impact on your body to a minimum. Fill out your landing cards early in the flight and have them ready with your passport and hotel accommodations printout so that you will have less hassle on arrival.

When traveling to Australia from North America, you cross the international date line, so if you leave the United States on Monday night, you will arrive on a Wednesday morning; it's not a typo that you completely skip Tuesday. Generally speaking, a passenger leaving New York should expect to be on an afternoon flight to Los Angeles and arrive in Sydney the morning after the next day. But don't worry; you'll get your lost day back when you return.

Day 3

Ideally, you want to arrive around early afternoon, so you can manage to stay awake for a few hours before succumbing to sleep. But even if you arrive in the morning, try and stay up all day. This will be tough, but it will help you enormously with jet lag. Westbound jet lag is reportedly not as bad as eastbound, but it depends on the individual, age, fitness level, and how used to travel your body is. Taking it easy and getting your bearings is the goal of today. Upon arrival, make your way to your hotel, which can be in the CBD, giving you the choice and location to go anywhere easily, or, if you have already narrowed down your choice of suburbs, try to find a small boutique hotel there.

Take a stroll around the neighborhood, find a little café, and soak up the atmosphere. Listen to the people around you, people-watch, and get a feel for what age groups and types of people live here. If you feel up to it, stop in at a newsagent to get a weekly pass for the local transportation system, hop on a bus into the CBD, and head straight to the top of the Sydney Tower. This might seem like a very touristy thing to do, but hey, you are a visitor and allowed the odd indulgence, and it will give you an idea of the layout of the city to help you get your bearings. Bring along this book with potential suburbs highlighted on the map in the *Prime Living Locations* section and see where they are in relation to the city center, the harbor, and the surroundings.

If you haven't already, confirm appointments with your potential or definite employer, real estate agents, and schools for the coming days, and then settle for an early dinner near the harbor, take in the views, and then head to the hotel for an early night with a copy of the local *Sydney Morning Herald*—not only to look at real estate listings but also to read local stories and soak up the different ways our language is used.

Day 4

This is a day of action: Ideally you will have set up some appointments with local real estate agents to show you around potential properties and will be meeting with the headmasters of a couple of schools in the corresponding areas. Stop into a local supermarket such as Coles or Woolworths, just to have a look at the products and prices; stop at some furniture and electrical stores to see if shipping all your old stuff is actually worth it; and get some local magazines, such as *Time Out,* at the newsagent to see what's happening in the city and surroundings.

Have lunch and plan coffee stops in the suburbs, maybe near the schools you are visiting, to get a feel for the people and the surroundings; try to imagine yourself living here. Does this suburb suit you? Could you imagine yourself here?

Day 5

Depending on how much you achieved yesterday, you will either need to spend another day in the suburbs or venture a little farther and have a look at the beaches and leisure facilities in Sydney. Hop on the bus to Bondi, have some fish-and-chips by the beach, and watch the surfers and lifeguards doing their thing. Even early in the morning you will see plenty of surfers, as many people try and fit in an hour in the waves before heading off to work. Not a bad way to start the day, is it?

Take a "commute" to Manly from Circular Quay and see if a daily ferry ride might suit you. Don't just saunter along the promenade but go into the side streets, look at the mix of houses and apartments, and imagine living here. It is easy to get swept away with the vacation feeling of Sydney and its surroundings. The sunshine, the beaches, and the many tourists give a slightly skewed view of what it is like to actually live here, with a daily school run, work, shopping, cleaning, and running errands, but try and detach and look beyond your first impression.

Day 6

Today you will venture outside Sydney. You've had a look at the CBD, the suburbs, and the beaches, and now it is time to have a look at the bush surrounding this big city.

It's up to you to decide if you want to rent a car or take the train, but ideally you'll head westward into the Blue Mountains by driving across the western suburbs of Sydney and reach Katoomba, where you might visit the Three Sisters monuments and see a typical mountain town. In the late afternoon, retrace your steps to Sydney. Throughout the expedition, keep the car filled with petrol (gasoline), as there can be long distances between stations in bush areas. Take lots of water and sun protection, look for the typical Australian bush vegetation, smell the eucalyptus trees' fresh aroma, see if you can spot a kangaroo or a koala, and enjoy the day away from the big city.

Day 7

Your journey is done, and you've seen the beach, the city, the bush, and the harbor. Well done! It's back to Sydney's international airport for the flight home. Keep in mind that heading west to east, you pick up a day crossing the international date line, so typically you will arrive in the States "before" you left Australia, according to the calendar. Flights often leave Sydney in the late afternoon or early evening, so you will fly through a shortened night and land in the afternoon of the day you left. Eastbound jet lag is usually deemed worse than westbound, so make sure you are prepared for "light duty" for a few days on your return, as you will feel a little disoriented at night when it's time to sleep.

TWO WEEKS

In this two-week itinerary, the first six days are the same as above, and on day 7 you leave Sydney for Canberra, Melbourne, and a day in "Tassie" (Tasmania) before heading back up the coast to Sydney. An alternative two-week itinerary is to take a week in Sydney followed by a few days on the Gold Coast, if you are considering it as a possible living location.

Day 7

Having spent the first six days duplicating the one-week itinerary by exploring Sydney, on day 7 you head to Canberra. Depending on your budget, you can take a car and drive to Canberra and then on to Melbourne; you can also take short flights between the cities, saving time and maybe money, if you opt for the low-cost carriers—but you will miss out on the scenic, if sometimes long, drive between the cities and all the small diversions that can be found along the way. This itinerary assumes you are happy to drive and are willing to put in the hours.

To Canberra, it's a solid half day's drive directly southwest. A good idea is to pick out a town like Yass along the way to have a typical Aussie lunch or snack. Travel down the "high street" (the main drag) of any small Aussie town and look for a pub with a back garden or a café. The outlying towns are also surprisingly well endowed with fairly good restaurants, offering a mix of light lunchtime snacks from healthy wraps to less-healthy but very yummy traditional savory pies with chips (fries).

You should arrive in Canberra in the late afternoon; there is a wide selection of good hotels in the Civic area. You might try a steak house if you are so inclined, as Canberra is a country town and the beef is quite good. A quick drive around Lake Burley Griffin will complete your initial familiarization.

Day 8

Today is a good day for some basic tourism, as you could use a day away from the car after your drive down to the Australian Capital Territory (ACT). You'll move around the city by car, but you can take in the Australian Parliament and the Australian War Museum or the National Gallery, the highlights in town. Visiting one in the morning and another in the afternoon will provide you with an excellent introduction to Australian culture and history, leaving you some time to meet with real estate agents and visit a school or two along the way. If you have some time, why not pop into the Canberra Mint, where they produce every coin in circulation in Australia?

Day 9

The final day in Canberra should include an exploratory drive around Kingston and Manuka suburbs with a late breakfast outside one of the many cafés, where you can watch the people of different nationalities walk past. With all the diplomatic missions around the city, there is a colorful mix of cosmopolitan living. After lunch, head south toward Melbourne, stopping in the picturesque and historic town of Beechworth for the night.

Day 10

Today, take it easy on the drive along the Hume Highway to Melbourne, but aim to be there in the early afternoon, giving you time for an initial look around the city. Once you have checked in to your hotel, I recommend either setting up a base in the CBD, as this is the ideal place to catch the trams leading out into the suburbs, or in one of your chosen suburbs, in a small and more budget-friendly boutique hotel. Once you have dropped off your car and bags, head up the Eureka Skydeck for a view across the whole of Melbourne, the breathtaking bay, and the surrounding peninsulas. Again, it is perhaps a little touristy, but you will get a feel for the city and its layout much better from above. Head out for dinner in one of the picturesque and hidden laneways, and take in the cultural buzz that is Melbourne.

Day 11

If you have made appointments to see houses and schools, this is the day for it. Check out the suburbs, walk along Chapel Street for some excellent shopping, and then have coffee or lunch in either Prahran, South Melbourne, or Victoria Markets, scouting these out as potential fresh produce shopping venues. Spend the late afternoon sauntering along the Yarra River or indeed St. Kilda

Beach, and maybe catch the penguins on St. Kilda Pier after sunset.

Day 12

Depending on the season and the day of the week, you may be able to catch a game or other sporting event at VFL Park for Aussie Rules football, the Melbourne Cricket Ground for cricket, the Flemington Racecourse for the iconic Melbourne Cup horse race or another daily event, or Melbourne Park for Australian Open tennis. In the early evening, hop on a local flight to Hobart, which will take you to the capital of Tasmania in less than an hour.

Day 13

Hobart is small and compact, and with a rented car it takes mere minutes to explore all the suburbs on a quick drive-through, allowing for breakfast and lunch stops along the way. While in the north, pop into the famed Museum for Old and New Art (MONA) and then spend the afternoon and evening exploring the small CBD and the picturesque fishing harbor, finishing with dinner in one of the many restaurants along Salamanca Place.

Day 14

You will be heading back to Sydney and the States today, but if it is Saturday, make sure you grab a quick bite at one of the many local produce stands at Salamanca Market before heading off to the airport. With many daily flights from Hobart to Sydney, there will be plenty of time to connect to your flight back home and a well-deserved rest on the flight; you have been to four states and four capitals this past week and have managed to get a brief overview of the many facets that make up Australia. Which one was your favorite?

ONE MONTH

On this itinerary, add on two extra weeks to the 14-day trip described above. Starting at day 14, you will visit the rest of Australia by plane, as there are vast distances to cover. You will take in not only the great living locations of the north and west but also a little extra tourism to the center of Australia at Alice Springs, home to the mysterious Uluru monolith.

Day 14

Instead of heading back home, in this itinerary you will go from Hobart directly to Brisbane. It's quite a scenic flight; try to get a window seat on the left side of the aircraft on the way north, as the views are generally better looking toward the land. On arrival in Brisbane, a taxi into the city is relatively expensive, so instead rent a car to use later to head down the Gold Coast. The late afternoon and evening of your arrival are spent strolling along the Brisbane River, taking in the sights in the CBD.

Day 15

This is your Brisbane exploration day, so your car will be heavily used. Take in some of the suburbs, planning a breakfast in Paddington, and then head northeast toward the airport and up the Bruce Highway toward the Sunshine Coast, stopping in Maroochy for some shopping. Swing back to the southwest and take in the classic northern suburbs. After lunch, head back briefly into the city to have lunch on James Street, and then out toward the Gold Coast along the Pacific Motorway, an hour south of the city, just in time for the evening meal.

Days 16-17

Two days at the Gold Coast are a must for some pure relaxation after all the running around. There are nearly 70 kilometers of exquisite beaches, with golf and casinos to add to the excitement. But sitting under an umbrella in the sun and dipping occasionally in the ocean might be just what you need, thinking through all the impressions you've accumulated so far. Meanwhile, in your daily walk or ride to the beach, you can pick up some real estate brochures to study between waves.

Days 18-19

Either fly to Cairns or take the overnight ***Sunlander* train** (www.railaustralia.com.au/sunlander.php) and pick out a Great Barrier Reef cruise from businesses such as **Reef Trip** (http://reeftrip.com) to take in the Great Barrier Reef with some classic snorkeling and diving options. The best way to see the reef is to stay overnight on a catamaran, but if you are on a budget, stay at a local hotel and take a day trip to the reef. More ideas on how to spend your time along the Great Barrier Reef can be found in the Moon guide Sydney & the Great Barrier Reef. In the evening, fly back to Brisbane.

Day 20

Today is essentially a travel day as you fly all the way to Australia's southwest coast; the five-hour flight will take up most of the day, even though you pick up two hours by flying west. Head to the beach section in Perth. Cottlesloe Beach is unbeatable for long white stretches of sand and views over Rottnest Island on the horizon. Check in to your hotel and spend the evening relaxing, as you've had hard "yakka" (work) the past few days.

Days 21-22

Your two days in Perth include a day by car exploring the environs of the city, particularly the north side of the Swan River and heading west from the CBD toward the beach suburbs. If you have made property, work, and school appointments, these are the days for those, and if you find some free time, pay a visit to historic Freemantle, which offers a lovely town center and port. On the second day, indulge in a Swan River wine cruise, which will stop in at a few wineries and is a lot of fun. Check out Captain Cook Cruises at www.captaincookcruises.com.au to arrange the cruise into the Swan Valley.

Days 23-24

In the early morning, it's over to the airport to catch the first flight to Adelaide. You'll spend two days here, with one day for exploring the suburbs, especially the western suburbs in the beach areas, and one day to visit the Adelaide Parklands, which form one of the most extensive urban park systems in the world. It's a good place to pick up some more exposure to sports, either with Aussie Rules football or cricket at the Adelaide Cricket Oval, depending on the season.

Days 25-26

The morning of day 25, head out to the Adelaide Airport and catch the first flight to Alice Springs. From there, visit Alice Springs and Uluru. While many people still think it's a great idea to climb Uluru, others think that you shouldn't; not only is it a sacred site to indigenous people, but also the views are not really that exciting. The exciting thing in this desert landscape is the view of the rock itself. So settle down and look at it at different times of the day. On day 26, if you are feeling ambitious, take a bus trip to the Olgas rock formations, which are eerie and magnificent. Alternatively, if you are not sick of flying quite yet, treat yourself to a helicopter flight across Uluru and the Olgas, or why not explore the area on a camel?

Day 27

Today you fly back to Sydney, and with an afternoon arrival, you can choose whether you want to head out to the beach, maybe climb the Harbour Bridge, do some shopping, or double-check on a suburb or two. Pick a hotel fairly close to the airport and take a taxi to your location of choice, or take public transit such as the express train to the CBD from the airport. You'll be the one to choose between a quiet meal near the hotel or something more adventurous by the water. If the weather is cooperative, try to make sunset at the Sydney Opera House the last thing on your list, as the sight of the sun going down behind the Harbour Bridge is just the image you want to keep in your head when you are back at home going through the hassle of moving.

Day 28

Return home, as detailed in the one-week and two-week itineraries.

Practicalities

ACCOMMODATIONS AND FOOD

Sydney

For an unforgettable stay, visit the **Park Hyatt** (7 Hickson Rd., The Rocks, tel. 02/9256-1234, http://sydney.park.hyatt.com), situated right below the Sydney Harbour Bridge with rooms overlooking the Opera House. Rooms start at $785 per night. For a family apartment option, try the **Goldsbrough Apartments** (243 Pyrmont St., tel. 02/9518-5166, www.oakshotelsresorts.com/Oaks-Goldsbrough) overlooking Darling Harbour. Centrally located and convenient, they offer more space than a hotel room, plus a kitchen for around $118 for a studio.

For a special occasion, go straight to **Quay** (Upper Level, Overseas Passenger Terminal, The Rocks, tel. 02/9251-5600, www.quay.com.au), voted one of the best restaurants in Australia. Overlooking the harbor, the food is simply superb. For a slightly less exclusive meal, don't miss **Mongers** (42 Hall St., Bondi Beach, tel. 02/9365-2205, http://mongers.com.au), an excellent fish-and-chips shop on Bondi Beach. Get the tempura prawns and eat them on a bench overlooking the beach.

Melbourne

For a luxurious inner-city stay with easy access to everywhere and views of the river, stay at **The Langham** (1 Southgate Ave., Southbank, tel. 03/8696-8888, http://melbourne.langhamhotels.com.au), from $295. Alternatively, get to know life in the suburbs and stay at the lovely **Georgian Court Bed & Breakfast** (George St., tel. 03/9415-8225, www.georgiancourt.com.au), with rooms starting at $85.

Have a sumptuous late breakfast at **8Days Café** (1184 High St., Armadale, tel. 03/9500-9711, www.8dayscafe.com.au), a light Japanese lunch at **Hako** (310 Flinders Ln., tel. 03/9620-1881), and a romantic dinner at **Café Di Stasio** (31 Fitzroy St., tel. 03/9525-3999, www.distasio.com.au), a tiny but superb Italian restaurant in St. Kilda, a stone's throw from the beach.

Brisbane and the Queensland Coast

For a luxury stay in the heart of Brisbane's shopping and dining mecca, Fortitude Valley, choose the **Emporium** (1000 Ann St., tel. 07/3253-6999, www.emporiumhotels.com.au), from $319. Have breakfast at **The Kettle & Tin** (2150 Given Ter., tel. 07/3369-3778) in fashionable Paddington, and dine at **Il Centro** (Eagle Street Pier, 1 Eagle St., tel. 07/3221-6090, www.il-centro.com.au).

If you are traveling up north to the Sunshine Coast, don't miss this gem of a bed-and-breakfast overlooking the Glass House Mountains: **Glass on Glasshouse** (182 Glass House-Woodford Rd., Glass House Mountains, tel. 07/5496-9608, www.glassonglasshouse.com.au), from $280 for two people.

Canberra

The five-star **East Hotel** (69 Canberra Ave., Kingston, tel. 02/6295-6925, www.easthotel.com.au) in Kingston is centrally located near the shops of Kingston and Manuka, as well as the government districts and museums, from $177. Alternatively, head south to Tuggeranong and find a spacious apartment in the new **Abode Hotel** (150 Anketell St., Tuggeranong, tel. 1300/122-633, www.abodehotels.com.au), which costs from $105.

For dining and a bit of predinner jazz, head to **Sage Diningrooms & Mint Garden Bar** (Gorman House Arts Centre, Batman Street, tel. 02/6249-6050, www.sagerestaurant.net.au), offering modern fusion cuisine, while **My Café In Manuka** (1/22-30 Franklin St., Griffith, tel. 02/6295-6632) is a perfect spot for breakfast or lunch plus a lot of people-watching and some after-lunch shopping.

For your overnight stay in Beechworth, go to **The Old Priory** (8 Priory Ln., Beechworth, tel. 03/5728-1024, www.oldpriory.com.au), an enchanting place that offers great value for money in a lovely setting with rooms from $70.

Hobart

For a perfect location and quirky history, head straight for the **Henry Jones Art Hotel** (25 Hunter St., Hobart, tel. 03/6210-7700, www.thehenryjones.com), by the fishing harbor, an old jam factory now completely refurbished and brimming with modern art, from $210. Alternately, head for the **Old Woolstore Apartments** (1 Macquarie St., Hobart, tel. 03/6235-5355, www.oldwoolstore.com.au), which offer a little more space for your money with just as much quirky history, for around $160.

For food, I highly recommend **Ethos** (100 Elizabeth St., Hobart, tel.

the Henry Jones Art Hotel in Hobart

Mealtime

Aussies eat breakfast and lunch at the same time as Americans do, although the portions are usually smaller. Aussies tend to eat more but smaller meals, although work life imposes a three-meal regimen on an increasing percentage of the population.

The morning break at work is not universal, but almost. Traditionally tradesmen called it a "smoko," but that word has all but died out. "Morning tea" or simply "tea" is served in offices and homes and consists of tea, coffee, and sometimes small cookies ("biscuits"). At primary schools it is often called "play lunch," and cakes such as lamingtons are typically served, along with juice. On the weekend, morning tea is often called "elevenses" and can include alcoholic beverages.

Afternoon tea is served in the "arvo" (AH-vo, meaning afternoon) and less common nowadays except for with hungry school-age kids, who will consume snack foods, dried fruit, and perhaps a "Milo" (mixed chocolate milk).

"Tea time" in Australia is not a time for tea; it is the evening meal, called "supper" or "dinner" in the United States, and also called "dinner" by an increasing number of Aussies. It is similar to the U.S. evening meal except that Aussies eat more meat than mainstream Americans and go easier on the pastas and breads. Some Aussies also cling to the tradition of a late supper, which can mean milk and biscuits, or other light fare, usually eaten just before bedtime or later in the evening.

03/6231-1165, www.ethoseatdrink.com) for unique takes on fresh and local produce and **Jack Greene Bar** (47-48 Salamanca Place, Battery Point, Hobart, tel. 03/6224-9655) for the best burgers in town.

Southwestern Australia

A hotel in a historic building offering short- and long-term rooms with access to kitchens and other day-to-day amenities right in Adelaide's CBD is **Adabco Boutique Hotel** (223 Wakefield St., tel. 08/8100-7500, www.adabcohotel.com.au), with rooms from $90. For some modern local Australian cuisine, complete with kangaroo steak and seafood from the coast all paired with local wines and overlooking the river, try **Red Ochre Grill** (War Memorial Dr., North Adelaide, tel. 08/8211-8555, www.redochre.com.au).

In Perth, for a unique and historic nonchain option, stay at the **Terrace Hotel** (237 St. George's Ter., tel. 08/9214-4444, www.terracehotelperth.com.au), a lovingly restored 1892 building centrally located in the CBD, from $180. For longer stays, families, or simply because you'd like more space and a kitchen, the CBD's **Fraser Suites Perth** (10 Adelaide Ter., tel. 08/9261-0000, http://perth.frasershospitality.com) are ideal. Services apartments have several room options, complete with living room and kitchen facilities, from $150 for a studio.

Eat out at the quirky and award-winning **Greenhouse** (100 St. George's Ter., tel. 08/9481-8333, www.greenhouseperth.com), or try the deli-wine bar-bistro **The Beaufort Local** (488 Beaufort St., tel. 08/9328-6299, www.beaufortmerchant.com) in fashionable Mount Lawley.

DAILY LIFE

MAKING THE MOVE

When we finally got the call that our visa to Australia had come through, we cracked open a bottle of bubbly. After months of filling out forms, answering awkward questions, numerous health checks, and copying and scanning countless documents, we felt we had conquered the mountain and had reached the summit. We were finally legal and allowed to move on to the next step of our adventure.

Considering Australia is a country of immigrants, with its original people, the Aborigines, only making up 2 percent of the population and the remainder either new immigrants or the descendants of earlier immigrants, you would think Australia would be an easy country to migrate to. Not so. After an initial flurry of allowing pretty much anybody into the country and even encouraging and paying them to come to the land Down Under after World War II—including the now famous "£10 Poms," assisting migrants not only from Britain who were encouraged to come and live in Australia—now the borders are tightly shut and numbers strictly controlled. Between 2014 and 2015 net overseas migration reflected an annual gain of 168,200 persons, 9.8 percent less than in 2013 to 2014, with the majority of immigrants coming from the UK and the majority of that quota going to the skilled immigrant sector.

Unless you hold a New Zealand passport, everyone needs a visa to get into Australia, and that is where it becomes complicated. I tried to count the number of different visas available to would-be immigrants and failed. With dozens of subsections for each visa, trying to understand the Australian visa system is a little like higher calculus—not impossible for some, but utterly mind-blowing to most of us. Here are some general guidelines that will make at least the gist of it a little clearer. It all depends on what it is you want to do in Australia.

Visas and Immigration

If you are just coming over temporarily to have a look, it's easy. If you hold a U.S. passport, you can get an Electronic Travel Authority (ETA) online via www.eta.immi.gov.au; it takes a few minutes and is valid for 12 months, allowing you to stay in Australia for up to three months once you have entered.

If you want to migrate longer term to work and you already have a job offer, or you have professional skills that are much sought after in Australia, such as those of a doctor, nurse, or engineer, it's also relatively easy, with either your employer sponsoring you and your family or you qualifying under the General Skilled Migration Program, the Employer Nomination Scheme, the Regional Sponsored Migration Scheme, or the SC457 Long Term Temporary Business Visa. If you have the skills and funding and the intention of buying or starting up your own business, your options are the Business Innovation and Investor Visa or the Business Talent Visa.

If you are coming to Australia in order to further your studies and are going to school, university, or a postgraduate research facility, you can apply for the Student Visa Program, which has several subsections covering the higher education sector, English-language intensive courses, primary or secondary school, and vocational training. Depending on the type of study, you may also be allowed in on a Visitor or Tourist Visa.

Under the Visitor Visa umbrella, you find the Working Holiday Visa, which allows, for example, students on a gap year to spend up to six months in the country doing light labor; the Investor Retirement Visa; and the Medical Treatment Visa.

If you are accompanying family, or you already have relatives in Australia who are willing to sponsor you, there are the Partner Visa and the Family Visa.

If you would like to set up home permanently in Australia and would like a Residency Visa, that can be achieved once you are in the country on a Long Term Business Visa and have worked for a couple of years in a Specified Regional Area. The process of obtaining permanent residency is very drawn out and can take months or even years; it is best done while here.

All Australian visa applicants must satisfy health and character requirements. The points table has recently been relaxed, but basically scores you higher points for younger age, better English language skills, higher professional experience, and academic achievements.

Visa fees vary widely and range from a mere $20 for a Visitor ETA to several hundred dollars for a long-term visa for the entire family. The fees change regularly, but up-to-date fees can be confirmed

Available Visa Programs

General Skilled Migration Program: The Skilled Independent Visa (Subclass 189) is a permanent work visa for individuals who have the qualifications and skills required to fill Australia's skill shortages. Applicants are required to obtain a minimum of 60 points on a point assessment. The assessment is such that applicants are required to be under 50 years of age and able to demonstrate that they have a qualification or skills in an occupation on the Skilled Occupation List (SOL). This visa does not require sponsorship.

Employer Nomination Scheme: The Skilled Nominated Visa (Subclass 190) is a permanent work visa for individuals who have the qualifications or skills that are needed by the Australian economy, but cannot meet the pass mark required to obtain a Skilled Independent Visa. Sixty points are required together with a nomination from a participating state or territory government.

Regional Sponsored Migration Scheme: Skilled Regional Sponsored Visa (Subclass 489) applicants must be prepared to live for two years and work for at least 12 months in a Specified Regional Area of Australia. A Skilled Regional Sponsored Visa is valid for up to four years and provides a pathway to permanent residency. You will need a minimum of 60 points and must either obtain sponsorship from an eligible relative living in a Specified Regional Area of Australia or nomination from a participating state or territory government.

457 Temporary Business Visa: The Australian 457 Visa (Temporary Business Long Stay) is a temporary work visa that allows employers to sponsor overseas workers to fill nominated skilled positions. The 457 Visa is currently the most common pathway of business sponsorship for overseas workers. Employers must meet specific sponsorship and nomination steps before the prospective employee can apply for a 457 Visa. This visa is valid for up to four years and work experience gained in Australia on this visa may lead to permanent residency either through sponsorship by an eligible employer or the General Skilled Migration Program.

Business Innovation and Investment Visa: The Australian Business Innovation Stream (Provisional) Visa is valid for four years, and visa holders may be eligible to apply for permanent residence after meeting the obligations of their provisional visa for at least two years. The Australian Business Innovation Stream Visa is a temporary visa for successful business owners who are under the age of 45. Applicants are required to demonstrate a successful business career with significant turnover and a commitment to owning a business in Australia. Applicants are required to submit a detailed business proposal with their visa application and demonstrate that they have sufficient assets to settle in Australia.

Applicants over 45 years of age but under 55 may qualify for the State/Territory Sponsored Business Owner (Provisional) Visa, which has a lower financial threshold. All applicants are required to lodge an Expression of Interest (EOI) and score at least 65 on the innovation points test.

Business Talent Visa: This visa requires state or territory government sponsorship. The Business Talent Visa is a permanent visa for the highest caliber of businesspeople

online at www.border.gov.au/Trav/Visa/Fees.

REQUIREMENTS FOR VISAS

Health and Character Checks

If you are applying for permanent residency or a long-term visa, you will need medical examinations and a "character" test. All applicants plus their spouses and dependents will be required to undergo an eye test, chest X-ray for those age 11 and older, an HIV test for those age 15 and older, and a TB screening for who are under the age of 55 and have sponsorship from a state or territory government. Applicants must be able to demonstrate that they have a successful business career and that their main business generated a minimum turnover of $3 million for at least two of the preceding four years. Applicants are required to submit a detailed business proposal with their visa application and demonstrate that they have sufficient assets to settle in Australia.

Retirement Visa: The Australian Investor Retirement Visa is a temporary visa that allows self-funded retirees to invest and spend up to four years in Australia. In order to qualify for an Australian Investor Retirement Visa, applicants must be over 55 years of age and have no dependents other than a spouse. Applicants must be self-supporting and be willing to make a significant long-term financial investment in Australia. Applicants require sponsorship from a participating state or territory government and will be required to make a designated investment in that sponsoring state or territory. The investment amount varies depending on where the applicant settles, and a reduced investment is available to applicants who settle in a regional area of Australia.

Working Holiday Visa: The Australia Working Holiday Visa gives visitors from certain countries casual work rights in order to supplement their travels. Work undertaken must be incidental to the main purpose of holidaying, and employment for more than six months with any one employer is not allowed. The application for a Working Holiday Visa must be made prior to reaching Australia.

STUDENT VISA SCHEMES

Higher Education: International students who have been accepted to study in a registered bachelor's degree, associate's degree, graduate certificate, graduate diploma, or master's by coursework are required to hold an Australian Higher Education Student Visa.

English Language Students: International students who have been accepted to study in a registered English language course in Australia are required to hold an Australian English Language Study (ELICOS) Visa.

Primary/Secondary School: International primary and secondary school-age students who have been accepted to study in a primary school course, a secondary school course, or an approved secondary school exchange program are required to hold an Australian School Student Visa.

Vocational Training: International students who have been accepted to study in a registered Certificate I-IV (except ELICOS) course, diploma, advanced diploma, vocational graduate certificate, or a vocational graduate diploma are required to hold an Australian Vocational Training Student Visa.

Postgraduate Research: International students who have been accepted to study in a registered master's degree by research or a doctoral degree are required to hold an Australian Postgraduate Research Student Visa.

those age 11 and older. Any serious long-term illness or condition in the applicant or dependents that would require special treatment or special schooling may disqualify you from the process.

In addition, police checks for the main applicant are necessary to prove that you are of "good character." You will need to provide a police certificate for each country you have lived in for a period of 12 months or longer in the last 10 years or since the age of 16.

Values Statement

Once you have proven that you are physically fit and of good character, applicants age 18 and older will also be required to sign a values statement when applying for selected visas. The statement requires applicants to confirm that they will respect the Australian way of life and obey the laws of Australia before being granted a visa. There are two different values statements. All provisional, permanent, and a small number of temporary visa applicants are required to have read or had the information contained in it explained to them before signing the values statement. This information is contained in the ***Life in Australia* book** (www.border.gov.au/Trav/Life/Aust/Living-in-Australia-values-statement-long). For all other temporary visa applicants, the Australian Values Statement is included in the general declaration section of their application form.

TAX CONSIDERATIONS

Australia has a complicated and intricate taxation system, where your residence status, together with your income and your country of origin, dictates whether or not and how much tax you will have to pay in Australia—and back home. Very generally speaking, if you are a resident, permanent or temporary, you will have to pay tax in Australia. But you may well qualify for a refund or a benefit called FEI (Foreign Earned Income). As all the factors differ from individual to individual, you should check with a specialist and your future employer before you set out.

Moving with Children

SCHOOLS AND THE SCHOOL CALENDAR

The biggest difference between the Australian school system and those in the Northern Hemisphere is the academic year: The school year starts in late January or early February and ends in December, for the summer holidays. There are two semesters, four terms, with a six-week break over Christmas, and three two- to three-week breaks between terms. Students attend school from Monday to Friday each week, with many schools having compulsory team sports events on Saturday mornings. School hours vary slightly across Australia but are generally from 8:30am to 3:30pm each school day.

Schooling in Australia, compulsory from age 5 to age 15 or 17, depending on the state you live in, starts with a kindergarten or preparatory year followed by 12 years of primary and secondary school. In the final year of secondary school, year 12, children study for a government-endorsed certificate that is recognized by all Australian universities and vocational education and training institutions, and which is a combination of exams and continuous assessment scores. This Senior Secondary Certificate of Education is also recognized by many international universities.

In addition, there are a number of government and private schools in Australia offering the International Baccalaureate (IB), a two-year pre-university curriculum for students age 16 to 19. For expatriates and children who may want to attend university back in the United States or elsewhere abroad, this is generally the more widely recognized option.

The vast majority of schools have uniforms, in both state-run schools and private schools. There are a number of

a school outing

private schools in each larger city, all charging fees according to the level, with higher years associated with more expensive fees. Also, if you are on a 457 temporary resident visa, you will have to pay a set fee for public schools. Only permanent residents get government schooling for free.

Usually expats have no control over when they have to move, and really there is no right or wrong time to start in an Australian school. If you do have a choice, take each child's history, level, nature, and flexibility into account. If they are young, it really doesn't matter that much, and they can enjoy school at any level, as long as it is not too boring or too demanding, considering that they are also coping with adjusting to a new life. If they are in the middle of an important stretch of schooling back home, consider whether they should finish it, whether it will benefit them just in case your stay in Australia is cut short and your child has to return to your home country's school system at short notice. Talk to the Australian school; they are quite used to newcomers and have plenty of advice on how best to slot them into the new system. Think about how long you are going to stay, whether the children are likely to finish school in Australia, or whether you are going to move again before they have completed specific milestones. Starting children at the right-for-you time, in the right school, and with the right frame of mind is a battle when moving countries. Take your time with the decision.

PREPARATIONS AT HOME

To ease children into a move abroad is not easy, especially if they have never moved before. They are going to lose their world, all their friends, their comfort zone, everything they know and love apart from you, and maybe even the family pet. Absolutely everything is going to be new to them.

Having moved countries five times with our daughter, I have found that it helped a lot when she knew someone in the new country—if not personally, then virtually. Nowadays, most people use Facebook, Twitter, or blogs, and they are a great way to meet potential friends. On several occasions I have found people on expat forums and asked them if they knew families with children of a similar age at the school my daughter was going to be attending, and I

The Points Table

The General Skilled Migration Self-Assessment test is a useful way to calculate your approximate score in the Skilled Migration Points test. This version dates to January 2013.

Visa applied for:

- Skilled Independent Subclass 189—no sponsorship required. You must have an occupation on the new Skilled Occupations List: 0 points
- Skilled Nominated Subclass 190—requires nomination by a state or territory government. You must have an occupation on the State/Territory Nominated Skilled Occupations List: 5 points
- Skilled Nominated or Sponsored Subclass 489—requires sponsorship by a relative living in a designated area or a state or territory government: 10 points

Age:

- 18-24: 25 points
- 25-32: 30 points
- 33-39: 25 points
- 40-44: 15 points
- 45-49: 0 points
- Under age 18 and over age 50 do not meet criteria.

English language skills:

- Less than competent English-speakers are not eligible
- Competent English, scoring 6+ in all 4 components of IELTS, or a passport from the United Kingdom, the United States, Ireland, Canada, or New Zealand: 0 points
- Proficient English, scoring 7+ in all 4 components of IELTS, or an OET B Pass: 10 points
- Superior English, scoring 8+ in all 4 components of IELTS, or an OET A Pass: 20 points

Overseas work experience: How long you have worked in your nominated occupation in the last 10 years?

- 8 years or more: 15 points
- 5 years or more: 10 points
- 3 years or more: 5 points
- Less than 3 years: 0 points

Australian work experience: How long you have worked in your nominated occupation in the last 10 years in Australia?

- 8 years or more: 20 points

- 5 years or more: 15 points
- 3 years or more: 10 points
- 1 year or more: 5 points
- Less than 1 year: 0 points

Qualifications:

- Recognized PhD: 20 points
- Recognized bachelor's degree or higher: 15 points
- Recognized trade qualification, including diploma or trade certificate completed at an Australian educational institution, or other award or qualification recognized by the skills assessing authority: 10 points

Australian educational qualification: Do you meet the requirements for the award of a degree, diploma, advanced diploma, or trade qualification that took at least two years of full-time study in Australia at an Australian institution, which are relevant to your nominated occupation and which were taught in English?

- Yes: 5 points

Professional year: Have you completed a professional year in Australia in your occupation following your studies (currently available for accountants, engineers, and IT professionals)?

- Yes: 5 points

Study in regional Australia or a low population growth area: Do you meet the requirements for the award of degree, diploma, advanced diploma, or trade qualification and (1) the qualification was not in English language proficiency, (2) the qualification took at least two years of full-time study in Australia, (3) the qualification was taught in English, (4) the campus of your institution is in a regional or low population growth area, (5) you have spent at least two years living in the regional or low population growth area, (6) you did not complete the qualification via distance education?

- Yes: 5 points

Designated language: Are you accredited as a paraprofessional interpreter or translator (level 2) by the National Accreditation Authority for Translators and Interpreters?

- Yes: 5 points

Partner skill qualifications: Is your partner under age 50, has competent English skills, and can pass skills assessment in an occupation on the applicable Skilled Occupations List for your subclass?

- Yes: 5 points

Support Organizations for Homesick Americans

There are a number of organizations where Australians and Americans meet up, and when you arrive, joining one is just about the best move you can make. The associations organize celebrations on U.S. holidays, education support for expat children (including courses on U.S. history and geography that expat kids will miss out on), and discounted tickets for "home leave" travel. Sometimes a friendly person who has "been through it" is just the friend you need, whether it's finding food ingredients, meeting business contacts, or just coping with the wonders of life in a strange land.

In most cities, the American Chamber of Commerce in Australia maintains an office and provides a valuable source of business contacts as well as opportunities for civic activities. The Australian American Association is in most cities, although in Sydney the American Society has traditionally been just as lively. In Sydney, the American Club on Macquarie Street counts mostly Australians among its members, but it has incredible views, great dining, and boardroom facilities. Each Thanksgiving, they serve a traditional turkey dinner—they provide the food, and you provide your Yankee, Yozzie, or Yank-curious Australian friends and family and carve a turkey they prepare. It's a lot of fun.

Also try these expat websites for contacts with others in the same situation:

- InterNations (www.internations.org)
- Sydney Womens International Club (https://swic.org.au)
- Sydney Americans (www.meetup.com/sydney-expat-americans/)
- ExpatForum.com (www.expatforum.com)
- Expat Arrivals (www.expatarrivals.com)
- American Australian Association (www.americanaustralian.org)
- American Women's Club of Perth (https://awcperth.com)
- Brisbane Women's Club (www.bwc.org.au)
- American Women's Auxiliary (www.awamelbourne.org)

usually found someone. When she turned up for her first day, she was looking for a specific person, someone she had already emailed with before, and someone who would, at least for the first day, look after her. Some of these initial friends turned into good friends, others went away, but overall, my daughter was not as stressed and worried as she might have been without already knowing someone.

You can also get pictures of the house you are going to live in, if you have one secured already. If you haven't, allow the children to design a flexible layout for their new home. Discuss colors and design ideas, and make concessions on an exciting toy, furniture, or poster for the room—something they can look forward to having once they move.

Look at websites together and learn as much as you can about your new destination. Make plans together, and discuss where you are going to go as soon as you get there, what you are going to see. Perhaps plan a visit to the nearest zoo as soon as you arrive to see the koalas and kangaroos. Maybe learn a few new key phrases, even if it is just "G'day, mate." Get the children excited about their new home, and treat it as an adventure rather than a challenge. If your children do not have a Facebook or email account yet, set one up with them so that they can keep in touch with all their friends from back home, regardless of the distance. They will have days when they will need to talk or cry to some of their friends rather than you.

Moving with Pets

Obviously you want to bring the dog or the cat. After all, they belong to the family. But this being Australia, it is not as simple as sticking kitty in the pet carrier and putting her on a flight. Australian animals have no resistance to the dreaded rabies virus, so the import rules are extremely strict, with numerous requirements before they're allowed to accompany you.

ELIGIBILITY AND VET CHECKS

Not all pets are allowed to enter Australia. You can bring cats and dogs, as long as they are older than six months and not of a restricted breed, such as a pit bull or other fighting-dog variant. Smaller critters such as hamsters, goldfish, turtles, and guinea pigs will have to stay behind. If you are moving to Australia from New Zealand, you are allowed to import certain exotic birds and even rabbits. Horses are allowed from a number of qualifying countries, but not from everywhere.

All pets must be microchipped as a means of identification, and it needs to be a microchip that can be read by an Avid, Trovan, Destron, or other ISO compatible readers. The microchip must be implanted before any further health and rabies testing takes place. Once the chip is in place, a vet can do rabies testing. The animal will have to have an up-to-date rabies vaccination within 12 months of moving to Australia. The vet who carries out the Rabies Neutralising Antibody Titre Test (RNAT) and completes the RNAT Declaration of the application form for an Australian Quarantine and Inspection Service (AQIS) import permit needs to be government approved in whatever country they are residing in. This test must be done at least 60 days and at most 12 months prior to your move. According to AQIS, 180 days must elapse from the date that the blood is sampled for the RNAT

It is possible, but complicated, to bring your family dog to Australia.

test (with a satisfactory result) before the animal can be released from quarantine in Australia.

APPLYING FOR A PERMIT TO IMPORT

Then, your animal needs a Department of Agriculture, Fisheries, and Forestry (DAFF) import permit. You can obtain and complete the permit online at www.daff.gov.au/aqis/cat-dogs/application, making sure you attach the following documentation: the RNAT Declaration signed and stamped by an official U.S. or Canadian government-certified veterinarian; the RNAT Laboratory Report; and a Private Veterinary Attendance and Treatment Declaration, completed by the person listed as the importer on the application form. You must provide Australian contact details—a physical street address and a telephone number. An address using a post office box, "to be advised," or "care of the animal quarantine station" won't be accepted—and a handwritten signature on this form. Furthermore, animals with ongoing medical conditions require a detailed medical letter from the veterinarian, plus full payment via the credit card payment form or check if not applying for the import permit through the eLodge system. This can be quite a lengthy and involved process, but either the experienced vet is able to help with all the documentation or you could enlist the help of a professional animal export person, who will see you through the entire process, complete with vet visits, form-filling, lodging, and getting the correct crate and airline tickets. This is what we did for our dog, and the peace of mind that all the correct steps were taken at the correct time, at a time that was already fraught with all sorts of moving-related upheaval, was well worth the nominal fee.

QUARANTINE

Once all the forms are submitted and you have the permit to import your animal into Australia, and further last-minute health checks have been passed successfully, the animal has been fitted with the right crate and has set off to the airport, the next worry on most peoples' minds is the quarantine. There are three official quarantine stations in Australia, in Sydney, Melbourne, and Perth. Obviously if you are moving to any of those cities, being close and able to visit will make things easier, but even if your animal is not in the same city as you, the handlers are so used to the processes that another short flight will not be too much trouble. Reserve a place for your pet as soon as you have the official import permit, to ensure you get a spot in the city of your choice. The length of quarantine depends on your country of export, but in most cases, especially if you are coming from a rabies-free country, it is one to three months, and pets seem to sail through it without too much trouble.

What to Bring

Moving is always a great opportunity to clean out your stuff, streamline your possessions, sell some, give some away, and yes, keep some as well. But with Australia's extremely strict import laws, have a good look at your possessions before you pack. The more you ship, the more expensive it will become, and the more potential problems you will have with customs. Also, take into consideration that many properties, rented or bought, come equipped with major appliances, and that the old sofa will probably look out of place in your new home. Also, your car is most likely built for driving on the right, not the left.

Electric plugs and sockets are different in Australia, and the voltage is different than in North America, so if you are unsure about that old blow-dryer or the electric toothbrush, get rid of it and get new gadgets when you get here. It will save you the irritation of having to buy and use adapters or voltage converters. Also remember that your belongings will be in the shipping container for a few weeks; if there is something you cannot live without for that length of time, and it doesn't fit into your luggage, it may be time for an upgrade anyway—buy another when you get here.

If you have garden furniture or other outdoor items, including walking boots, tents, and plant pots, it is best not to pack them, as customs will most likely pull them out and charge you for destroying them. Trying to import even the smallest amount of dirt, however innocent or unintentional, is very much frowned upon by Australia's custom officials.

MOVING TO AUSTRALIA CHECKLIST

Six Months Before the Move

- Check out schools in Australia.
- Review your relocation package, if you have one, and determine what expenses will be paid by your company.
- Start a log of moving expense receipts; some may be tax deductible.
- Get written estimates from moving companies, including their written commitment of pickup and delivery dates. Get references. Check the limits of insurance they offer, and if it covers replacement costs.
- Purchase additional insurance if necessary.
- Arrange for a storage facility if you plan to store any of your belongings. Again, check on insurance.
- Check that your pets' vaccinations are up to date.
- Arrange an export service for pets and automobiles, if needed.
- Get your medical and dental records prepared for transfer.
- Put your house on the market for sale or rent.

Two Months Before the Move

- Secure temporary or permanent accommodations in Australia.
- Enroll your children at your chosen school.
- Contact your bank to arrange transfer of your accounts; order checks with your new address; clean out your safety deposit box.
- Submit change-of-address forms to the post office; mail postcards to friends and creditors.
- Give your day care center proper notice of withdrawal.
- Contact schools and arrange for transfer of student records.
- Contact your doctors to double-check that medical records are ready to go.
- Change your insurance policies on property, cars, and health.

- Organize all important documents in a fire-safe box. Include school records, home purchase and sale papers, wills, marriage and divorce papers, pet documents, financial records, stock certificates, Social Security cards, birth certificates, and passports.
- Give notice of resignation to any clubs, organizations, or volunteer activities you belong to.
- Cancel newspaper subscriptions, and change your address for any magazine subscriptions you intend to keep.
- Arrange for hotels, rental cars, or temporary housing as needed.

Four Weeks Before the Move

- Take a ruthless walk-through to determine what you really want to take with you.
- Tag the rest of it and hold a garage sale, or call a charity to pick it up.
- Clean out club, gym, and school lockers; pick up all dry cleaning.
- Arrange for disconnection or changeover of utilities.
- Have measurements taken of the rooms in your new residence and use floor plans to determine where everything will go.
- Begin packing less-used items. Number and label each box, and keep an inventory.
- Retrieve and return all borrowed items from neighbors and friends; return library books.
- Clean out the cupboards and plan remaining meals so you can pack what you don't need, and don't buy any more perishables than you have to.

One Week Before the Move

- Make an inventory list of all items going with you personally. Keep valuable and irreplaceable items such as jewelry and heirlooms with you, not movers.
- Confirm arrangements and dates with moving and storage companies.
- Confirm arrangements with auto and pet transportation companies.
- Confirm hotel, rental car, or temporary housing accommodations.
- Disassemble furniture or other items.
- Sell your car.
- Be sure to check yards and sheds for all items to pack.
- Inform friends and relatives of your forwarding address.
- Take pictures of furniture or get fabric samples for anything you will want to reference for color or decorating before your goods are delivered to your new home.
- Set aside a box of cleaning supplies and the vacuum cleaner.
- Have cards and gifts ready for the kids to give to their friends, complete with the new address and social media contacts.

One or Two Days Before the Move

- Clean and defrost refrigerator and freezer.
- Withdraw cash needed for the move, and convert currency.
- Reconcile and close bank accounts, unless you will be using another branch of the same bank.
- Conclude financial matters relating to the sale or rent of your home.
- The movers or you should complete packing of all household goods for the move.

Moving Day

- Confirm delivery address, directions, and delivery date with the movers.
- Carefully supervise the move. Make sure boxes are clearly marked and your instructions are understood.
- Clean the home and check the entire grounds before leaving.
- Check the thermostat and make sure the temperature is set appropriately. Make sure all windows and doors are closed and locked, and all appliances are turned off. Leave your forwarding address, garage door openers, and any keys, if agreed to, for the new owners or renters.
- If your home is going to be vacant when you leave, make sure a relative, neighbor, or real estate agent has the keys and can contact you. Also, notify your insurance agent and police department that the home will be empty.
- Meet up with friends, relax, and look forward to your adventure. It's really happening.

Arrival Day

- Get a new SIM card at the airport or get a new cell phone, and let friends and family and your moving company know your new number.
- Check to make sure all utilities are on and working properly.
- Let family members or friends know you have arrived safely. Check in with your employer and real estate agent to confirm itineraries.
- Check in with the moving company to confirm the exact date of arrival of your container.
- For any airfreighted boxes, supervise the moving crew on the location of the furniture and boxes. Begin unpacking necessary basics first—kitchen utensils, bath toiletries, and so on.
- Go over the bill of lading from the moving company very carefully before signing; check for damaged items first, as it is usually binding once signed.
- Try to stay up until bedtime. It will help you cope with adjusting to the new time zone. Explore at least the block around your new place and point out exciting finds to the kids. You have arrived in Australia!

One Week after Arrival

- Get a tax number in Australia and register with your local embassy.
- Look into buying a car.

- Organize school uniforms for the children.
- If you have a pet in quarantine, go and visit so they know they're not alone.
- Meet the neighbors.
- Check out some local sports clubs and log on to an expat forum or join the Australian American Association in your city. It's time to make new friends.

SHIPPING OPTIONS

Required Customs Documents

If you are moving with some or all of your belongings, enough to require professional shipping or airfreight, the company you hired will supply you with all the required paperwork. You will have to declare any items made from wood, animal parts, shells, or other natural materials such as rattan. You will also need to declare anything valued over $1,000 and anything new, such as still-boxed electrical items. There is a comprehensive guide booklet issued by the customs authority of Australia with more details; download it from www.border.gov.au/LegacyPagesandAboutUs/Documents/docimpdecguide.pdf.

Prohibited Items

Australia is an island and has an ecosystem that could be severely harmed by introduced organisms, be it a bacterium or a beetle, that we sometimes are not even aware that we're carrying. Therefore, there are plenty of prohibited and restricted items on the import list. Here are some to be aware of:

- Pharmaceuticals, unless prescribed and accompanied by a letter from your doctor
- Animals
- Animal products
- All food items, fresh or dried
- Plants, soil, seeds
- Untreated wooden items

If you are bringing, for example, a decorative item made from wood bought on vacation, it needs to be declared and inspected on arrival, and it may be taken from you if it's deemed potentially harmful to the fragile Australian ecosystem.

HOUSING CONSIDERATIONS

Today's technology is extremely helpful for hunting for a home from abroad. Most property companies have excellent websites with information on houses and apartments to rent or to buy, all with details about what is included and what isn't, pictures of the properties, and floor plans. With Skype and emailed photos and videos, a spouse or family member abroad can get involved in the house hunting process once you're here.

Australia's main cities have a wide range of architecture and structural variety. Cities are brimming with Victorian row houses, art deco apartment blocks and villas, classic styles, 1950s modernist architecture, and modern apartment blocks with all conceivable amenities. The typical Australian home is a detached single-story house that often looks tiny from the front but is built on a deep roomy lot. Front gardens often precede the entrance, fences surround the property, and out back there is often decking and space for outdoor entertaining, facilitating Australians' love of barbecues and eating alfresco.

Big-city apartments often come with attractive views.

Housing Options

APARTMENTS

Housing prices are high in Australia, and many people consider apartment living a viable alternative, especially the young professionals who tend to gravitate toward busy city centers full of cafés, restaurants, and easy access to outdoor life. Apartments, often called "flats" here, come in all shapes and sizes, including one-room studios, large duplex penthouses with pools and rooftop gardens, modern shiny high-rises in the Central Business District (CBD), and suburban flats in art deco villas. Equally diverse is the condition these apartments are in. In the old days the norm was a basic kitchen with a single stove element, a refrigerator, no heating or air-conditioning, a simple tiny bathroom without a shower; these are still around today, but increasingly apartments have been modernized. Modern apartment buildings come with parking; older apartment blocks in the suburbs often have, if you are lucky, a space allocated by the side of the road.

It pays to shop around. Even if a building looks old-fashioned on the outside, it might well have been nicely renovated, keeping old features but also boasting modern amenities. On the other hand, many new high-rises suffer from thin walls and low water pressure. Being wary, taking your time, and asking the right questions are more important in finding an apartment than in a detached house; remember that you are living in a place literally surrounded by other people that can easily become a nuisance.

Think about the floor you are going to live on. On the ground floor you may not have anyone living below you complaining about your walking around early in the morning, but you may be more vulnerable to burglary and street noise; on the top floor you may well have the view, but you'll pay top dollar for it. Are you bringing the family pet? That is one of the first questions to ask, especially when you are renting, as many apartment buildings have a no-pets policy. A goldfish is fine, but a dog above ankle-height will probably not be.

Short-Term Apartments

If you're taking your time looking for the perfect home, in the country on your own and waiting for the family to follow later, or in Australia only for a short-term contract, consider living in a serviced apartment with short leasing terms. While these are more expensive than regular apartments, they often come fully furnished, with amenities such as a gym or pool access and someone to clean either daily or weekly. These "apart-hotels" are often centrally located, convenient for work and city-center attractions, and as such at least save money and time on the commute.

SINGLE-FAMILY HOMES

Single-family houses are the vast majority of Australian homes. Once outside the CBD with its apartment buildings and the inner suburbs with their town houses and Victorian row houses, you'll find the suburbs sprawling with detached, fenced, mostly single-story houses set just off tree-lined residential roads. As mentioned before, from the street these houses often look smaller than they are due to the width-to-length ratio, but the majority are relatively small, especially when compared with suburbs in the United States. Every city has wealthier suburbs with houses of any size, but when there is a sea or a river nearby, prices skyrocket.

The farther you go from the CBD, the more affordable the prices are, and the larger the lots become. Before you start house hunting, you need to decide on whether you want the convenience of city living or suburban life with easy access to the countryside and larger gardens.

What is included in a house and its state of modernization varies widely, from old-fashioned and dilapidated to highly modern and with everything included. Older models might have a traditional furnace for heating, but still not be upgraded to air-conditioning. As house ownership is very common, you will find few suburbs or even streets where no updating is going on. Many owners buy their houses to improve them and then sell them or rent them out, and many beautiful old buildings might be quaint from the outside but have ultramodern amenities inside, including, increasingly, air-conditioning. Outdoor entertaining space is key to Australian life, and most houses will have a deck or barbecue area outside, often with retractable roof to enable enjoyment of the outdoor space year-round.

If you have pets, you will find that even if you are renting, house landlords are much more accommodating than in apartments. Most lots are separated from the neighboring properties with fences or walls, so garden areas are quite safe for pets and kids.

STUDENT ACCOMMODATIONS

It is common for Australian students to live at home for the duration of their studies, and halls of residence are not as common as in other countries. But they do exist, and there are student houses and apartments for sharing. All universities offer assistance when it comes to students who need to find a place to live, and many have an agreement with rental agencies where all types of accommodations are available to rent. Landlords are either vetted or at least supervised. Australian universities are popular with overseas students, and increasingly universities are building housing near their campuses with a range of student accommodations.

Boarding schools for younger students are usually private schools, often single-sex and pricey. Boarding options are either full-board, in which students only go home during the holidays or less, and semiboarding, where students go home on the weekend. Students are often from families living overseas or from remote rural regions of the country with no access to schools.

ROOMMATES

Popular with young professionals who don't have the means to buy, sharing houses or apartments is common and possible in major cities, but less common in rural areas. As long as sharing or subletting is allowed in your rental contract, it is an easy way to share the rent, utility bills, and cleaning. It is easier to share with people you know, work with, or at least have common interests with, but for newcomers there are plenty of advertisements in the large daily newspapers, such as the *Sydney Morning Herald* or the Melbourne's *The Age* looking for people to share. Then it is just a matter of going for interviews and hoping that the people and the place suit you.

Renting

If you are in Australia for a relatively short period of time or are on a temporary visa and not allowed to buy, or simply want to familiarize yourself with the lay of the land and find the right place before you buy, renting is the best option. Traditionally renters have been seen as inferior to homeowners, but this outlook is fading. Increasingly, young professionals rent until they can afford to get on the property ladder, or even just choose to rent. With Australia's inflated property prices, renting is the only option for many, and rental properties are increasingly difficult to find, especially in popular inner-city suburbs.

No flat or house is ever going to be ideal in terms of location, price, and amenities, so compromises based on your budget will be required. The important thing is to focus on the aspects that are important to you, and "don't sweat the small stuff." Once you see the flat or house you like, take action; don't wait for the market to change, as a good apartment won't stay on the market for long, and prices change only gradually. Keep in mind that negotiating on the rent is frowned on in Australia. It's not unheard of either, but it is easy to offend a landlord unless you're well versed in the culture.

Especially in the inner city, listen to the noise inside the unit, and try to imagine what the noise will be like during commuting hours. Ask about water restrictions, and test the showers, taps, and toilets. Specific things to look for:

- Water pressure
- Adequate number and placement of electrical outlets
- Reputable cable TV provider
- Quality Internet access: if it is provided via DSL, make sure you are close to the local telephone office, as the speed depends on the distance
- Air-conditioning unit noise, and location of vents

- Privacy from noisy neighbors

Make sure you know as much as possible about how it will feel to live here. Other questions to ask:

- What rules and restrictions are in place? Ask for a copy of the bylaws or house rules to determine if you can stick to them. There's no point in paying extra for a flat with a swimming pool if your kids can't swim in it.
- Are there many move-ins and move-outs per year? These are disruptive, and lots of movement could be a sign of trouble.

Green Living and Energy Efficiency

Australia is an ecofriendly country with a strong emphasis on recycling, preservation, and environmental protection. Here are some typical tactics.

Solarize: Install a solar hot-water system and a solar heating system if you want heat. Although solar systems cannot heat a home in cold parts of the United States, they do well in Australia.

Awnings: Put broad awnings on your home to shade it from the fierce Aussie summer sun, providing some relief from harsh sunlight as well as cooling the house.

Window placement: Large vertical windows facing north (compared to south, as in the Northern Hemisphere) maximize warmth in the winter when the sun is low and are shielded from the light when the sun is high in the summer.

Lightbulbs: Compact fluorescent lightbulbs last as long as five years.

Electronics: Turn off computers and other "stand-by" electronics while you're at work. Most people keep their home computers on during the day; this adds to the load on the electricity system, and during peak capacity times, your power company may have to use greenhouse gas-emitting coal-fired electricity to keep the power on. You can reduce this by turning off stand-by electronics such as chargers, computers, and iPods.

Recycle: Every major city has a recycling program; get involved in it. Create a compost heap in your backyard using vegetable matter, grass clippings, leaves, and so on. Rather than burning or tossing, you can renew your soil with the compost after a few months using an inexpensive composter.

- Is there enough closet space and storage space? Will you have to buy wardrobes and storage containers?

- Is there enough outdoor space? Is the outdoor space safe for your family? Are there enough barbecue spaces, chairs at the tables, and laundry lines?

- How good is security? Are there locks on the main doors, and an intercom to buzz guests in? Guards are very rare, except at the largest or most high-end buildings.

- What are the maintenance arrangements? Is there someone associated with or employed by the property who can handle small repairs?

- What will the commute be like? How far is it to public transportation? How long is the commute to the CBD? Are there dedicated school buses, or will the kids walk to school or have to use public transportation—or worse, be driven? Generally speaking, the farther you are from the city, the better the rail transit becomes over buses.

REAL ESTATE AGENTS AND LEASING

Trying to find a property for rent generally involves a little legwork. Walk through the neighborhood you're interested in; not only will you get a feel for the area, see what kind of people live there and what amenities there are, but also you can look in real estate agencies' windows and get a feel for pricing. Many agents' windows are split between buying and renting, which makes it easy to compare prices. You can submit your name with a wish list, for example that you want a two-bedroom, two-bath unit in a specific area, along with your budget. The agent will notify you if something suitable comes on the market, or get the Saturday newspapers and go through the ads. The weekend sections are always brimming with real estate listings, and from the listings you can get onto the agents' websites, such

You can browse photos in the windows of real estate offices.

Common Australian Housing Terms

In housing, Australia sometimes shows its British heritage, and some terms may be unfamiliar to newcomers from the United States and other regions. Here's a glossary of typical terminology:

- **agent:** realtor
- **building society:** savings and loan bank
- **conveyance:** due diligence or inspection period
- **flat:** an apartment
- **exchange contracts:** following agreement on price, the term for making a real estate contract
- **garden flat:** ground-floor apartment with a courtyard area
- **ground floor:** In Australia, the ground floor is considered a distinct floor; a high-rise has a ground floor and above it a first floor (which would be the second floor in the United States).
- **let:** rent ("flats to let" means "apartments for rent")
- **settlement:** real estate closing
- **solicitor:** commercial lawyer
- **strata unit:** condominium
- **unit:** apartment

as the excellent **Domain** (www.domain.com.au), which lists rental and sale properties by neighborhood, price, and size. Listings usually come with a good selection of photographs and a floor plan. One thing that makes house hunting a little more complicated from afar is that you generally cannot make an appointment to view a place but have to go on prearranged viewing dates, when several interested parties will show up at once to be shown around the house.

FINDING A PLACE ON YOUR OWN

Going it alone? Ask acquaintances and colleagues, look in shop windows for ads, and read through the Saturday papers. Many supermarkets have notice boards where people advertise accommodations and apartment sharing opportunities in the nearby area. Walk through the neighborhood and look for "to let" and "for rent" signs; often there are even ads pinned to trees.

MOVING IN

Before you sign up and get packing, make sure you check and test everything in your new place and let the landlord know what's wrong. Check all the light switches, toilets, and showerheads. Try out the range and other appliances, and open and close the doors and windows. Look into the cupboards, closets, and fireplaces if you have them. Ask about maintenance agreements, gardeners (many rental properties with gardens have a gardener provided by the landlord), fire safety checks (these should be done once a year), garbage collection dates, and laundry room access. Ask also about pets, and check little things such as whether you will be allowed to put picture hooks into the walls; some landlords can be extremely fussy.

If you are already settled with your belongings from home, either hire a local moving company for the day or rent a truck to move your things. Sometimes rented trucks include the driver and another person to help you carry things, but these can be pricey. If you are still waiting for your stuff from overseas, make sure you advise the shipping company of your new address to ensure correct delivery.

Buying

Owning your own home will make you feel at home in your new country, but if you are coming over as a working expat rather than a permanent resident, it is not as straightforward as simply buying a house. You are allowed to buy residential property if you are either an Australian citizen or are married to one, if you are here on a permanent resident visa, or if you are a citizen of New Zealand; if you are here on a working visa or temporary resident visa, you are not allowed to buy in Australia. However, there can be mitigating circumstances, such as your employer putting your case forward, or you can plead your own case as to why you want to buy property. In those situations, your application goes to the Foreign Investment Review Board and is individually assessed. Even if you are permitted to buy a home, you will be required to sell it again when you leave Australia.

PRICES

Australian housing prices are horrendously high, with the median capital city price around $695,000. Invariably, the farther outside the city center you look, the larger the plots and the properties and the lower the prices. In Melbourne, just 20 kilometers from the CBD, you can buy a four-bedroom house with access to a golf course for around $500,000; the same amount would not get you a two-bedroom apartment anywhere in the inner suburbs. But it is worth looking around, and there are plenty of properties that need work done and are priced for less, as long as the new owner is willing to modernize the property. In 2016 the Australian housing market fell for the first time in three years. But there is always an element of risk involved, especially if, as an expatriate, you can't control when you buy and sell.

REAL ESTATE AGENTS AND CONTRACTS

The first thing to remember is that real estate agents work for the seller, not the buyer, so they are in no way interested in getting the best deal for you. They also tend to multilist, meaning one property may be listed with several agents; in that case the commission has to be shared, so they don't tend to be that keen on showing you the multilisted properties and tend to promote those exclusively listed with them. Ask for all properties that fit your requirements. You can, of course, do it on your own without a real estate agent. But what you do need is a conveyancer (a lawyer who specializes in the legal aspects of buying and selling real estate) or an attorney to deal with the legal aspects for you, and a mortgage broker to sort out your financing, unless you are in the happy situation to be able to pay cash.

Buying a home comes with all sorts of added costs to be aware of. Australia has the Stamp Duty, a tax of around 1.5 to 7 percent of the purchase price, depending on the state and on any discounts you might be eligible for. In South Australia though, Stamp Duty is going to be phased out completely by July 2018. First-time buyers—including you, if this is your first property in Australia—are eligible for a Stamp Duty discount, for example. There is also the land transfer fee, an average of 0.5 percent of the purchase price; inspection and survey fees, depending on the size of the property and the depth of the survey; legal and mortgage fees, plus insurance and moving costs.

Once you have found your property,

Look for realtor signs when house-hunting.

have done the math as to the total cost, and have agreed on a price, both parties, the seller and the buyer, sign a contract that needs to have been checked by your conveyancer before it's signed. After that, you have two or three business days, depending on the state, as a cooling-off period, during which you may change your mind. You will also need to pay the prearranged deposit, often around 10 percent of the purchase price.

If you intend to buy your property via auction, which is extremely popular in Melbourne and Sydney, you need to have done all the legwork before you raise your hand to bid: the surveys, setting up your financing, and knowing the neighborhood and the true value and condition of the property. If you have a twitchy finger or easily get carried away in the competition of bidding, or if you're abroad, you can use a buyer's representative for a small fee who can find a suitable property for you, bid for you at the auction, and then negotiate the sale for you.

Some of the largest real estate agents are **Century 21** (www.century21.com.au), **Domain** (www.domain.com.au), **Realestate.com.au** (www.realestate.com.au), and **LJ Hooker** (www.ljhooker.com.au).

COMMUTING

Where you are going to rent or buy your property very much depends on how easy it is to get to work every day. Unless you intend to be close to the city center and walk to work, in which case you will be able to draw a circle of a specific distance around your house, you will need to either jump in the car or on public transportation and try out the timing, crowdedness, and ease of connections at the time you would normally leave for work and return home. Make sure you also test the train or tram before and after the most obvious one, as sometimes a five-minute gap can make a huge difference in finding a seat or your stress level. Studies have shown that commuting 30 minutes or less is best for overall happiness, so try to stay within that perimeter when you are house hunting.

NEIGHBORS

It is difficult to check out the neighbors before you commit to a new house, but you can try. If you have decided on a specific apartment building, ring a few doorbells, ask what it is like to live in the building, and sit outside to see who comes through the door: families, singles, or older people? If you like a specific neighborhood, do the same; sit in a café and see who's around. Check how many houses are for sale or for rent and how many are currently being worked on, which indicates how much people care about their property. Also try to visit at different times of the day; 10am can give you the wrong idea of how busy it gets at rush hour or at school times, or how loud it is in the evening.

SCHOOLS

Your main schooling decision is whether you want your children to go to public or private school. If you opt for a public school, learn about the catchment areas of each school; if you live within a public school's catchment area, the school must take your children, but it doesn't have to if you live even a few meters outside it. Private schools will take you wherever you live, as long as your children fit their criteria and you are willing to pay the fees. Finding the right school is never easy, but Australian schools publish their annual results and rankings quite regularly online, and apart from knowing someone who is at the school, these rankings are the best measure of a school's quality.

Just as you should do a trial run of your daily commute to and from work, you should check the daily school run. Some schools have school buses, but do they stop near your home? Are your children old enough to use public transportation, or will one of you have to drive them there and pick them up? How long will it take? How big a priority schooling is can affect your process: Do you find a place to live first, look at the commute, and then look for schools, or do you find the school first, and take it from there?

INSPECTIONS

When buying a house, make sure you have it inspected. In Australia, it is up to the buyer to have a building or strata inspections, while a termite or pest inspection is compulsory in some states. The cost of a structural inspection is around $500, a strata inspection (which looks at legal and managerial aspects of a building) is around $250, and a pest inspection is another $250. However, the cost also depends on the size of the property. It is generally wise to organize these inspections to forgo future problems. In many cases, if problems are detected, it is possible to negotiate with the vendor to have these problems either fixed before the sale or alternatively agree upon a reduction in the purchase price. Your conveyancer will have plenty of regulated contacts and can organize the inspections for you before you go and make an offer. However, is not unheard of that buyers organize inspections after they have made an offer on the property and then to pull out or reopen negotiations if problems were found. Once you have signed on the dotted line, you only generally (varies from state to state) have a two-day cooling off period during which you are allowed to change your mind and pull out of the deal.

If your building has a residents' association, you are likely to meet board members in an interview before you buy; be sure to ask them about the reserve funds—there's no better way to gauge a well-run association than whether they have made any provision for future expenses.

NEW VERSUS RESALE

You will probably be looking at buying an existing house. New housing is only for those willing to live a great distance from the city. These days new construction is prohibitively far away unless your employer is based in a remote area away from the CBD. If this applies to you, by all means look at new homes. Construction costs are high, and you will pay 10-30 percent more for a new home than for a comparable resale, but you have the opportunity to configure the house according to modern needs rather than adapting to the way people lived in the early or mid-20th century.

If you are looking for something closer to the CBD but the inventory doesn't fit your needs, there is always the option of remodeling. If you do a remodel:

- Get three written estimates from contractors.
- Get references from the contractors and be sure to call them. Ask about timeliness; contractors are chronically overbooked.
- State the job as accurately as possible in the contract, and provide drawings, pictures, or schematics when possible. Make sure that the contract states exactly what is to be done and how change orders will be handled. In a dispute, your extra efforts will pay off; otherwise you may be labeled a "pushy foreigner," and it's tough to win sympathy from a judge or an arbitrator if that label is successfully strung around your neck.
- Never pay more than half up front, and try to pay just the cost of the raw materials at first.
- Check your contractors' license, and get every permit required without exception. As a foreigner, you can't fight city hall.
- In your contract, clearly state the penalties for late completion, and enforce them.

FINDING THE RIGHT HOME

Even if you know the area well, finding the right home is never easy, and being new to this country, you will need some help. Ask potential friends and acquaintances in the city you are moving to for advice on suburbs, check expat forums on the Internet, and by all means enlist the help of a real estate agent. However, there are a few things to do before you select a realtor, because they specialize in very small areas. You have to do the work of reducing a wide range of possibilities to an area sized to fit an agent's expertise.

Drive the neighborhoods. If you are not driving, use public transportation, and take note of the time it takes. Walk the main areas to see if you like them, but more importantly, make sure you will be able to get to them quickly enough after work to enjoy them.

List your family activities, and match them with neighborhoods. If you're religious, is there good access to a suitable religious venue? If you want to visit the beach a lot, how will you get there, and how will your kids get there?

Look at the schools. If you plan on private schools for your kids, try out the commute. It's not much fun for a 13-year-old to start a daily commute at 6am. If you are going public, look at the local primary and high schools. Older buildings can be daunting learning environments. Information on school performance is available from the state department of education, so check that as well as activity programs when school is in session, holidays, and after school. Kids will often measure the quality of their home by proximity to their good friends, and parents often measure a good home by the happiness of their children.

Consider safety. Ask friends, and look online. Look beyond raw statistics to the type of activity—burglaries, robberies, or violent crimes.

See for yourself. Once you've narrowed your focus to two or three neighborhoods, go there and walk around. Are homes tidy and well maintained? Are the streets quiet? Pick a warm day if you can and chat with people working or playing outside. Are they friendly? Are there children to play with your kids?

In general, it's reasonable to give yourself six months to buy a home: 90 days to get familiar with what you need, 30 days to find the ideal place, and 60 days for closing.

FINANCING AND MORTGAGE ISSUES

The first thing to do is to determine your borrowing power. In Australia, this is generally around three times your annual salary. Use a mortgage calculator such as those at **MoneySmart** (www.moneysmart.gov.au/borrowing-and-credit/home-loans) to look at your payment options based on current rates. Remember that sensible advice is not to overextend yourself, and stick to a maximum monthly mortgage payment of around 30 percent of your after-tax income. It is easy to get carried away, especially with low interest rates and interest-only mortgages available.

Mortgages are generally available at 5- to 30-year terms, and are available at fixed or adjustable rates (ARM). There are real estate-oriented banks called building societies that tend to have a good range of products; St. George Bank is probably the best known of this type. If you are looking to stay in Australia for less than five years, the adjustable rate is probably a good option for you if the rate is lower, as there is often a five-year lock-in period before the rate floats. Loans are in Australian dollars, so keep this in mind if your company pays you in U.S. dollars or another currency. Typically, credit conditions are comparable to those in the United States, but as a rule real estate prices are higher compared to average household income, so you may find yourself borrowing more than you are accustomed to.

SELLING

When it's time to leave Australia again, you may be in a rush to get the house sold, and with a job change and moving arrangements, you may not have the time to get the sale accomplished as quickly as you would like to. The good news is that closing is often done remotely, and you can sign the papers wherever you happen to be.

To help you get the most out of the sale of your house, a few things will help speed up and ease the sale:

Smart pricing. Ask your agent for a range of fair market values, and set your starting price at the lower end, and then try to hold firm in negotiations.

Make your home ready for showing a week before you show it. Get an inspector from the pest company to come by and treat the house, and have your own inspector come in and do a presale inspection so you can handle small repairs while you are still around, to make sure the work is done right and at a fair price.

Be as flexible as possible about showings. This means getting out of the house at a moment's notice. You should never be around when potential buyers visit; it distracts them.

Be ready to deal with a low offer. Never refuse to negotiate.

Be ready. Know the name and contact info for your real estate attorney, appraiser, home inspector, mortgage loan officer, title company, insurance consultant, and moving company.

Know the comparable sales numbers in your area. If possible, go ahead with an appraisal, which will cost you less than $500 but will give you a strong negotiating tool to improve your price or speed up negotiations.

Household Expenses

Generally speaking, if you're renting a place, you are responsible for all utilities unless they are advertised as included, which is rare except in roommate situations or renting a room in someone's house. Expect to pay a deposit for each utility; some utilities allow you to pay a deposit in installments over 2-3 months. You don't need to register for mail service unless you are forwarding mail, in which case you should visit your post office to file a change of mailing address.

Consider paying your utility bills electronically. When you move, you have to contact so many new and current service providers, and eliminating the paper makes it much easier.

Some questions to ask before you move in:

- Are there jacks for cable TV and broadband Internet, and where?
- Are there enough phone jacks?
- Does the home or flat have DSL already wired in from a company such as Big Pond? Does it have a LAN for linking computers?

Electricity, water, and gas are paid quarterly. These utilities for a two-bedroom apartment in Sydney will cost $400-600 per quarter, depending on the size of your family and the supplier. In addition to electricity, there are council rates, which are taxes that run approximately $300-400 per month for a standard two-bedroom apartment in a good suburb of Sydney. These taxes are related to land value and remain reasonably steady. Condominium fees, known in the United States as maintenance fees or homeowners' association (HOA) fees, are called "strata rates" in Australia. These typically run $300-1,000 per quarter and cover garbage collection and property maintenance.

Electricity and gas have been

Water Efficiency

Australia is extremely dry, and severe water restrictions may become crueler. Here are some things you might install or see already in your home.

Use less water by installing a water-saving showerhead—these restrict water usage to nine liters per minute. Another water-saving device is a two-button flush toilet, with the second button for the less-intensive flush needs.

Use gray water, which is wastewater from the washing machine, shower, bath, or sink—everything except the kitchen and toilet. You can put in a gray-water treatment system that allows you to collect, treat, and store gray water. There are no restrictions on the use of gray water during water restrictions, so you can use this to save a cherished garden or lawn when everyone else's is browning into dust. You can't pipe gray water directly into the garden; you need a treatment or irrigation system. If you don't treat the water, you have to use it right away.

deregulated in Australia (except in Western Australia), and you may choose the old monopoly, Energy Australia, or a competitor such as Jackgreen, Origin Energy, or AGL. **AGL** (www.agl.com.au) is the largest, with more than six million customers for gas and electric services. Water service is supplied by the state governments, and accounts are set up and managed online through each state water board.

There are many Internet, TV, and phone packages to choose from. Companies such as Telstra, Optus, AT&T, iinet, and Virgin Media all offer competitive bundles, with competition being fierce, so shopping around will pay off. Depending on Internet usage, packages cost roughly around $120 per month, which would include Foxtel (cable channels in addition to the local free TV channels). These packages tend to ask for a lock-in period of usually 24 months, but can also be agreed upon for periods of 6, 12, or 18 months. Prices will vary accordingly.

There are companies who provide help with cleaning and ironing from $73 for a two-hour regular service and $26 per hour thereafter. For one-offs, a three-hour service is around $165, with $40 per hour thereafter. The prices vary slightly from city to city and suburb to suburb.

LANGUAGE AND EDUCATION

When I first arrived in Australia, I remember being baffled by a news report about hundreds of "thongs" washing up on a beach in Northern Australia. Rather than skimpy underwear piling up in the sand, the story was about flip-flops, popular footwear that Australians call "thongs." If you thought they spoke English here, well, officially, yes, they do, but the Australian version of the language can mystify native English speakers from other countries.

Standard British and American English is completely understood by Australians, and they understand most American idioms due to the popularity of American content on Australian TV, but Americans can struggle to follow an everyday Australian conversation and Australian expressions. Even newspaper headlines, news reports, and shop-window displays can leave a newcomer somewhat perplexed. The Internet is an excellent resource to figure out the most commonly used idioms and terms.

Most people find the Australian accent and intonation both charming and endearing. The slight raising of the voice at the end of the sentences and the constant abbreviations make everything simply sound cute; even a city like Brisbane is reduced to "Brissie." However, although endearing, the language can also have its pitfalls for newcomers.

Learning the Language

Spend even a brief time on a bus, train, or tram and you'll truly appreciate the variety in the Australian dialect. You'll barely understand some people, with the thick accent, distinctive drawl, and slight upward inflection at the end of sentences that sounds like they might be asking a question. Others have a barely noticeable accent, and most people are somewhere in between. Like anywhere, differences in language use are usually connected to education and social class, even though Australians will insist their society has no class differences. One thing most Australians have in common is the almost inevitable shortening of every expression. An avocado becomes an "avo," a tradesperson becomes a "tradey," a U-turn is a "youie," and football is "footy," and your cookie should normally be a biscuit, but is turned into a "bikkie." Even your name is not safe and will inevitably be abbreviated.

Aside from the Australian dialect itself, which can vary among cities and states and by social class, Australia has three types of language differentiation: slang expressions that are common to nearly all Australians; rhyming slang, which crosses social and geographic boundaries and is virtually impossible to comprehend; and Strine, the "ocker" accent and vocabulary that at times feels like a whole new language, replete with unique expressions and words.

SLANG

Not all Australians use Aussie slang extensively. You may have to wait to hear your first "g'day," and like all slang, phrases common in one generation do not always carry over to the next. Aussies do not really call each other "cobber" except on rare and often ironic occasions, despite the universal presence of the word in dictionaries of common Aussie slang. *Righto* is also fading out, although it has been popular for several generations. Words like *swagman* and *billabong* that feature in popular songs like *Waltzing Matilda* are no longer in common usage.

But mastering slang—at least understanding it—is essential for following even average-length conversations of moderate complexity. Get a decent online or printed dictionary of slang and read it through once, have a giggle, and familiarize yourself with the sound of the phrases and words. A good example is **Koala Net** (www.koalanet.com.au/australian-slang.html).

Next, keep an ear out for unusual words from Aussies you know, write them down if you like, and look them up—having a smartphone with an app or

Flip-flops are better known as "thongs" to Aussies.

at least the Internet handy is very helpful at times. You'll find, for example, that some cases of slang are impossible to figure out logically, and some seem to be real words in their own right. A news report might describe someone being "king hit"; no amount of rational analysis would tell you that it means being knocked out cold.

In general, the use of Australian slang words by new arrivals is a no-no; it's just too difficult to understand the nuances, and a well-meant phrase can easily be offensive. Generally speaking, the use of diminutives and basic words like *g'day* are safe to use when around your "mates," but any more than that is often misinterpreted as insulting.

Certain words in common usage elsewhere should not be used in Australia: *fanny, root* (as in "root for the home team"), and *bung* (as in "I bunged my car right into the wall"). These have vulgar meanings in the Australian idiom. *Bastard* can be a term of affection in Australia, but avoid trying to use it unless you really know the people well.

Rhyming Slang

The prevalent rhyming slang of Australia needs to be explained to be understood. For example, to "have a Captain Cook" is rhyming slang for "have a look." Rhyming slang is often combined with the diminutive: *Yank* rhymes with *septic tank,* which becomes *seppo,* a derisive slang term for Americans. *Trouble* becomes *rubble,* then *Barney Rubble,* which becomes *barney,* so that a "friend in barney" needs your help. A *bone,* from *dog and bone,* is a phone; a *Noah,* from Noah's Ark, is a shark; and so it goes in every increasing circles. It is colorful and can only be learned by example.

Strine

Beyond Australian slang, which is common to most Australians, there is an extensive vocabulary delivered with a strongly drawled accent known as Strine. Someone who speaks Strine is an "ocker" (OCK-ah). Strine is known as Broad Australian English and generally reflects the working class. The classic ocker says "yous" for the plural of *you,* "good on ya" for "well done," and "me" instead of "my" as in "tie me kangaroo down, sport."

LANGUAGE SCHOOLS

Standard English is universally understood in Australian life. While some care must be taken to learn the considerable vocabulary of Australian idiomatic speech and Strine, language classes for newcomers focus almost entirely on people from non-English-speaking countries.

Education

Australian education has a good reputation worldwide. Schools and universities are administered at the state level, and government funding varies, but it is always on the national government's agenda. Australia is one of the most popular countries to study abroad at the university level, as the combination of easy living and great facilities draws thousands of international students to some of the best universities in the world.

COLLEGES AND UNIVERSITIES

Australia has an impressive ratio of universities and other higher education facilities to its population, and the number of students who seek higher education is steadily increasing. In Australia, the basic structure of postsecondary education includes graduate education, professional education, undergraduate education, known as "uni," and the Technical and Further Education (TAFE) system, or "tech." Tech draws students aiming to work in trades and in some cases professionals, especially those looking for specialized courses, for teaching certificates, or for continuing education credits.

University in Australia is generally three years for an undergraduate degree in arts or sciences, with an additional year required for an honors degree. Professional degrees such as law and medicine are also three-year programs. Most major universities offer an option for students to take a combined undergraduate and professional degree program simultaneously, and students who select, say, arts and law, for example, graduate in five years with two degrees, a bachelor of arts (BA) and a law degree (LLB). Professional degrees are usually accompanied by additional postgraduate study via internships or six-month law training at the College of Law before professional certification is issued.

Admissions are handled centrally for Australian students through the University Admissions Center. The UAC processes all high school test scores against program quotas established by the universities and then checks the personal preferences of the students before determining where they will study. Foreign students can apply directly to a school, which gives them more freedom to choose and follow their own path.

Student Housing

It is quite common for Australian university students to live at home with their parents, so student accommodations are not in demand. Some universities provide no halls of residence at all; other have limited space, and others are expanding to offer student housing on campus and also access to self-catering shared houses and apartments. But space is limited, and putting your name down immediately

the main quadrangle of the University of Sydney

after gaining admission gives you a better chance but is no guarantee.

Universities all offer roommate-finding help as well as bulletin boards, which support "flat wanted" and "flat to let" notices. Financial assistance for housing is sometimes available in the form of work-study programs or grants. Additionally, large-scale apartment complexes catering to students are typically run independently of the university but closely align themselves in terms of making information available on the university website.

Australian National University (ANU) in Canberra is a significant exception and offers a number of residence halls; it is also highly welcoming for international students.

Financing

Australian students have their postsecondary education subsidized by the government, as do permanent Australian residents; international students will have to pay their own way and must pay their full tuition in advance. Fees for residents are capped at around $10,440 (in 2016) per year, and set in three categories, depending on the field of study: Band 1 includes national priority subjects, where there is a national shortage in qualified professionals in those fields (education, nursing, humanities, foreign language, social studies, and the arts) and is capped at $6,256. Band 2 includes fields such as mathematics, statistics, computing, health, engineering, and is capped at $8,917, and Band 3 is capped at $10,440 and covers subjects such as law, medicine, dentistry, veterinary science, accounting, and economics.

All universities and other postsecondary education providers have the option to set their fees from zero to the maximum, and while some are leveled just below the maximum, most charge full fees.

Fee-paying students may be able to defer payment of all or part of their tuition fees using the FEE-HELP government loan scheme. This is an interest-free, income-based loan that students do not have to pay back until their income reaches a certain level. But there is a limit on how much students can borrow; for 2016, the limit is $99,389 for Bands 1 and 2, and $124,238 for medicine, veterinary science, and dentistry.

INTERNATIONAL UNIVERSITY STUDENTS

Australian universities offer all their programs to international students. In an Australian university, basic university degrees are three-year programs with a degree in arts, science, health, education, social studies, or business. A fourth year may be taken as an honors year. Typically, students take several subject concentrations in year one and become focused on a single subject by the third and final year. Undergraduate degrees may be combined with professional degree studies so that double degrees such as a BA-LLB may be earned over five years by applying law courses as elective courses within the arts degree program. Similarly, medicine and veterinary studies can be taken directly after high school.

It is also possible for American students to apply through overseas study schemes such as **Education Abroad** (www.educationabroadnetwork.org), which offers students the opportunity to study in Australia for a semester or a full year, rather than completing their entire studies abroad. These organizations also help with the visa, finding accommodations, and health insurance.

International students need to pay their full university fees in advance; living expenses can be estimated at around $16,000 per year.

The Old School Tie

Australians mostly believe that they live in a firmly egalitarian society. So why are so many children—up to 40 percent in some cities—sent to private schools?

The decision to send children to private school is primarily for religious reasons, with the majority of students attending private Roman Catholic schools. Many parents assume that superior education is available at expensive institutions with smaller class sizes and more freedom in the curriculum. Statistics show that for secondary education, where government-run schools' enrollment is decreasing, private schools are gaining. Parents seem happy to send their children to a state primary school, but for secondary education increasingly prefer private schools.

Undeniably, elite Australian private schools offer some professional and social advantages that are supposedly declining in importance but in reality cannot be ignored. There is great value in making connections by being part of a notable and recognized school, having learned its values, and having made friends and acquaintances there. Students who attend these institutions will find some advantage in building their careers as well as social connections. It is often said that great students will succeed in any school, but middling students benefit from the associations formed at elite schools and their clubs or activities.

In a globalized economy the marginal advantage of "the old school tie" is increasingly debatable, but it's a fact that the most influential jobs around the world are filled through connections, and however cliché it might sound, it is still very much about who you know as much as what you know. And that's where a good private school gives students a head start.

Transferring Credits

Australian universities are internationally accredited, and credits are generally transferable. There are sometimes credit-hour adjustments made with respect to converting Australian semester credits to quarterly credits at other institutions, and individual institutions will make determinations on how Australian classes apply toward specialized requirements such as required courses in a major concentration.

Tuition

International students are not subsidized by the federal government and can incur fees up to $30,000 per year for a degree program. Most universities offer scholarships and also operate job banks. In a job bank, local employers, including the university itself, government, and private enterprise will list available jobs for students and graduates. These job banks are typically online or published on a physical bulletin board, often by a university department or at the student union building. International students are not eligible for the Commonwealth Supported Places (CSP) subsidy program or for the FEE-HELP (Higher Education Loan Program) loans, but they can receive grants and scholarships as financial aid.

STUDY ABROAD

Many Australian universities offer a study-abroad year or semester. These are full-fee opportunities, typically taken after a year of university, and require maintaining passing grades plus proficiency in English. Specialized course loads offer opportunities to study Australian history, culture, business, health, or education subjects, and internships are sometimes made available to extend the experience.

PRIMARY AND SECONDARY SCHOOLS

Schooling in Australia, compulsory from age 5 to age 15 or 17, depending on the state, starts with a kindergarten or preparatory year followed by 12 years of primary and secondary school. In the final year of secondary school, year 12, children study for a government-endorsed certificate that is recognized by all Australian universities and vocational education and training institutions. This Senior Secondary Certificate of Education is a combination of exams and continuous assessment scores and also recognized by many universities in other countries.

All states have recently switched from a three-term to a four-term system. Typically students have two weeks off in April, July, and late September, followed by six to eight weeks in the summer (Jan.-Feb.).

For many years Australian students were allowed to leave school after year 10, typically to join apprenticeships for the trades or jobs in factories. As global competitiveness increases, educators have been encouraging students to stay in school longer and to complete year 12, at times even hatching plans to pay parents to keep their children in school, although the debate is raging about the utility of forcing youths who do not want to be at school to stay at school to potentially disrupt those who want to be there.

For expats, apart from the dilemma that the school year ends in December and universities in the Northern Hemisphere start in September, one of the potential areas for trouble is having children complete high school in Australia and then apply to universities in the United States and elsewhere without the benefit of a traditional high school grade point average. Since Australia does not issue traditional grades but rather bases university entrance on scores achieved in comprehensive examinations taken at the end of year 12, the incompatibility of systems can create confusion. However, the SAT exam is offered in major cities, and non-Australian universities are becoming more adept at evaluating international student applications.

Public Versus Private Schools

About one-third of Australian students in secondary school attend private school. Most of these are Roman Catholic schools, and about one-quarter attend mainstream Protestant religious schools. The remainder attends secular private schools. For many years, the Australian government has subsidized private school education, so fees have historically been well below what they are at comparable private schools in the United States. Annual tuition for the average year 12 student averages around $25,000, and boarding fees can push this up considerably.

Boarding is less popular than it used to be, except for students from remote country areas and expat students whose parents live abroad. Typically, private schools have slightly longer holiday periods, stronger academic results, smaller class sizes, and more religious education. Private schools continue to offer some limited benefits in social status, although the gap is closing as the country continues to become more egalitarian. Many employers offer subsidies, and the schools themselves offer numerous scholarships based on merit or need.

The majority of Australian state schools are coeducational, but a large number of private secondary schools are restricted to either boys or girls, although coed is becoming more popular. Typically, primary school is mostly coed, and all universities are.

Most schools have a strict uniform policy.

Study Requirements

In Australia, secondary school students have core requirements in mathematics and, not surprisingly, Australian history and literature that are more rigorous than studies in these areas in other countries. Australian students receive less education in foreign literature and history than they would, for example, in the United States. Expat parents often supplement secondary school with special lessons in language or history, typically offered by a private tutor or through a local expat association such as the American Australian Association.

Uniforms

The vast majority of Australian state and private schools use student uniforms, and even if they don't, they have a specific dress code. Uniforms tend to be more formal at private schools, which often have fairly ornate dress uniforms, sports uniforms, and different winter and summer uniforms. Winter uniforms typically add a blazer, cardigans or pullovers, scarves, and ties; the summer uniform tends to be shorts and short-sleeved shirts for boys and dresses for girls. Each school has its own uniform policy and typically makes arrangements with local retailers to supply uniforms; a thriving secondhand market exists at most schools. While the debate rages about the use of uniforms, it is generally agreed that wearing a uniform relieves the peer pressure about what to wear and whether it is fashionable enough.

HOMESCHOOLING

Homeschooling is growing in popularity in Australia, but the numbers are still minimal, less than 2 percent of schoolage children nationwide. Homeschooling is regulated at the state level, and states require registration and a description of a program of studies. There are local service providers who assist with program development. For families in extreme rural communities, the Royal Flying Doctor Service allows their radio network to be used by the School of the Air, which educates children in remote parts of the Outback with transmissions, one-on-one phone calls, Internet, and correspondence, managing for more than 60 years to bring education even to those thousands of miles from the nearest school.

Students can pursue university studies after homeschooling through the Open Training and Education Network (OTEN) program offered through TAFE colleges, essentially the same as correspondence or online study. Students over age 25 can apply as "mature age" students, in which an interview is typically substituted for scores on standard exams.

The **Home Education Association Australia** (www.hea.asn.au) is the major association promoting homeschooling and offering information about options and requirements.

HEALTH

Generally speaking, Australians are a healthy lot. Life expectancy at birth is 80 years for men and 84 years for women, giving Australian the seventh longest life expectancy in the world. Infant mortality is 3 deaths per 1,000 live births—impressive statistics that surpass those of the United States and most other nations. On the other hand, Australians love red meat and are infatuated with junk food; recent statistics show increasing obesity in adults and children, along with worrying numbers of diabetes cases, with an estimated 7.5 percent of the population affected.

No matter what your personal lifestyle and eating habits are, there is no avoiding the doctor, especially when you have kids. It is usually the first thing on any new expat's to-do list: find a local clinic and sort out medical coverage, because it is only a matter of time before someone comes down with something.

Australia's health care coverage includes both a public and private system. Medicare, the public system, is paid for by taxes and covers most of the costs of basic care and prescription medicines. The private system takes care of the remainder: treatment in private hospitals, ambulance trips, dentist visits, eyeglasses, and other treatments such as acupuncture.

Types of Insurance

PUBLIC VERSUS PRIVATE CARE

Some countries have a government-run health insurance scheme; others encourage citizens to take out private insurance. Most expatriates negotiate private health care into their work contracts as a priority, making sure that wherever they go they are covered. In Australia the majority of people rely on the public health care system, called Medicare, but many supplement this with a degree of private health insurance. Others, mostly high-income earners, are encouraged through tax breaks to rely solely on private insurance.

Medicare

It seems that in Australia everybody has Medicare: You will be asked when you make an appointment with the doctor, and you'll be asked when you open a bank account, as the card is frequently used as an everyday means of identification. But while Medicare is available to all permanent residents of Australia, it is not available to expats who reside in Australia on a temporary residence visa.

When you first arrive, you can either check with your employer or directly with **Medicare** (www.medicareaustralia.gov.au) as to whether you might be eligible for either full coverage or reciprocal care under an agreement Australia has with several countries.

Instituted in 1984, Medicare is funded partly by general government resources and partly by income taxes. High-income earners are subject to a tax surcharge to persuade them to take out private insurance. To avoid this extra levy, you have to apply for an exception and complete a form confirming that you have private health insurance. As of 2016 the surcharge starts at income levels of $90,000 for singles and $180,000 for couples and families, but as tax rates change regularly, you are advised to check the current rates when you arrive.

If you are eligible for Medicare, it is a great scheme that allows you access to consultation fees for doctors, including some specialists; tests and examinations needed to treat illnesses, including X-rays and pathology tests; eye tests performed by optometrists; most surgical and other therapeutic procedures performed by doctors; some surgical procedures performed by approved dentists; specified items under the Cleft Lip and Cleft Palate Scheme; and specified items for allied health services as part of the Chronic Disease Management Plan. It does not cover private patient hospital costs; general dental examinations and treatment; ambulance services; home nursing; services such as physiotherapy, occupational therapy, speech therapy, eye therapy, or chiropractic services; glasses or contact lenses; hearing aids; the cost of prostheses; medicines, which are covered by the Pharmaceutical Benefits Scheme; medical and hospital costs incurred overseas; medical costs for which someone else is responsible; medical services that are not clinically necessary; surgery for cosmetic reasons only; and examinations for life insurance, superannuation, or membership of a friendly society. For more details check with the federal **Department of Human Services** (www.humanservices.gov.au).

Neither does Medicare necessarily cover all the cost of any treatment or consultation. You are covered if you're taken into public hospital care, but Medicare generally only pays around 75 to 85

Royal Flying Doctor Service

Living in the Outback means living away from civilization and the essential conveniences it offers. No supermarkets around the corner, schooling via the radio or Internet, and no hospitals nearby. This is the case today; now imagine living like that a century or more ago. Just one of many case studies is the tale of a young stockman, Jimmy Darcy, who fell off his horse in 1917 in the remote region of Kimberley. Suffering from a broken leg and with head and internal injuries, he was driven 75 kilometers to the distant telegraph station, only then to be operated on by the postmaster, receiving instructions via telegraph in Morse code from Perth. His operation was a success, but, alas, by the time the doctor from Perth had arrived seven days later, Jimmy had died from complications. The story fuelled John Flynn, a minister of the Presbyterian Church, into action. He thought medical services should be made available to those in the stark Outback. In 1912 he set up the Australian Inland Mission, but a letter from a medical student with an interest in aviation presented the idea that doctors in airplanes might provide the solution. Flynn started campaigning for an aerial medical service, but the idea was shot down due to safety concerns. Later, Flynn met Hudson Fysh, a founder of Qantas, then the Queensland and Northern Territory Aerial Services and later Australia's global airline, and in 1927 Australia's first aerial ambulance service was created.

The service progressed steadily, with farmers in the bush using their radios to arrange consultations and with doctors and local contractors providing pilots and planes for doctors to get to distant cattle stations for emergencies.

Today, the Royal Flying Doctor Service owns a fleet of 66 fully instrumented modern aircraft, with some 150 pilots flying the equivalent of 25 round-trips to the moon annually in their quest to care for more than 250,000 patients who live in regions too remote to access local clinics.

percent of doctors' consultation fees and other treatments. Most Australians have private insurance to cover the remainder.

HOSPITALS AND CLINICS

In Australia there are public and private hospitals, with the public hospitals funded jointly by the federal government and state or territory governments, and administered by those regional governments. Generally speaking, the health care system is the same throughout the country, but regional variations exist.

In the public hospital sector, there are the large general hospitals that cover maternity, infectious diseases, psychiatry, rehabilitation, pediatrics, and geriatrics. There are also specialized hospitals and clinics that focus further on pediatrics, oncology, eye problems, and the like.

The quality and number of good hospitals and clinics depends on where you are. Cities are exponentially better equipped than the less densely populated regions of Australia, and there are many of those. There is a severe shortage of qualified staff willing to move to more isolated regions—so much so that the government is actively inviting and importing qualified staff for those areas, such as Western Australia and the Northern Territory.

In addition to trying to provide more staff and facilities to the remoter areas of Australia, many people depend on the famed Royal Flying Doctor Service, which provides medical services in the remotest areas, either on the spot or to evacuate patients to the nearest hospital by plane.

INTERNATIONAL COVERAGE

For the first six months of your stay in Australia, you may well be covered under a reciprocal care agreement between Australia and your country, depending on what passport you hold. Australia has reciprocal agreements with several countries, including the United Kingdom, Ireland, New Zealand, Sweden, the Netherlands, Finland, Belgium, Norway, Slovenia, Malta, and Italy, but not the United States. If you are a student, you are expected to take out private health insurance, usually Overseas Student Health Coverage (OSHC), before you enter Australia to ensure you are covered from your arrival. Universities often have agreements in place and will be able to help you, but note that OSHC does not cover dental care, optometry, or physiotherapy.

Pharmacies and Preventative Medicine

PHARMACEUTICAL BENEFITS SCHEME

Part of Medicare, the Pharmaceutical Benefits Scheme (PBS) is a system that subsidizes the cost of prescribed medications obtainable from a pharmacy (sometimes also called a "chemist"). If you qualify for Medicare or are from a country with which Australia has a reciprocal agreement, you will automatically qualify for PBS, which means you will pay a maximum of $38.30 for each medication on the prescription, although the amount you pay for each item varies according to the medication. Also, some medications are not covered under PBS, and you will have to pay the full amount. Further subsidies apply for low-income

Australian Medical Terms

"Two cultures divided by a common language" is something Aussies say, referring to Australia and Britain or Oz and the United States. It is relevant in medical treatment. A few tips and translations:

- A nurse is often called a "sister."
- A doctor's office is called a "surgery."
- A Band-Aid is called a "sticking plaster."
- When you feel sick, you "feel crook."
- Don't say "fanny"; say "bum," as "fanny" is a vulgarism.
- A tampon is a "sanitary napkin," which may be why many Aussies say "serviette" instead of "napkin."
- Alternative medicine is called "herbal medicine."
- Some call a car accident a "bingle."
- A pharmacist is a "chemist."

A good place to check out regional variations is the **ABC Australian Word Map** (www.abc.net.au/wordmap).

Go to the chemist to have your prescriptions filled.

families, students, pensioners, and the unemployed.

MEDICAL RECORDS

Medical records were formerly maintained via a national electronic scheme called HealthConnect, now being superseded by the Australian government's individually controlled electronic health (eHealth) record system, which was launched in July 2012. The eHealth system is intended to facilitate the flow of information without compromising the privacy of health records. To register and find out more about the system, see **eHealth** (www.ehealth.gov.au).

VACCINATIONS

For children under age five, the recommended vaccination schedule according to the Australian government is as follows:

- Birth: hepatitis B
- 2 months: diphtheria, tetanus, pertussis, polio, Hib, hepatitis B, pneumococcal
- 4 months: diphtheria, tetanus, pertussis, polio, Hib, hepatitis B, pneumococcal, rotavirus
- 6 months: diphtheria, tetanus, pertussis, polio, Hib, hepatitis B (or at 12 months), pneumococcal, rotavirus

- 12 months: measles, mumps, rubella, Hib, hepatitis B (or at 6 months), meningococcal C
- 18 months: varicella, pneumococcal
- 4 years: diphtheria, tetanus, pertussis, polio, measles, mumps, rubella

Children under age seven are automatically registered with the Australian Childhood Immunization Register, which tracks and updates vaccinations either at birth or once they have received any type of vaccination from an Australian doctor. Childhood vaccinations are covered under Medicare, if you qualify.

ALTERNATIVE THERAPIES

Alternative and complementary medicine (ACM), covering different and varied branches such as natural therapies, holistic medicine, naturopathy, complementary medicine, herbal medicine, nutrition, massage, and homeopathy, has reportedly been used by some 50 percent of Australians to gain more control of their health and well-being. The trend and the industry

Traditional Aboriginal Medicine

The Aborigines are the indigenous people of Australia and are thought to have arrived in Australia some 50,000 years ago, although some research indicates it could be much earlier than that. There were countless separate seminomadic bands all over Australia, Tasmania, and the Torres Strait, with hundreds of languages and dialects in use. The individual groups were as different from each other as their different languages suggest, but one thing they all had in common was a love and knowledge of the land, its flora and fauna, and a holistic approach to life and health. Where Western medicine looks for symptoms and tries to remedy the illness, the Aboriginal approach is to understand not only what is wrong but also why it is wrong, looking not just at symptoms but at the entire picture, including the patient's family, spiritual and physical health, and everything around that could have caused the illness.

Unfortunately, as the Aborigines did not write down any of their knowledge and everything from medicines to history was passed along via singing and dancing, and since that lifestyle is slowly vanishing, a lot of the information on natural remedies has also been lost. It is known that the different groups used a wide variety of medicines, including massage, amulets, squashed witchetty grubs, soaked bark, leaf sap, and berries, utilizing the ingredients found around them and their knowledge of the powers of the indigenous plants.

Many of the traditional remedies have now been recognized and utilized by modern society, such as tea tree oil, which was commonly used on wounds and is today widely acknowledged for its strong antiseptic properties. It is used now in skin preparations for acne, to clear fungal infections, and as a scalp remedy. The eucalyptus tree, so much part of Australia, has seen its oil enter nearly everybody's medicine cabinet, and it is known to work wonders for colds and throat and sinus infections. Less commonly known and available mixtures include the emu bush, whose leaves have been found to have strong antibiotic effects; crushed witchetty grubs, the rather large larvae of the cossid moth, which the indigenous people in central Australia used to place on burns and wounds, but now they are more known as a protein-rich source of bush food; and the hop bush, whose mashed up roots were used on cuts, stings, and for toothaches.

While sadly a lot of traditional knowledge is not retrievable, some ingredients of the indigenous Australian health regime are being actively promoted, such as the kakadu plum, a rich source of vitamin C, antioxidants, and bioactive substances that was traditionally used to prevent illness among the Aborigines and is now promoted as a superfood.

are steadily increasing, and every large city in Australia offers a range of therapists providing a wide range of therapies. To search for a practitioner near you, try the **Australian Health Directory** (www.healthdirectory.com.au), which has access to both general and complementary medicine practitioners around the country.

Environmental Factors

AIR QUALITY AND SUN INTENSITY

Australia is famous for its Slip, Slop, Slap campaign (slip on a shirt, slop on sunscreen, and slap on a hat) and the dire statistic that Australia has the highest skin cancer rate in the world. Australians are four times more likely to develop skin cancer than any other form of cancer, and approximately two in three Australians are diagnosed with skin cancer before the age of 70, according to the government's Department for Health and Aging. This is partly due to the depletion of the ozone layer above the Antarctic, and while it is tempting to soak up the sun, especially after some gray days, always wear sunscreen and reduce the amount of time you spend in direct sunlight. An unfortunate twist in avoiding the sun is the fact that Australians suffer from low levels of vitamin D; to synthesize vitamin D, the body requires 15 minutes a day in the sun. The best advice is to be sensible, avoid the sun between noon and 3pm, and wear sunscreen.

As a whole Australia continuously ranks high among nations for clean air, but this is partly due to it being one of the least densely populated countries in the world. When you look at Sydney and Melbourne, Australia's most populous cities, the statistics are slightly less impressive and subject to seasonal variations, with air quality worse in winter, due to temperature inversions and popular wood-burning ovens that raise the amount of particulate matter in the air. Sydney has also been called the allergy capital of the world, probably attributable to the voluminous green spaces and parks everywhere, which increase the pollen count at certain times of the year to uncomfortable levels for allergy sufferers. Parkland also offsets air pollution, however.

WATER QUALITY AND CONSERVATION

Throughout Australia the tap water is safe to drink and is fluoridated in most parts of the country to combat tooth decay. That said, water is still a scarce commodity in the driest inhabited country in the world. Yes, Victoria has recently suffered devastating floods, but just a few years ago southwest Western Australia, southeast South Australia, Victoria, and

Smoking rates are declining in Australia.

northern Tasmania suffered from the longest recorded draught in history. Water is not a commodity to be taken for granted here.

Water restrictions are regular features of the summer months, sometimes even in the cooler months, and water conservation is a keen topic in houses. Most toilets come with standard half-flush and full-flush options, and people are encouraged to use a four-minute timer for their showers.

SMOKING

Smoking is rapidly declining in Australia, from 45 percent of men and 30 percent of women in the 1970s to 18.3 percent in men and 14.1 percent of women in 2011-2012, with rates at present around 16.3 percent, one of the lowest in the world. Smoking is banned in all enclosed public places and offices, and only a few pubs and hotels still allow smokers a secluded enclave. Legislation differs from state to state, but since December 2012 all cigarette packaging is a uniform olive color with large and dramatic health warnings on them with the brand's name in small generic lettering. It is hoped that this change in advertising will further push the percentage of smokers below 10 percent.

WASTE MANAGEMENT

Just as Australia has a sensible approach to the country's water management, the approach to waste is also advanced. Depending on the individual local government, each household is given at least two containers for weekly collection, one for normal trash and one for recycling; in some areas households also receive an extra bin for garden waste. Regular container checks aim not to punish but to educate people as to what can be recycled and what can't. A recent survey in some of Melbourne's suburbs found that 20 percent of "normal" waste could have been recycled. Many local governments also have a policy that households can phone twice per year to have bulky items such as furniture picked up. Nicer items often get picked up by neighbors, with old TVs usually the only thing left at the curb; in this way people aren't compelled to dump items illegally. Check with individual local governments for their policies.

Health and Safety

ACCESS FOR PEOPLE WITH DISABILITIES

In general, most Australian public facilities are well equipped when it comes to accessibility for those with mobility difficulties. Parking, toilets, and ramp accesses are well marked and plentiful, and all major cities and many states produce maps and websites listing their services. Local governments issue parking permits for the disabled. Companion cards are issued to prove that the holder requires a carer to attend community activities, so a second ticket can be issued without charge. Melbourne public libraries, for example, are equipped with recharge points for electric scooters and wheelchairs. Facilities and assistance vary from state to state; check with the local government for details. Another good website is the **National Information Communication Awareness Network** (www.nican.com.au), which aims to give full information on recreation, tourism, sports, and the arts for people with disabilities.

POLICE

Law enforcement in Australia is provided at the state and territory level, and there is also a national police force, the Australian Federal Police, responsible for investigation of offenses such as drug trafficking, counterfeiting, money laundering, illegal immigration, crimes against national security, and crimes against the environment.

The police forces of each state and the Northern Territory are responsible for dealing with crimes under state and territorial laws. Policing in the Australian Capital Territory is handled by the Australian Federal Police. Police are generally armed and have a relatively broad range of powers for crime prevention. Local police numbers differ from state to state. If you phone 1234, you will be directed to the nearest police station; in an emergency, the national emergency line is 000 from a landline or 112 from a cell phone.

Dial 000 from a landline for emergency services.

CRIME

Like every country, Australia has crime, and at times it can seem that this is all that is covered in the news. Though, when properly analyzed, the rates are generally better in Australia than in the United States, and much better when it comes to serious crimes such as murder (1 in 100,000 in Australia, as compared to 4.5 per 100,000 in the United States). Robberies are reported at 58 in 100,000 in Australia, compared to 113 in 100,000 in the United States, as per 2014-2015 statistics.

Common sense should be paramount: Don't leave your handbag or cell phone unattended, lock your car and your house, avoid walking the streets late at night, and look after your belongings even more carefully when visiting tourist areas. Poorer suburbs tend to have worse crime rates than wealthier neighborhoods, but wealthier neighborhoods attract more break-ins. Nationally, more crimes are reported in the Northern Territory, and the fewest are in Victoria and Tasmania.

In case of an emergency, call 000 from a landline, or 112 from a cell phone.

FIRES AND EMERGENCIES

In Australia, fire and paramedic services are combined into individual state emergency response systems, accessible via the national emergency numbers: 000 from landlines, 112 from cell phones, and 106 for TTY, teletypewriter, or text phones for the hearing or speech impaired. It is not possible to contact emergency services using text messaging (SMS).

Fire is taken very seriously in Australia, with an average of 52,000 bushfires per year, some 50 percent of which are found to have been deliberately lit or suspicious. In 2009 Victoria experienced the worst bushfires in the country's history, leaving entire communities wiped out and 209 people dead. Bushfire is an annual threat that kills people and destroys homes, businesses, farms, and animals. There are daily warnings in the summer season, when people living in or near the bush, even on the outskirts of towns and cities, are encouraged to have a fire plan in place and a ready-made container of documents and valuables along with a change of clothes packed and ready for evacuation if necessary.

SURF AND SAIL RESCUE

Going into the water in Australia can be a dangerous undertaking, with strong riptides, undertows, and a wide variety of nasty creatures. This is where the famous Aussie lifeguards come into play. The Surf Life Savers are a mix of paid lifeguards and enthusiastic volunteers organized in 313 clubs with more than 167,000 members throughout Australia. They have saved more than 630,000 lives since 1907 and aided countless victims suffering from shark bites, jellyfish stings, and other painful encounters with not-so-cuddly creatures. Surf Life Savers also run Westpac Life Saver Rescue Helicopters, the world's longest-serving search-and-rescue helicopter service, with helicopters stationed in every state. The helicopters are also used for shark patrols during the southern summer months (Oct.-Apr.), scanning the waters in particularly affected regions, but also watching out for other dangers. Australia has threatening wildlife and riptides on the coast, so drowning is a very real danger, and it is advisable only to swim at patrolled beaches between the flags.

POISON CONTROL, BITES, AND STINGS

Australia has some of the most poisonous spiders, snakes, and toads in the world. Why exactly Australian critters have evolved to be so toxic and vicious is not completely understood, but it pays to be alert. In the cities you are generally a lot safer than in the countryside; the riskiest places are in bush with plenty of undergrowth. But one of the most poisonous spiders, the funnel web, is actually indigenous to Sydney. In the outer suburbs you may have snake encounters, and once you leave the relative safety of the cities, be wary. The best way to protect yourself is to know your enemy. While it might not be great bedtime reading, get a book on local spiders and snakes and learn to recognize them, because once you've been bitten, time is of the essence. Call the Poison Information Centre at 131-126, state your emergency, and they will provide you with antivenin. Don't panic—of all the countless spiders in Australia, only three can actually kill you (the funnel web, redback, and white-tailed), and only one unfortunate person has died from a spider bite since 1979.

EMPLOYMENT

Many people's dream of life in Australia begins when they meet relaxed, cheerful, funny, and interesting Australians traveling abroad. But work life in Australia is very different from holiday life. Far from being a country of irrepressible individualists, this is a highly conformist country when it comes to the workplace. That can actually be good news for a newcomer; it is easier to pick up the work ethic, office style, and nuances in colleagues' and bosses' behavior.

The key to finding work as a new arrival is to quickly study and understand Australian behavior and which rules can be bent and which must be observed. Finding work also involves overcoming the prejudices that Australians have about foreigners, especially Americans. Once you have assimilated the basic Australian work ethic, you'll find that work in Australia is structured much as it is in the United States and that your credentials will be understood and appreciated by potential employers.

Newcomers will often find work in the health sector, mining industry, and in managerial levels in banking, law, finance, engineering, and hospitality. For short-term jobs, there is plenty of seasonal employment in the fruit orchards and vineyards. If you have money and a well-thought-out business plan, entrepreneurs can also do well here.

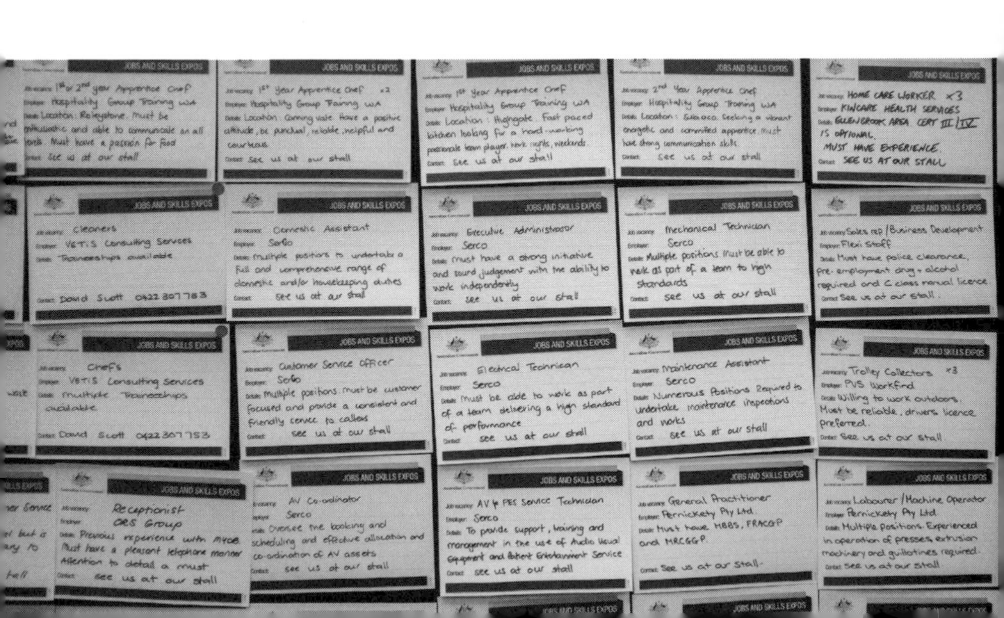

The Job Hunt

The basic resources for job hunting are the Internet and newspaper ads. Major newspapers run the most job ads on Saturday. The best way to get a job is often through a personal connection, and it is easier to make that happen today than in the past.

As soon as you know you are ready to move to Australia, if you don't already have a job or don't have local contacts get an account on a social networking site like **LinkedIn** (www.linkedin.com) and build a profile expressing your interest in Australia so that recruiters doing keyword searches can find you. One option is to join, among other profession-specific groups, the group LinkedIn Open Networkers (LIONs) to start the process of hooking yourself up to the hundreds of Australian recruiters that use the service. You will need to sort through a lot of spam to get useful job leads, but it is an option that has worked for others immigrants. LinkedIn Open Networkers, as a rule of membership, accept invitations from anyone, even if you don't have a prior relationship established.

Within a few weeks of joining, you should have 50-100 direct contacts in Sydney and Melbourne and up to 20,000 indirect contacts. Use that as a base to get your résumé out and begin discussions. All industries are represented, and LinkedIn users are generally very helpful as long as you are friendly in your approach and offer the possibility of returning the favor at a later date.

Depending on the type of job you are looking for, Twitter may also be helpful, at least in establishing new contacts that may then lead to job opportunities. In addition to social networking activities, you can try contacting recruiters. At the executive level, there are companies like **Boyden** (www.boyden.com), while **People Bank** (www.peoplebank.com.au) handles middle management, and companies like **Finite IT** (www.finite.com.au) and **HealthStaff Recruitment** (www.healthstaffrecruitment.com.au) specialize in IT and medical careers, respectively. The website adzuma.com.au publishes career and job offers across the country.

YOUR CV

Although the term *résumé* is generally understood, a résumé is called a CV (for curriculum vitae) in Australia, and it is generally longer and more important than the résumé for a U.S. job search. Australia is a small country, so an avalanche of 1,000 CVs landing on a manager's desk for a job opening is unheard of, and each submission will generally be given more attention.

Cover letters are still essential in grabbing that initial interest of a potential employer and making a good first impression; do not assume in a blind job application that sending a generic CV will do. Your CV can follow the same format as in the United States, but tone down the self-praise, as this is frowned on in Australian culture. Instead of emphasizing your individual achievements, focus more attention on the achievements of the group or the brand, and highlight it if you have worked on a top brand or for a top company in your field. Let the names of your employers and your positions tell the story of your personal excellence, and keep the descriptions of your job summaries factual as to your duties rather than your achievements. Pictures are not necessary, nor are high-end graphics, although good-quality paper and envelopes are still impressive if you are sending a hard copy.

Your academic achievements will be important to your prospective employer, so don't minimize them.

After you've rewritten your CV for the Australian market, the most important task is to put it in the hands of headhunters and friends who can distribute it. The best jobs will be advertised on "the bush telegraph" (word of mouth), either formally or informally, before they are posted on company websites or with third-party services. With Aussies, always politely ask permission; never just spam-deliver your CV to people.

INTERVIEWS

Firms rarely hire people based on overseas interviews except for specialized industries with shortages, such as hotels, cruise ships, nursing, and IT, where an overseas human resources firm will handle interviews. For most assignments, the interviews will take place in Australia.

Punctuality is highly prized, as is efficiency in providing extra hard copies of your CV. Formal business attire, generally conservative, is appropriate for interviewing, although offices tend to be business casual in daily attire. Generally, Australians prefer a low-key approach to speaking about past accomplishments; any hint of bragging or superiority is generally an interview killer.

Employers expect candidates to be friendly, cheerful, and demure in interviews. Australian employers consider a good fit with existing staff to be an important consideration, and interviews are generally more successful when the candidate lets the employer lead with questioning. Except for very small firms, questions about benefits should be reserved for a later interview with HR.

WHAT EMPLOYERS WANT

Foreign employees are especially valuable in the medical professions. Foreign workers help fill general shortages and add expertise in specialized areas, often through exchange programs; large-scale project management, where specialized experience in big projects will give foreigners an edge over locals; university posts, where specialization in subjects not widely taught in Australia leads to invitations for visiting fellowships; primary and secondary education, although often this involves work in the Outback, where many Australians choose not to work; and IT, where there is a chronic shortage of workers.

There is a special category of visa, the 457, which expedites granting visas for skilled foreign workers. The government maintains a list of professions and trades where shortages exist (www.visabureau.com/australia/skilled-occupation-list.aspx).

In the part-time or seasonal labor markets, foreign workers are popular candidates for work in summer beach resorts and for winter skiing jobs. Luxury hotels and cruise lines also experience chronic shortages of trained staff and welcome foreigners, although the pay can be low.

Seasonal workers should keep in mind that Australia has a much lower standard rate for tipping; 10 percent is considered a very adequate tip in most circumstances, and tips for housekeeping services are not common.

WORK CULTURE

Australians are patriotic but aren't especially verbal or boastful about it. Accordingly, Aussies appreciate foreigners who approach Australia with affection, admiration, and a desire to assimilate. This kind of new arrival is considered a great asset. Anyone who comes here seeking to impose their culture on Australians is going to have a hard time. That applies to companies as well.

What you wear, how you act toward

Doing Business in Australia

With a generally relaxed attitude to life, Australians also tend to be a little more casual when it comes to work. For example, everyone is on a first-name basis. The most junior employee calls the general manager by a first name. Addressing someone as "Mr." is done in jest, but not necessarily out of respect. You call your doctor "Angela" rather than "Dr. Smith." Even the prime minister is generally referred to by first name rather than family name.

Appointments are usually made after there has been a phone call and agreement to meet. A "cold call" or meeting set up without some sort of introduction is not favorable; the introduction can be as simple as "so and so told me to give you a call." Who you know is important—more so than your position or job title.

Meeting agendas are only drafted for formal meetings that require minutes, and while a meeting will have a chair, there is a general lack of meeting structure: no formal facilitation to keep the meeting moving and no time allocation for each item of business to ensure that the meeting stays on time. As a result, meetings frequently run late and don't always get all of the items addressed in an equal manner. Also, coffee meetings are a normal part of business in the cities and are considered a legitimate way to have a meeting.

others, the hours you keep, and the way you approach your work are important in every respect for finding and keeping a good job.

Dress

Australians generally dress casually in light clothing because of the warm weather and the historical rarity of air-conditioning. However, as a general rule in offices people dress business casual, but this differs from industry to industry. In upper management, banking, or law, or to meet with high-flying clients, as a rule the dress code is a sharp suit. British-style formalism still permeates the banking business, for example, and barristers still wear black robes and white wigs in court. There are regional clothing variations; in Melbourne, for example, black is famously popular, while in Brisbane, mostly due to the sunnier climate, colors are more prevalent. Depending on your rung on the ladder, a suit is still essential in management for women and men, while younger colleagues can get away with more casual attire.

Professional Conduct

In business Australians are famously nonconfrontational. Words like *reconciliation* and *arbitration* are a part of daily life. Aussies like harmony at home and at the office.

In light of that, Aussies also like to kid each other all the time, and insults are seen as a form of affection. You will find yourself tested, perhaps in a job interview, speaking with a recruiter, or in the job itself. Someone might call you "another stupid bloody Yank," which will sound like an insult, but it's really just a test. You might reply, "that's right; they asked me to come to keep you company." Never take an insult; throw it right back, but paint a smile on it and make sure everyone can see that you are playing along and assimilating.

Australians are highly egalitarian, and while respectful toward the boss, they aren't obsequious and you shouldn't be either. Neither can they stand the office snitch; it's all about the team, so don't become the one who tells on someone else, no matter how much you want to please the boss.

Most people work in the Central Business District (CBD) of a city.

Generally, Australian workers tend to take public transportation and arrive at work on time. They tend to leave on time too and place a high premium on getting the job done efficiently while in the office. Untidy desks are not appreciated, five-minute calls should take five minutes, and 10 o'clock appointments should begin at 10 o'clock, not five minutes after.

However easygoing and focused Australians may seem, the American approach of telling it like it is or barging in and grabbing the bull by the horns tends not to go down well. Bite your tongue, take it a little slower, and go with what the team decides until you find your niche, have been accepted, and may be able to take it farther. Remember that tall-poppy syndrome: Australians don't like those who stand out from the team. Obviously there are promotions and the corporate ladder, as in any workforce, but unless you want to make firm enemies, bide your time.

Labor Laws

Generally speaking, Australia has a strong tradition of employee rights and employer responsibilities. In the past 30-odd years, the Labor Party has been in power in most Australian states and in power at the federal level about 60 percent of the time. The general drift of legislation has been to expand and safeguard worker rights.

The doctrine governing employees is a set of laws known collectively as the Fair Work Act, which has replaced the controversial WorkChoices, a single nationwide industrial relations structure that replaced a collection of federal and state systems that had evolved over the years. An Australian Fair Pay Commission sets minimum standards in areas such as pay, hours, and leave.

Fair Work started in 2009 and has revisited and revised the various labor laws with an aim of better productivity and output. The Fair Work Australia Commission carries out a range of functions related to minimum wages, employment conditions, collective bargaining, strikes, dispute resolution, termination of employment, and other workplace matters, generally providing a safety net for workers.

FAIR WORK AUSTRALIA PROVISIONS

In Australia, the Australian Fair Pay and Conditions Standard operates in five areas relating to pay, hours, and leave. There are five basic provisions that form a minimum standard for Australians.

Hours

Australians work a maximum of 38 hours per week, although this can be averaged over a 12-months period. Employees can be asked to work "reasonable" additional hours and can refuse "unreasonable" requests. Reasonability is based on health, safety, hours previously worked, the operational structure of the business, and the amount of notice given for the request. Overtime is generally paid at twice the hourly rate and usually welcomed in small doses by Aussies.

Annual Leave

Australians are entitled to four weeks paid annual leave. Part-time employees earn leave proportional to the number of hours they work, but casual seasonal workers do not earn paid leave. Workers who regularly have shifts on Sunday or public holidays receive an extra week of leave. Employees can also request to "cash out" up to two weeks of their leave every 12 months to earn extra money instead of taking holidays, but employers are not required to agree to this. An employee's entitlement to annual leave accrues progressively during a year of service according to their ordinary hours of work and accumulates from year to year.

Personal and Caregiving Leave

Australians are entitled to 10 days of paid sick or caregiving leave each year, with caregiving limited to an immediate family member or member of the household. This leave accumulates, and there is no limit on the amount of sick leave that can be accumulated or used in a given year. There are limits on caregiving leave (10 days per year), but two unpaid days of extra caregiving leave per emergency occasion are available.

Parental Leave

Australians are entitled to up to 52 weeks of unpaid parental leave, which can be taken by one parent or shared. It is taken at the time of birth (or adoption of a child under the age of five). Any employee who has worked for 12 months in full-time, part-time, or in some cases casual employment for an employer is eligible for parental leave, and in this case even small businesses are covered by this provision. Mothers are also entitled to six weeks of paid maternity leave immediately following the birth of a child, if they have accumulated 12 months' service with an employer.

Minimum Wage

The Australian Fair Pay Commission is responsible for establishing the federal minimum wage, classifications, and pay scales in the Australian Pay and Classification Scales, as well as the timing and frequency of pay reviews. The commission also sets minimum wages for trainees, apprentices, and juniors, but all adult full-time workers must be paid the federal minimum wage even if their job is not covered in a commission classification. The federal minimum wage is

Business Lunch

In a business setting, there's nothing more awkward than a business lunch in a country where the customs and the food are foreign. Here's a guide to what the locals say and eat after they say g'day:

- **arvo:** afternoon
- **barbie:** barbecue
- **courgette:** zucchini
- **fine, thanks:** good
- **John Dory:** local white fish
- **mince:** ground beef
- **prawn:** shrimp
- **rissole:** sausage-filled pastry
- **schooner:** a 21-ounce beer, the standard Aussie size
- **seppo:** American
- **serviette:** napkin
- **sarnie:** sandwich
- **snags:** barbecued sausages
- **ta:** thank you
- **tea:** dinner
- **tucker:** food
- **yobbo:** lout; rude person

Tipping 10 percent is considered just fine, thanks.

Wine is still quite acceptable at Aussie business lunches, if no one is driving; the safe practice is to drink water.

Bringing a customer home for dinner is rare these days, but bringing a colleague home is less so. Nowadays, people meet at restaurants for dinner, but entertaining colleagues at a Sunday barbecue at the boss's place is still quite common and, though casual, is rarely optional.

currently $17.70 per hour, or $672.70 per week, and is generally increasing by 3-4 percent per year.

Apart from the minimum wage, the sky is the limit when it comes to potential income. In 2015 the top-earning areas in Australia were the eastern suburbs in Sydney, New South Wales, with an average taxable income of $177,514; and the lowest was Delungra, New South Wales, with an average taxable income of $21,691.

Self-Employment

Australia does not have a strong entrepreneurial culture in comparison to the United States, but it is generally more open to self-employment and entrepreneurialism than Europe. The climate for self-employment is generally improving; many financial institutions, for example, are making it easier to obtain mortgages and other consumer finance based on self-employment. The gamut of self-employment opportunities includes:

- Sole traders or sole proprietorships, such as consulting
- Small start-up businesses, such as services
- Franchises
- Large start-up businesses, such as manufacturing

Generally speaking, the sole-trader route is only viable in the case of a wealthy private individual who can qualify for a business investor visa, or for the spouse of someone coming in on a business or professional visa. In this sector, there are opportunities to affiliate with larger firms as a "business finder," including headhunters and financial services firms. One route that has been popular with expats is to establish a real estate practice catering to other expats; again, this is typically the case when the businessperson has obtained a visa through a spouse. This is viable only in Sydney and Melbourne.

In Australia, an investor or business owner can obtain a (provisional) visa (subclass 188) on the strength of an investment in Australian bonds or a business. Provisional business owner visas allow a person with business interests in the country to obtain a multi-entry visa, which can be converted to permanent residence by applying for a Business Innovation and Investment (Permanent) visa (subclass 888). The visa will also extend to a spouse and children under age 18.

The visa (subclass 188) includes four streams: The Business Innovation stream is for people with business skills wanting to establish a new or existing business in Australia and who have been nominated by a state of territory government. The Investor stream is for people willing to make a designated investment of at least $1.5 million in an Australian state or territory and maintain business and investment activity in Australia. The Significant Investor stream is for people able to invest at least $5 million into complying significant investments in Australia; and the Premium Investor stream is for people willing to invest at least $15 million into complying investments in Australia.

Australia maintains a fairly robust government support system for planning small-business activities, including seminars on starting businesses. Financing is just as tough to find in Oz as anywhere else and maybe harder, as Australia has a highly risk-adverse banking culture on smaller investments. The federal government maintains a small-business office, the **Small Business Development Corporation** (www.smallbusiness.wa.gov.au), with field officers who answer questions and give local presentations.

One of the best routes to starting a business in Australia is franchising, which is a growing field and one foreigners often have excellent results with, as many of them involve international brands. The franchising route requires up-front investment, and they generally require a long-term commitment to be financially viable. The **Franchise Council of Australia** (www.franchisebusiness.com.au) offers information on more than 4,382 franchises, which typically involve up-front payments of $20,000 to $250,000. The business categories of franchises are primarily food, consumer goods, and services.

FINANCE

The people of Sydney did not have a currency but worked with handwritten notes, a certain amount of rum, and barter until 1813, when then Governor Macquarie shipped some 40,000 Spanish silver Maria Theresa dollar coins Down Under in a bid to create a more civilized society. Holes were punched in these large coins, creating two new coins: the holey dollar and the dump. Since then, the Australian currency has become part of a steady and healthy economy. The Australian dollar sometimes approaches parity with the U.S. dollar, but exchange rates vary. In the early 1970s the Australian dollar was worth as much as US$1.50, and by the mid-1990s was worth around US$0.50. Those are the extremes, and in recent years the Australian dollar has generally been valued at US$0.70-0.85.

Following the global financial crisis, even Australian interest rates have dramatically dropped, with the average at around 3 percent on higher investments of around $10,000. Shares earn you a little more, but there is always a risk with the market still being volatile. If you have the residency and the money, the Australian property market is always a good investment, especially if you will live in the house while you are here, but like anywhere in the world at the moment, the return on investments, after tax, is not as exciting as it once was and should be approached with caution.

Moving to another country is a major undertaking that may or may not include a higher income and a better standard of living. While Australia certainly has a high standard of living, a move here won't necessarily involve a higher income, and it can cost you quite a bit to get here. A move from the United States to Australia may require at least $5,000 for the shipping container, another $3,000 to bring the dog, a deposit on your rental property, initial outlays for extra furniture, car rental, school administration fees, and many more initial moving costs depending on your particular needs.

Cost of Living

Living in Australia is not cheap, even if the high standard of living makes it very livable; the quality of life here comes at a price. The 2016 Mercer Worldwide Cost of Living Survey rated Sydney and Melbourne as Australia's most expensive cities, with Sydney 42nd and Melbourne 71st on the worldwide list, a dramatic drop in ranking due to the depreciation of the Australian dollar against the U.S. dollar.

HOW MUCH MONEY DO I NEED?

Minimum Standards

In Australia, rent is quoted by the week, and the budgeting described here follows this pattern. Outside Sydney and Melbourne, life can be relatively affordable, but a good basic standard is to use $600 per week as a starting point for a minimal lifestyle for an individual, and add one-third for Sydney and Melbourne or about 10 percent for the other major cities. This would cover a modest shared flat in an accessible, relatively safe outlying suburb, basic utilities, a public transit card for commuting, and food and low-cost entertainment. This includes an allowance for a broadband Internet connection that will cost about $30 per month, but this will enable you to connect to Skype, often the expat's best friend for international communication.

Average Standards

The average weekly expenditure in Australia is around $2,200 per household. This estimate includes home loans or rent at an average $600 a week, followed by food and eating out at $400, and insurance and other financial services at $200. Utility bills have risen steadily since 2006. (For a small 85 square meter apartment the monthly utilities of water, electricity, and gas cost around $220 per month. For a telephone, TV, and Internet package allow around $70 per month.) These numbers mean it costs an average household around $100,000 per year to live in Australia.

Luxury Standards

Where luxury standards are involved, the sky is the limit; you could easily spend the annual budget of a small country on a nice house by the beach. More realistically, $1,500 to $2,000 per week can get a very nice house or apartment within easy reach of the city or the beaches in any of the country's major cities, including Sydney. Typical water, electricity, and gas bills for a house with four bedrooms would cost around $400-500 per month. TV, telephone, and Internet packages with extra TV channels included are available from around $100 per month. Add $500 per week on food and drink, plus around $400 on eating out; if you

Comparing the Cost of Living

Every few years, Mercer Consulting releases a study showing the comparative cost of living in various cities around the world. The factors that determine a city's ranking are the relative strength of its currency against the U.S. dollar in the 12 months between ranking, and price movements over the 12 months as compared to those in New York City as the base. Ranks can also change based on the movement of other cities in the ranking list. The ranking of the previous year is given in brackets.

City	Ranking (as of 2016)
Sydney	42 (21)
Melbourne	71 (47)
Perth	69 (48)
Canberra	98 (65)
Brisbane	96 (66)
Adelaide	102 (71)

Sample Prices for Everyday Items

- 2 liters of orange juice: $4.80
- 1 liter of full-fat milk: $1.46
- 1 kilogram of carrots: $2.50
- 1 kilogram of potatoes: $1.95
- 500 grams of lean ground beef: $5
- 1 loaf of white sandwich bread: $2.99
- 8 rolls of 2-ply toilet paper: $6.60
- 24 cans (375 ml) of Coca-Cola: $17
- 6 free-range eggs: $3
- 500 grams of aged cheddar cheese: $7.48
- 1 725-gram box of Kellogg's Cornflakes: $4
- 1 Mars bar: $2.20
- 1 can of dog food: $2.26
- 200 milliliter bottle of Head & Shoulders shampoo: $7.04
- 500 grams of butter: $2.60

have kids going to private school, two cars, and hobbies such as tennis or golf, costs would be about $200,000 per year, or nearly $4,000 per week, not including vacations.

MONTHLY EXPENSES

Housing and Utilities

Some expatriates have housing provided by their employers or get a housing stipend; if not, housing will be your biggest monthly expense, because Australian accommodations, rented or purchased, are expensive. In cities such as Sydney and Melbourne, a comfortable and reasonably spacious family home will cost at least $1,000 per week anywhere near the city center. Utilities are also quite expensive, although shopping around and switching suppliers can be worthwhile, as there is competition, including discounts to encourage you to change providers. As a general guideline, plan to spend around $350 per month on electricity, water, and gas; $70 on telephone and Internet service; and if you want cable TV, around $100 per month. Gas for the car costs around $1.15 per liter in August 2016.

Food and other Necessities

When it comes to groceries, it pays to shop around. The two main supermarket chains are Coles and Waitrose (Safeway is part of Waitrose), and each has a loyalty card scheme to woo the customers. There is also the low-cost and no-frills Aldi, which can help reduce costs if you buy in bulk. There are Costco big-box stores in Sydney, Melbourne, and Canberra, but these require a membership.

As a general guideline, and if you are trying to buy seasonal and local products as compared to trying to find brands you recognize from back home, around $350 per week should feed a family of four. Wine and other types of alcohol are quite

Coles is one of Australia's major supermarket chains.

pricey, but again, shop around or order your favorites by the box and you'll get better deals. A drinkable bottle of wine costs over $15 and a six-pack of beer around $30, although there are always discounts and "clean skin" shops that sell wine without labels, generally of good quality and a lot cheaper. Eating out depends on where you go, but you can get a cup of coffee for $4, a substantial breakfast for $18, and a main course for dinner in a decent restaurant for around $30, accompanied by a glass of wine for $9.

Medical

Health care is said to be free because everyone is covered under the government Medicare scheme, but there are certain limitations: If you are not a permanent resident, you cannot apply for Medicare coverage, and Medicare does not necessarily cover all the cost of treatment or consultation. Medicare covers public hospital care but only pays 75 to 85 percent of doctors' consultations and other treatments. Most Australians have private insurance to cover the remainder, and higher-income earners are encouraged through taxation to opt for full private health insurance. A basic doctor or dentist consultation costs around $75 per visit, and depending on your private health insurance, you can probably claim all that back. What type of coverage you buy depends on your family status, age, existing conditions, and other factors, but most expats who come to Australia to work try to negotiate at least basic private coverage into their contracts.

Schooling

Whether you opt to send your kids to state or private schools, you have to pay tuition fees, although these are waived for 457 visa holders in some states such as the ACT and Tasmania. Roughly speaking, private independent nonreligious schools are the most expensive, with annual fees up to $20,000. Add to that the cost of uniforms, books, excursions, calculators, laptops, and other necessities and school costs can be around $25,000 or more per year per child. Faith-based private schools are more affordable, but even state schools, for those who are not permanent residents, can incur fees up to $10,000 per year. If you are opting for boarding or semiboarding schools, costs are higher.

Entertainment and Travel

An average cinema ticket will set you back around $16, a fitness class membership around $20 per week for unlimited group classes, and membership to a gym around $70 per month. Reasonable seats at an Australian Rules football game will cost around $45 per person.

Daily travel will set you back around $3 per trip on a tram, bus, or other public transportation for the shortest distance, with discounts if you buy passes. Air travel can be expensive, although domestic flights can be cheap, from $55 one-way between Melbourne and Adelaide, for example, on one of the domestic low-cost airlines such as Tigerair.

Shopping

Ask any American expatriate living in Australia and they will tell you that clothing is very expensive; most buy their clothes online and have them shipped or brought over by friends. You can expect higher prices for manufactured goods as well as clothing—20 to 30 percent more than in the United States is a rule of thumb. But there are also many bargain shops around that are especially useful when you're first setting up a home, including Target, Kmart, IKEA, and Big W, all selling household goods; some sell clothes as well at good prices. Shopping malls are a growing phenomenon, especially in the suburbs, where supermarkets and bargain shops mingle with mass retailers and designer goods. Food courts and kids entertainment areas are provided, making a trip to the mall an easy way to stock up on everything.

For fresh produce, the true essence of relaxed Aussie-style living is to patronize the farmers markets, where seasonal fruit and vegetables and other goods are available from stalls operated usually once a week. The crush of people and the dazzling array of fresh food make these a must. Credit cards are widely accepted, although American Express less so.

In the suburbs most shops close by 6pm; they are open late only on Thursday nights, typically until 9pm. Most shops close on Saturday afternoon and all day Sunday, which makes the cities peacefully quiet as the nation turns to sports and barbecues, although this is rapidly changing as a way to keep life in the CBD, with cafés and shops opening on the weekend more and more.

Specialty meat, fish, and fruit and veg shops still exist, although they are rarer each year. The fruit and veg shop is also called the greengrocer, especially among older people.

Electronics are quite expensive here, as are cars. Serious consideration should be given to bringing computers, music

shopping mall in Melbourne

players, and similar items with you when you make the move, despite the need for an electric plug adapter. Cars are generally 20 percent more expensive than in the United States, and unfortunately it can be difficult to import your U.S. car. The best you can hope for is a company car, or a car allowance from your employer to help defray the initial expense. Personal car import approval is only given by the Department of Infrastructure to migrants with full residency visas or Australian or New Zealand nationals who are of driving age in Australia. Holders of retirement or long term/business 457 visas will have to prove that they are a resident in Australia before they will be granted permission to import their car. The vehicle also needs to meet a set number of standards before permitted. Generally speaking, a left-hand-drive vehicle can be registered in most states only if it is more than 30 years old.

Banking

Australia is very much a card-oriented society. Even for a cup of coffee, cash rarely changes hands. Bills are paid online, and it's easy to transfer funds. Setting up a bank account that provides for all your needs is a vital first step when you move to Australia.

OPENING AN ACCOUNT

If you already bank with an international bank such as HSBC, it is easier to open an account in Australia, as they can later connect your existing accounts. With the competition among Australian banks, however, it is still easy enough to open an account. You will need to bring photo ID, and your passport is acceptable. You have to either make a deposit or prove your regular income, such as with a salary slip from your employer; and you must provide proof of your address. This is usually the most difficult to obtain for new expats, especially if you have not found permanent accommodations yet or have not yet received a utility bill. The bank will usually accept verification of an address from your employer.

INTERNATIONAL ACCOUNTS

International banks don't tend to have truly international accounts unless you opt for offshore tax-free accounts. In all other cases you still have an account in your home country and a new one in Australia. They can be linked online, but to transfer money from one account to another you will still have to apply for, and pay for, a telegraphic wire transfer. If you do not have an account in Australia but want to send money home, you can do so at the post office and services such as Western Union, found in all major cities.

CURRENCY

The Australian currency is the Australian dollar, which in recent years has been near parity with the U.S. dollar. Coins come is denominations of 5, 10, 20, and 50 cents and $1 and $2, and bills are in denominations of $5, $10, $20, $50, and $100. Each note is a different color and size to allow the visually impaired to distinguish them. Since September 2016, the $5 notes also have raised bumps to distinguish them further. Australia was the first country to have notes made from plastic, or polymer, making them longer-lasting and more difficult to counterfeit. They also survive an erroneous stint in the washing machine rather well.

Most banks offer all the usual services.

ATMS, CREDIT CARDS, AND CHECKS

ATMs are widely available, although availability decreases in relation to distance from larger towns and cities. Using these machines you can withdraw cash, deposit cash and checks, and often pay bills. Checks are still used, but not widely, and they are not generally accepted for personal payments. The majority of transactions are done either through electronic transfers online or by bank card. Even savings accounts have cards with the Visa logo on them, and although they're not credit cards, they can be used as debit cards in shops and restaurants and for online payments. Many shops have the Visa payWave system installed, in which you simply wave your card in front of a sensor; for purchases under $100 you don't have to sign or use a PIN.

If you are in Australia and don't yet have access to a bank account but don't want to carry wads of cash around, another option is a multicurrency prepaid card. These cards, usually linked to Visa or MasterCard, are like deposit accounts; you deposit cash and then access it through the card. Products from providers such as **Cash Passport** (www.cashpassport.com/multi) allow you access to your money online and in several countries, making it much safer than carrying cash when you're traveling.

Taxes

The good news is that Australians pay only federal income tax, and there is no need to file state or local tax returns. The bad news is that Americans still have tax obligations when they live outside the United States and have to file U.S. tax returns. Tax rules in other countries vary.

AUSTRALIAN INCOME TAXES

Australian taxes are filed by October 31 each year, based on the July 1-June 30 tax year. When arriving in Australia, you need to obtain a tax file number (TFN), which you can get online from the **Australian Taxation Office** (www.ato.gov.au) or at a local tax office. The nine-digit tax file number is one of the most important things to have in Australia; without it you are taxed at the maximum rate, 45 percent. Income is counted from all sources, including salary and investment returns.

Income taxes for salaried workers are collected on a pay-as-you-go basis, so in many cases filing a return will get you a refund.

The regulations concerning taxes for the self-employed can be complicated, especially for a newcomer. In Australia, 90 percent of self-employed people use a registered tax agent to help them through the tax maze and ensure that they pay the minimum amount possible. However, there are distinct advantages to being self-employed, such as the possibility to claim allowances in the form of business expenses, including telephone bills, travel to and from work, and work clothes or uniforms. There is also the option to delay between making profits and paying tax on them. One of the pitfalls of being self-employed is that you have to organize paying your own "superannuation" or pension fund to ensure that you receive a large enough pension to live off of once you retire. But, if you are self-employed, you can claim a tax deduction on those superannuation contributions. At the time of writing, if a self-employed person earns

Tax returns are due by October 31 each year.

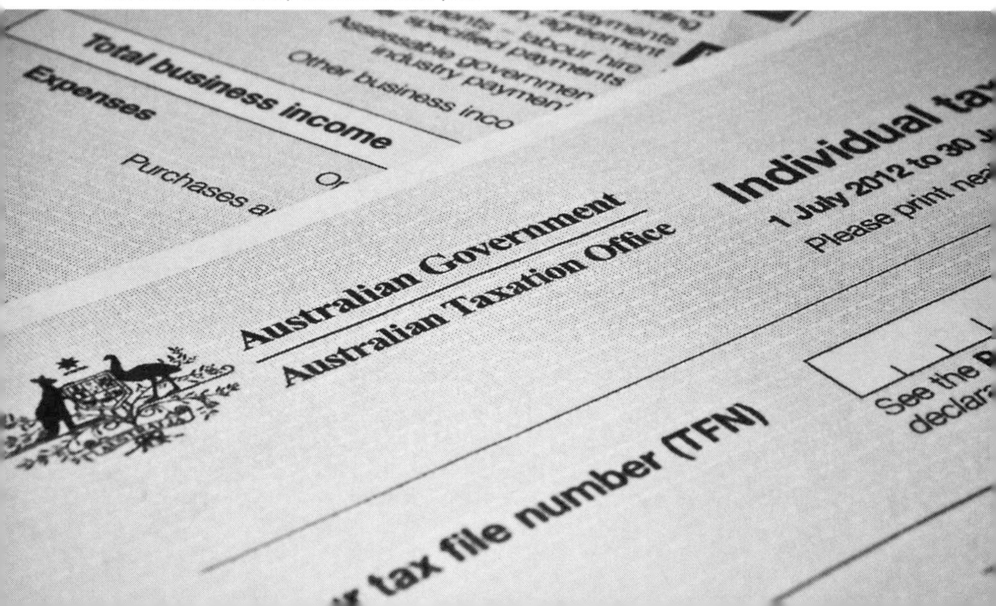

less than $46,920 per year, the option of making after-tax contributions to a superannuation will also qualify them for co-contribution from the government.

SALES TAX

Australia has a general sales tax, called the Goods and Services Tax (GST). This rate is set at 10 percent and applied by merchants to almost all transactions, although services are currently exempt from GST. This revenue, like income tax, is collected by the federal branch of the government and then shared with states on a negotiated basis; states in turn fund local governments.

Investing

SUPERANNUATION

If you are 18 years old or older and earning more than $450 per month, your employer is legally required to pay an additional 9.5 percent (in 2016) of your income into a "superannuation" or pension fund. Superannuation, abbreviated to "super," is a private pension fund that employees can either manage themselves or have managed by the state. The fund can be subsidized by additional voluntary contributions, which might have tax advantages, and it is available to casual workers and full-time and part-time employees. The self-employed and nonresidents are not required to pay into a fund. From 2016 to 2019 an increase will be gradually implemented in super payments from 9.5 to 12 percent.

THE STOCK MARKET AND MUTUAL FUNDS

Stocks and mutual funds are broadly similar to the U.S. market. The Australian market has less liquidity than the U.S. system, and stocks are generally more volatile. There are several types of mutual funds available: closed-end funds, funds, and index funds. Since Australians are forced to save money for retirement but have some discretion as to how it is managed, Aussies have more invested in

"Super" or Superannuation

It may sound complex, but superannuation, usually abbreviated to "super," is a pension scheme similar to the 401(k) system in the United States. In Australia, your employer has to make a contribution to your superannuation scheme at least once every three months. Individuals can make contributions that are tax-deferred. Your super is managed by one of more than 300,000 superannuation funds operating in the country, of which about 300 are major outfits with more than $50 million in assets. You choose the manager of your funds. The employer contribution in 2016 is 9.5 percent. You can begin to access the funds as early as age 55. The super is, in fact, a super way to manage a pension plan. The government offers guaranteed pensions (based on a means test) to all older people, and a pensioner receives the employer's compulsory contributions to superannuation, plus, of course, the voluntary contributions made by the employee.

mutual funds than any other country in the world.

Reportedly, Australia has one of the highest rates of share ownership in the world, with around 40 percent of Australians as shareholders. If you are thinking about investing some money in shares, the process is pretty straightforward. To get a feel for how certain shares are performing, you can join websites such as www.australianstockreport.au, which send you regular newsletters letting you know about the daily happenings on the stock market. There are also blogs and forums where individual traders and investors can get information. Generally speaking, you can start dealing in shares with $1,000 or more. You can place bids either in person, over the phone, or through an online broker. The brokerage fee for an investment of $1,000 is approximately $20. Fees decrease as the investment amount grows. For example, an investment of $100,000 would have a brokerage fee of around $100.

If you'd rather invest in mutual/managed funds, you can compare the top funds in Australia on websites such as www.investsmart.com.au/managed-funds.

COMMUNICATIONS

Australia is isolated from the rest of the world by vast oceans, and even within the continent, distances can make communication a challenge. The original inhabitants of this vast land, the Aborigines, had complex ways of communicating. There were originally around 250 indigenous languages, although most have disappeared and the great distances and sparse populations meant that most communities never had the opportunity to meet or talk to one another. The distinctive Aboriginal visual art was also a means of communication; the myriad symbols have meaning and convey a message, perhaps about the history of the community, a special event, or specific useful information such as good hunting areas or the location of water. The Europeans brought their own means of communication, and by 1854 there was a telegraph line from Melbourne to Williamstown. It was just 20 kilometers long, but the feat paved the way to further advancement.

Today, you can generally expect top-level telephone, Internet, and television services thoughtfully provided even in remote areas, although service bundles can be confusing and sometimes not well constructed. Increasingly you can get personally configured packaged products to suit your needs. Phones, computers, and other electronic devices are expensive here, and customer service will feel slow

and unresponsive for anyone used to the American way of doing things. It pays to shop around, as many companies offer similar services at different rates; competition can be fierce and deals can be found. If you are renting your housing, your landlord may have an existing deal for some or all of these services, but you can ask to change companies if another suits you better.

Telephone

Australian telecommunications were deregulated in 1995, and now several dozen companies provide services. Telstra and Optus are the main landline phone companies. Telstra, the government-owned phone company, is used by the vast majority of Australians, often simply because they had service set up before deregulation. Telstra also has the broadest coverage in outlying areas.

Generally speaking, for a basic Telstra plan, expect to pay $50 per month with unlimited local calls, but a $0.45 fee for timed mobile and international calls and $1 per long-distance call and $0.36 per minute for calls to Telstra mobile phones (capped at $1 for the first 20 minutes) and $0.36 per minute for non-Telstra mobile phones (capped at $2 for the first 20 minutes). International calls start at $0.39 for the call, plus $0.21 per minute.

INTERNATIONAL VALUE PACKS

A must for international calling are value-pack options, especially if a lot of your calls will be to family and friends overseas. If you are a subscriber to an eligible Telstra landline, for $15 per month you can get unlimited calling to the United States. Optus offers the World Saver Calling option to be added to your existing plan for $5 per month, reducing calling rates to the United States from $0.18 to $0.02 per minute.

CALLING CARDS

Telstra has a wide range of prepaid or billable calling cards, which can be used remotely, but the long-distance calls are charged at a premium, $0.21 per minute to the United States plus a $0.49 connection charge per call.

You can get other international calling cards online, such as **OzPhoneCard** (www.ozphonecard.com.au), that promise calls to the United States as low as $0.04 per minute with no connection charges through Chinese or European vendors. How reliable and legal these are, however, cannot be guaranteed.

a public phone booth in Melbourne

Area Codes and Networks

For telephone calls, Australia has a short and easily remembered system of calling codes. Area codes are organized by state, with some exceptions around border areas. Mobile phones have their own area code, 4. When dialing from inside Australia, you add a 0, so that Sydney phone numbers are dialed using "02."

AREA CODES

- 2–Central East: New South Wales, Australian Capital Territory, parts of northern border areas of Victoria
- 3–Southeast: Tasmania, Victoria, and parts of southern border areas of New South Wales
- 4–digital GSM mobile phones
- 7–Northeast: Queensland
- 8–Central and West Region: South Australia, Northern Territory, and Western Australia

NETWORKS

For mobile calling, Australia has three networks that work with a wide variety of devices, and your U.S. device may function if you have an international roaming plan; check with your service provider. When you move here, it may be possible to keep your existing phone, if it's unlocked, and simply buy a new SIM card from your new carrier. Optus, Telstra, and Vodafone operate the networks GSM-900; GSM-1800; 3G WCDMA; HSDPA-850, 900, and 2100; and 4G LTE 1800.

SKYPE

For long-distance service, most expats use **Skype** (www.skype.com). It is a voice over Internet protocol (VoIP) service that offers free unlimited computer-to-computer calling and cheap calls from your computer to a landline (as low as $0.03 per minute). Most computers these days have microphones and cameras built in, or you can buy a small USB camera-microphone set. Apple users can use iChat, similar to Skype.

MOBILE PHONES

The large mobile companies are Optus, Virgin Mobile, Vodafone, Telstra, and 3. Telstra is by far the biggest, although the others are well-known, except perhaps 3, which is part of Vodafone.

Mobile phone service generally comes with a subsidized phone and a contract. A Telstra package with a 24-month contract and a midrange phone is around $40 per month, which includes $35 for voice and $5 for data. Usage costs $0.76 per minute and $2 per MB, and $0.25 per SMS text message. Australians have widely adopted text messaging to keep mobile costs down.

Customers typically buy their phones through the carrier, but you can also buy only a service plan with a new SIM card to use in an existing unlocked phone. Ringtones are widely available and are easy to download.

Another option is a prepaid mobile phone, which can be purchased outright with no contract for as little as $29, depending on the phone. You can add a service plan, which usually comes with $10 of call credit and six months of network access. You can fill your account with as much credit as you like, and usage costs $0.38 per minute for calls, $2 per MB for data, and $0.25 per text message. You can buy specialized plans that optimize text messages, and calls and texts to numbers on the same carrier are highly discounted. Some packages offer unlimited calls and texts to a calling circle of up to five numbers on the same network.

BRINGING YOUR EXISTING PHONE

Australia uses the same 900 MHz and 1,800 MHz GSM technology found in most countries except North America and Japan. Some American GSM phones designed for 1,900 MHz can handle standard GSM. 3G and 4G services are also in use, both via Telstra.

A typical CDMA phone from the States will not work here, although some will—check with your service provider. The good news is that GSM is getting more popular in the United States, so there's a chance that a handset will work in Australia if it's unlocked. Almost all phones sold in the United States are locked to the providers who sell them. Some phones can be unlocked for a fee by the U.S. provider, and others can't be unlocked. You must arrange this before you leave.

If you have an iPhone, whether it will work in Australia depends on whether it is GSM or CDMA. The iPhone 6 is widely available in Australia and will cost around $929.

If your phone can be used here, when you arrive, **Telestial** (www.telestial.com) offers an Australia SIM card with free incoming calls and local-rate outbound calls, all prepaid and with no contract. You start with a local Australian number and a $10 airtime credit and minutes cost $0.49. For unlocked 4G phones, most airports have a small Optus store where you can purchase a local SIM card under a 12-month bring-your-own-phone plan starting from $30 per month, including 200 MB data and $200 in credit, two-minute standard national calls at $2.15, and text messages at $0.25. Double-check the 4G compatibility of your phone, as not all 4G devices are compatible with the Optus 4G network.

Internet and Postal Services

INTERNET

The largest provider of Internet service in Australia is Big Pond, a Telstra service, which offers both DSL broadband or broadband over cable when bundled with the Foxtel cable TV service. Big Pond also features wireless broadband and satellite broadband service in remote areas.

Broadband via DSL starts at $30 per month on a 5 GB plan, and up to $90 per month for 500 GB of data usage. You must sign a 12-month contract. Special offers may discount up to half the monthly cost for the first year of a two-year contract. Home networking systems for up to five computers are available free from Telstra.

For remote areas, broadband satellite is the way to go. It requires a dish, and for a midrange 2 GB data transfer plan, the monthly cost is $250 and $0.15 per additional MB. It might sound extremely expensive, but if you intend to move into the Outback away from city life, this is the only option.

POSTAL SERVICE

The postal service, Australia Post, has improved its services from the dreadful state of years past. There are quicker alternatives: For bills, pay online; for greetings, use email.

The cost of postage is incredibly complex, determined by size, weight, thickness, and destination distance. Sizes come with unusual codes: DL (110 by 220 millimeters), C6 (114 by 162 millimeters), C5 (162 by 229 millimeters), C4 (324 by 250 millimeters), and B4 (353 by 250 millimeters). A standard envelope, the DL size, of standard thickness, weighing 20 grams, and traveling within Australia costs $1 for nonguaranteed first-business-day service, or $5.75 for express mail that is guaranteed the next business day. Internationally, a postcard will cost $2.75 and will arrive in 3 to 10 working days. Packages over 20 millimeters thick, weighing more than 500 grams, or larger than 260 by 360 millimeters are considered parcels. A 500-gram package that is a small standard-package size of 22 by 16 by 7.7 centimeters will travel Sydney to Melbourne in up to three business days for $7.45, or $10.20 for Express Post, guaranteed the next day.

FedEx shipping is available for international shipments only.

Australia Post for all postal essentials

Media

Australia's cultural exports are well-known around the world, remarkable considering Australia's small population. Many financial observers around the world get daily market updates from Sydney, and a string of programs from Australia have been adapted for American audiences, such as *Wheel of Fortune* and *A Current Affair*. Australian content transfer has become particularly acute since Rupert Murdoch's News Corp. acquired 20th Century Fox in 1984. The Fox and Fox News networks have become recognized around the world along with Aussie-owned premium services such as SkyTel, the main satellite television service in Australia.

NEWSPAPERS

Australia has a robust and competitive newspaper market, although the general decline of newspapers in the Internet age has been felt here as well. Expats will be surprised by the variety of newspapers available, their competitiveness, and the racy, lurid style of their mix of content.

The two newspaper empires are the Murdoch and Fairfax chains. The Murdoch tabloid style will be familiar to readers of other Murdoch papers such as the *New York Post* or London's former *News of the World*. They are sensationalist, rough-hewn, conservative, and aimed at the mass market, and generally have the largest circulation. The *Herald*

Sun in Melbourne and the *Telegraph* in Sydney are the leading Murdoch tabloids. The Fairfax chain produces the broadsheet-style *Sydney Morning Herald* and *Melbourne Age.* They are generally the number-two papers in circulation numbers but have better advertising rates reflecting their more upscale readership.

In addition to the local papers, Australia has two national newspapers: *The Australian,* a broadsheet published by Murdoch, and the *Australian Financial Review,* a daily financial tabloid published by Fairfax. Large Australian cities have 3-4 daily papers to choose from, excluding the free city weeklies and weekly community "advertisers."

RADIO

Australia has a relatively quiet radio market due to its small population and conservative licensing policies. Few stations were launched between 1932 and 1976, and only a limited range of stations can be supported by the small population, especially in rural areas. In the cities, FM has a mix of formats ranging from religious stations to alternative rock. News and opinion stations tend to exist mostly on the AM band. National radio networks are built around key radio brands Fox, Nova, Mix, and others, which have affiliates in all the major cities. Talk radio is dominated by four stations owned by the Fairfax media empire.

The Australian Broadcasting Corporation (ABC, or "Aunty") is government-owned but quite independent of government influence. It produces a news service, a country-music radio network (DiG Country), a classical music service, and Radio National, similar to NPR in the United States. SBS radio is the multicultural radio service broadcasting in major immigrant languages. A number of religious broadcasters appear on the dial, primarily fundamentalist Christian.

Station identifiers begin with numbers that reflect the station's state, so 2MMM is the Triple M station in Sydney, 3MMM is in Melbourne, 4MMM in Brisbane, 5MMM in Adelaide, and 6MIX in Perth.

TELEVISION

Australian over-the-air television consists of five national networks. The ABC is the government-owned channel; it runs a service like BBC or PBS, offering serious fare that includes many documentaries.

SBS is the multicultural television service that grew out of a desire by the government to explain the first national health scheme to new immigrants. It shows multilingual programming, including foreign films, news with a stronger international component, and international sports such as soccer.

The three commercial networks are the Seven, Nine, and Ten networks, named for the channels they occupy on the VHF band. The Nine Network, controlled by the Packer family, has consistently been the market leader, especially in sports, while the Seven Network has been its most persistent rival. The Ten Network was launched in the 1960s to increase local content, and it consistently trails in ratings. All commercial networks broadcast a mandated percentage of local content, but they also tend to purchase syndicated foreign programming to save on costs. Most well-known U.S. shows appear on these networks.

CABLE AND SATELLITE

Foxtel is the primary cable and satellite broadcasting system in Australia. It is a joint venture between Rupert Murdoch's News Corp., Consolidated Media Holdings (owner of the Nine Network), and Telstra. Foxtel produces standard cable service, a high-definition service, a mobile service featuring 12 channels that can stream on wireless devices, an on-demand service, and a DVR-like personal digital recording service called Foxtel iQ.

Basic Foxtel service starts at $26 per month for 45 channels, including Discovery, CNN, CNBC, and Fox Sports News. Platinum packages cost from $135 per month, and include all channels from news to drama, kids' channels to sport. Multiroom access is available for an additional $15 per month per outlet, with a one-off fee for the box, if you choose a different package.

The Foxtel service serves more than 1.6 million homes, or about 25 percent of the population, compared to cable's 90 percent permeation in the United States.

MAGAZINES

Australia has a relatively vibrant magazine market despite its small population. The primary chains are the Fairfax magazines and ACP. Most well-known international titles are sold as Australian editions produced under license, so local content is more heavily featured. Prominent magazines include *Women's Weekly, Woman's Daily, Cleo, Cosmopolitan, New Idea, Ralph, FHM, Rolling Stone,* and *Better Homes and Gardens,* plus plenty of gossip magazines, while Time Inc. offers titles such as *People* and *Money.* As with a lot of things, there are some unusual aspects to Australian media, so the popular women's magazine *Women's Weekly* is a monthly magazine, and *Women's Daily* is a weekly.

A couple of good travel magazines are the *Australian Traveller* and the *International Traveller,* the former giving expats great ideas on where to go to explore their newly adopted country.

Magazines are under pressure from the Internet, both in advertising and circulation, and Australian magazines increasingly represent the interests of the advertisers who fund them. Extensive product placement and advertiser-friendly story lines have become more common.

TRAVEL AND TRANSPORTATION

Traveling to and within Australia can be a challenge, if only in terms of distances. From Europe, flight times including stopovers add up to 24 hours. Most travelers choose to enjoy a couple of days in Dubai, Singapore, or Hong Kong to break up the long journey. From the East Coast of the United States, flights take around 19 hours, but potential stopovers are the South Pacific islands, which take the edge off the long trip.

And, once you arrive in Australia, it can often take a while to drive from one city to another. On a map it might look like Sydney is just around the corner from Melbourne, but it's at least a 10-hour drive. Considering the distance between Sydney and Perth, with so little human settlement in between, air travel is clearly the way to go.

Domestic flights are more relaxed than international travel, and you can even bring your bottle of water onboard. There are domestic quarantine laws, so no fruit, vegetable, or plant matter can be carried from state to state. Sadly, rail travel is not really an option, but again considering the vast distances, it would be time-consuming.

It is not as easy as it might seem to

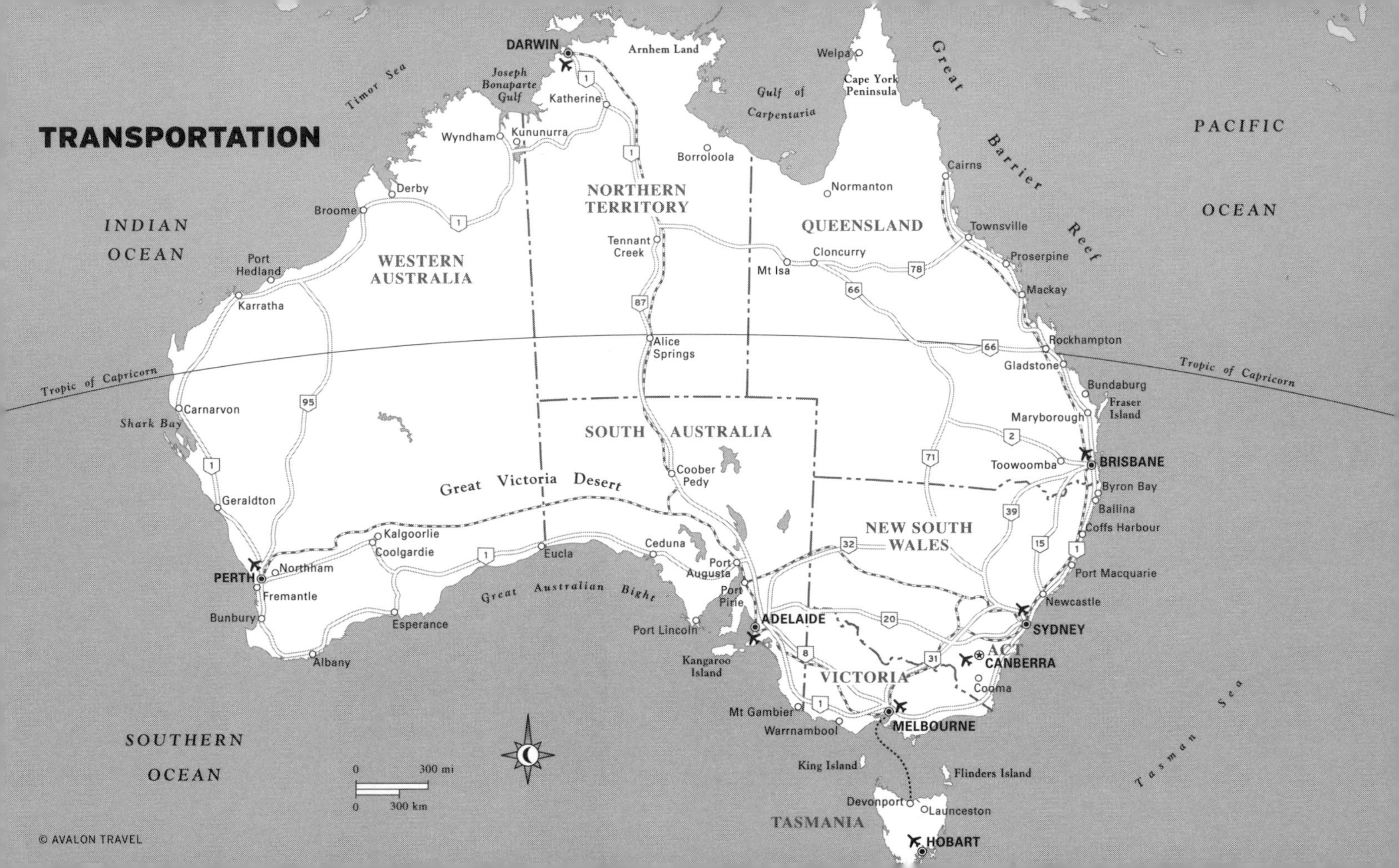
TRANSPORTATION
INDIAN OCEAN
Timor Sea
Joseph Bonaparte Gulf
DARWIN
Arnhem Land
Katherine
Wyndham
Kununurra
Gulf of Carpentaria
Welpa
Cape York Peninsula
Great Barrier Reef
PACIFIC OCEAN
Borroloola
Normanton
Cairns
Derby
Broome
NORTHERN TERRITORY
QUEENSLAND
Townsville
Tennant Creek
Cloncurry
Mt Isa
Proserpine
Mackay
Port Hedland
Karratha
WESTERN AUSTRALIA
Alice Springs
Rockhampton
Gladstone
Bundaburg
Fraser Island
Maryborough
Tropic of Capricorn
Carnarvon
Shark Bay
SOUTH AUSTRALIA
Toowoomba
BRISBANE
Byron Bay
Ballina
Coffs Harbour
Port Macquarie
Great Victoria Desert
Coober Pedy
Geraldton
Kalgoorlie
Coolgardie
Eucla
Ceduna
Port Augusta
Port Pirie
NEW SOUTH WALES
PERTH
Northham
Fremantle
Bunbury
Esperance
Albany
Great Australian Bight
Port Lincoln
Kangaroo Island
ADELAIDE
Newcastle
SYDNEY
ACT
CANBERRA
Cooma
VICTORIA
Mt Gambier
Warrnambool
MELBOURNE
King Island
Flinders Island
Devonport
Launceston
TASMANIA
HOBART
Tasman Sea
SOUTHERN OCEAN
0 300 mi
0 300 km
1
95
87
78
66
71
2
39
15
32
20
31
8

explore this vast country, even if you live here; many people wait until they retire, buy an RV, and hit the road. They are called the gray nomads, and you'll see bumper stickers such as "Spending the Kids' Inheritance" along the highway.

Air

There are more than 600 airports in Australia, from simple landing strips in the Outback to busy international airports. Sydney's Kingsford Smith Airport is undoubtedly the busiest, followed closely by Melbourne. Sydney's airport, eight kilometers from the city's Central Business District (CBD), saw some 39.7 million passengers in fiscal 2015, with 25.9 million domestic passengers, 13.7 million on international flights, and the remainder on short regional hops. U.S. citizens coming through the airport ranked number 5 of nationalities in transit. The airport hosts 45 airlines and 40 percent of all international airline passengers, and it has flights to 49 international, 21 domestic interstate, and 23 regional New South Wales destinations. With direct connections to most regional airports, it is also usually the first stop for U.S. visitors and expats arriving in Australia, considering that 28 worldwide countries offer direct connections to Sydney.

From North America, the major carriers to Sydney are American Airlines, Air Canada, Delta, United, and Qantas. Flight time from LAX to Sydney is around 13 hours, but you lose a day crossing the international date line; you get it back on the trip home. These flights are often overnight, allowing you to arrive first thing in the morning, with connecting flights at the ready. Fares range from $1,500 round-trip in economy to $5,000-10,000 round-trip in business class, and at least an extra 50 percent more for first class. From New York City, deals can be had for around $1,500 round-trip, with the trip taking around 22 hours; more comfortable business class costs from $7,000 round-trip. Travel from the U.S. East Coast involves at least one stop.

Flying to Australia is never cheap,

the Customs and Border Protection checkpoint in Melbourne's airport

Airline Loyalty Programs

Qantas Frequent Flyer (www.qantas.com.au): There are four membership levels: Bronze, Silver, Gold and Platinum. You earn a minimum of 1,000 points for every eligible one-way flight taken on Qantas, with percentage bonuses applied if you fly Premium Economy, Business, or First, depending on your membership level. You progress to a higher membership level by earning status points, which you can only earn on eligible Qantas and Oneworld alliance airlines (American Airlines, British Airways, Cathay Pacific, Finnair, Iberia, JAL, LAN, Malév Hungarian, Royal Jordanian, and S7), Air Pacific, Jetstar Airlines (limited to Starter Plus, Starter Max, and Business max fares only), or QantasLink services. There are some 500-plus partners with which you can earn points, including banks, hotels, restaurants, and supermarkets. Priority check-in and lounge access are some of the privileges, plus reward flights.

Oneworld privilege (www.oneworld.com): Not a bonus scheme in its own right, members of participating airline schemes have their rewards and privileges extended throughout the alliance, which includes Air Berlin Top Bonus, American Airlines AAdvantage, British Airways Executive Club, Cathay Pacific Marco Polo Club, Finnair Plus, JAL Mileage Bank, Iberia Plus, LANPASS, Qantas Frequent Flyer, Royal Jordanian Royal Plus, and S7 Priority. The three status levels are Ruby, Sapphire, and Emerald, awarding various levels of benefits including priority check-in and lounge access across the member airlines' facilities.

Virgin Australia Velocity Frequent Flyer (www.velocityawards.com.au): Earn points on flights with Virgin Australia, Virgin America, Virgin Atlantic, Virgin Samoa, Singapore Airlines, Air New Zealand, Etihad, Delta, Hawaiian Airlines, Skywest, and Airlines PNG. An added bonus is that you can pool your family's points together and thus redeem awards much quicker, and as a Gold or Platinum member you are guaranteed up to four return economy Reward Seats for an annual family trip.

but deals can be found if you are flexible and travel outside Australian school holidays and major national holidays. There are a handful of competing domestic budget airlines that occasionally have fare wars. Tigerair and Jetstar are cheap domestic airlines that forgo comfort and always sell one-way tickets. The longest domestic flight is Sydney to Perth ($150-250), which takes five hours, so not getting fed is a small sacrifice. Prices vary by airline and destination, and regular fare sales show lively competition. As a rough guide, if you shop around and are willing to fly at the less popular times of day, you'll spend a maximum of $150 for flights between Melbourne and Sydney (one hour) or Sydney to Brisbane (two hours). Booking online allows you to compare prices more easily at a glance.

Websites such as **WebJet** (www.webjet.com.au) or **Flight Centre** (www.flightcentre.com.au) have fare deals from Australia.

Train

Although there is a national rail system and you can travel the length and breadth of the country, connections to points outside the larger cities are difficult. If you are interested in a slow but scenic journey, rail travel may be a good option. The **Great Southern Rail Company** (www.greatsouthernrail.com.au) runs trains such as the famous *Ghan* from Darwin to Adelaide, which takes three days to cross the continent, traveling via Alice Springs. A Gold Single Cabin for one adult costs $1,819 one-way. *The Indian Pacific* runs from Sydney to Perth via Adelaide in four days, three nights along the longest straight piece of rail track in the world, the 478 kilometers of the Nullarbor Plain in Western Australia. *The Overland* connects Melbourne with Adelaide in luxury ($179 one-way in a premium seat). These journeys are for vacation time; on a nonvacation schedule, Brisbane to Sydney (from $50) takes 14 hours on **CountryLink** (www.countrylinl.info), a rail company that connects various parts of New South Wales and Brisbane, Canberra, and Melbourne.

Within the large metropolitan areas, commuter services are excellent with local train systems, light-rail (in Sydney), an extensive network of streetcars (in Melbourne), and buses (Canberra has commuter bus services rather than trains). Adelaide even has a free metro and bus service that loops around the city center.

Bus

Buses and commuter public transportation are regulated at the regional or state level. Every city has an extensive network of buses, and in larger cities like Sydney, buses run around the clock. On some lines you buy tickets before you enter the bus, and others have ticketing onboard, but this varies from city to city and even within the same city.

There is also interstate bus travel on so-called "coaches," which are comfortable buses, designed for longer journeys with restrooms. The main operator is **Greyhound Australia** (www.greyhound.com.au), offering overland coaches connecting most major cities, although you may have to change and reconnect. One of the longest journeys available is from Broome to Darwin, around 27 hours and costing $284, which is more than a flight would cost; a coach journey from Sydney to Melbourne costs around $120 and takes 13 hours. Greyhound does not serve all destinations but partners with local operators to get you there eventually. Long-haul routes are cheapest but also the longest and least comfortable way to travel across the continent.

Ferry

Commuting by ferry is slightly more glamorous than by a bus or a train. Floating past some of the world's prime real estate, the Sydney Opera House, and Sydney Harbour Bridge is hard to beat. You can also commute across the water in Adelaide, Brisbane, Perth, and various points in Victoria. Ferries feed into other modes of public transportation and tend to start at 5am or 6am and in most cases run until after midnight. As with other modes of public transportation, ferry timetables are widely publicized, tickets come in single-ride to annual passes with many other options, and there are discounts for students, disabled people, and pensioners.

Ferry fares vary by city and the length of the commute; for example, the regular Manly ferry in Sydney Harbour costs $7.80 one-way, while the fast Manly ferry costs less than $9 one-way, with the fast one being quicker than any comparable bus trip. Generally speaking, if you have a ferry stop near you, it's quicker and more economical than the bus.

Some longer commutes are possible by ferry, most notably the ***Spirit of Tasmania*** (www.spiritoftasmania.com.au), which leaves Melbourne for Devonport in Tasmania daily in winter and twice daily in summer. The trip takes 14 hours and can get rough, but while there is no cost advantage over flying, with fares from $89 one-way, it does allow you to take your car.

Commuting by ferry can feel like a vacation.

Car

DRIVING

Australians drive on the left side of the road. It is surprisingly easy to get used to; just practice a little first off the main roads. The big cities have rush-hour traffic problems, and you are better off reading a book on the bus than being stuck in traffic twice a day. If your home is not on a public transit route, you will have to drive or carpool. Many main highways have dedicated carpool "express lanes" for vehicles with two or more passengers. Another possibility to avoid traffic congestion is to negotiate flexible work hours, arriving before or after rush hour.

Apart from driving on the left, the rules of the road are similar to most countries. Speeding incurs hefty fines and up to three points on your license, depending on your speed, and once you have accumulated 12 points, you lose your license. Speed limits are 50 to 60 km/h in cities; highways and expressways allow speeds up to 120 km/h and sometimes 130 km/h. In residential areas, speed limits are 20 km/h in speed-reducing areas; nears schools it is always 40 km/h; and on unmarked roads, when there are no speed-limit signs, the limit is 50 km/h.

The blood-alcohol limit for drivers in Australia is 0.05 percent, with a zero limit for drivers with learner status. On weekend nights police often set up roadblocks and perform breath tests randomly, handing out immediate penalties.

Many cities have at least one toll road or bridge; tolls are currently an average of $4.50 per journey and fines for nonpayment are steep and increase by the day. A transponder that you place in your windshield can be purchased online from **eWay** (www.eway.com.au) for an $10 initial setup fee, and then you pay as you go; these can be requested when you rent a car, making toll payment automatic and stress-free. The system works nationwide.

Getting out of the cities is worthwhile, but Australia does not have an extensive road system, and you have to plan your journey carefully and with safety in mind. Distances can be vast, and petrol (gasoline) stations can be far and few between once you hit the Outback. On long roads fatigue can be an issue, and kangaroos hop across or sit in the middle of the road, creating a hazard. If you are even slightly unsure about where you are going or driving long distances, plan to take the trip together with a second car in case of a breakdown or problems. Get your vehicle's roadworthiness checked before you set off, take potential climate issues into account, pack plenty of water, and take a GPS receiver or a high-frequency radio if you are traveling to remote regions. Always lock your car; opportunists are always around to steal it or what's in it. Park in well-lit areas, and if you feel the part of the city you're in is unsafe, park in a secure lot. The Northern Territory has the highest crime rate, so if you are hitting the Outback, take extra precautions there.

Driver's Licenses

Driver's licenses are handled by the states, and each state and territory has slightly different rules. You need a valid driver's license to drive, and the minimum age is 16 in some states, 18 in others. Visitors are allowed to drive on a valid overseas license together with their passport or an International Driving Permit for the duration of their stay; if you are in the country on a temporary visa, the same is true as long as your driving license is in English or you have an International

Driving Permit. If your license is not in English, you have to get an official translation, obtained through your embassy or a National Accreditation Authority for Translators and Interpreters (NAATI) accredited translator; you then have to carry your license, the translation, and your passport when you're driving. If you are in the country on a permanent visa, you are allowed to drive on your own license for six months from the date you first entered Australia, if your permanent visa was issued prior to you entering the country. If you are having the permanent visa issued while you are already in the country, you can drive on your original license for six months after you receive your permanent visa. To obtain a local state license, you will have to prove that you have held your license for at least three years after your 18th birthday, and it must not have expired. Some license holders may have to take a written test, which you are allowed to retake if you fail and which also comes in a number of different languages. You are charged a fee each time you retake it. You will have to pass a simple eye test. If you hold a license issued by an exempt country, as defined by each state, you will also have to take a road test.

If you intend to get a new license in Australia or have a teenager in tow who is likely to take up driving, again, the rules vary from state to state. The minimum age to start learning is generally 16, when you will have to take a written test at a testing center. If you fail, you can retake it as many times as necessary, but you will pay a fee each time. When you pass the test, you are issued with a learner's permit and "L" plates. Equipped with those, you can either enroll in a driving school or persuade an experienced driver with a valid license, not necessarily an Australian one, to teach you. You get a logbook and must complete a total of 120 hours under supervision, driving in various situations, heavy and light traffic, day and night, dry and wet weather, and on different roads. After this you take the formal driving test; if you pass, you are given red "P" (for "probation") plates to be displayed for one or two years, depending on the state, and then a green "P" plate that you display for another few years before finally receiving a permanent full driving license.

The process of obtaining a driver's license is long, drawn-out, and costly. Learners and probationary drivers are regulated under a different set of rules, such as zero tolerance for blood alcohol. If you have a valid license from another country, use it and only get a local license if you have to.

If your overseas driver's license does not have your picture on it, get an International Driving Permit, which will have your picture; otherwise your license might be questioned.

Rules of the Road

Driving on the left side means that you enter the ubiquitous roundabouts (traffic circles) going left, yielding to vehicles coming from the right. Apart from stringent alcohol limits, low speed limits, and strict penalties on breaking either one, most traffic rules are the same as in other countries, with common sense, defensive driving, and good manners being most important. Where most newcomers have trouble is street parking. Signs are quite unlike those anywhere else and take some getting used to, traffic wardens are everywhere all the time, and parking fines can be high. As a general guideline, speeding fines range from $100 to $3,500 plus demerit points on your license; parking tickets can be as high as $160. A good idea is to obtain the driving test booklet from the traffic authority in the state where you live to get familiar with the traffic signs and general rules of the road.

In Melbourne, the infamous "hook

Road signs in Australia take some getting used to.

turn" is confusing for newcomers, even those from New South Wales. The hook turn is a turn that involves crossing tram lines. It requires you to stop in the left-hand lane when you want to turn right, wait until there is no oncoming traffic and the light has turned red, and then hurtle across the tracks while avoiding the trams. Confused? You will be; nothing but practice can help you with this one.

RENTING, LEASING, AND BUYING A CAR

Renting a Car

With distances what they are in Australia, car ownership is quite common, with nearly one car per adult, but if you choose to live in the CBD or inner suburbs of any of the major cities, there isn't any need to own one. Commuting is easy on public transportation, shops are generally nearby, and for weekend exploration it's easy to rent a car. There are even schemes such as **Flexicar** (www.flexicar.com.au) in Melbourne and Sydney that allow you to pick up a car by the side of the road for anything from an hour to three days; it is as easy as picking up a shared bicycle in large cities, and rates range from around $10 per hour to $65 per day.

Longer-term renting it straightforward, with most of the large international companies present in Australia. You might find, however, that local rental companies have a price advantage, with many companies specializing in, for example, luxury cars, camper vans, pickups, or 4WD vehicles and offering better deals as they go. Long-term car rental works out cheaper than short rentals, with prices sometimes as low as $30 per day, depending on the car.

Third-party insurance and a collision damage waiver should be included in the rental agreement, but the deductible varies widely from company to company and state to state, so make sure you are getting a good deal and feel safe before you sign. In some states you might find a distance restriction, basically discouraging you from taking the car out of the state or driving across the continent. If this is your intention, be clear about it beforehand, as any breach of the rules might result in your insurance being invalidated and you being charged large penalties.

Buying a Car

Buying a car in Australia is not cheap, but depending on where you live, it may be a necessary expense. To reduce costs, it pays to look for locally produced models from companies such as Holden (General Motors) or Ford, as spare parts are easier and cheaper to come by. Imported cars are not only slapped with import tax but are difficult to find parts for; expensive cars are also levied an additional luxury tax. Cars are much smaller in Australia than in the United States, and 4WD vehicles are not common. The most popular car in Australia is the Holden Commodore, first manufactured in 1978.

Good websites for car-buying advice, for both certified dealer purchases and private purchases, are the **National Roads & Motoring Association** (www.mynrma.com.au) and **CarsGuide** (http://carsguide.com.au). As a general price guide, a used Holden Commodore sedan, which has a six-cylinder 3.6-liter engine, with around 80,000 kilometers on the odometer, will cost around $15,500; an equivalent new version is $32,000. On the luxury side, a used six-cylinder three-liter Audi A5 with 73,000 kilometers on the odometer costs around $45,000, and an equivalent new convertible will set you back up to $130,000.

Vehicle registration must be renewed annually with state traffic authorities, and you must provide proof of current third-party insurance. Technical inspections, carried out at authorized service centers usually displaying signs stating that they deal with "Pink Slips," are compulsory in most states and territories. If you are buying a car privately, the seller needs to sign the back of the registration document, and you need to register the change of ownership at your state's motor-vehicle registry, paying a set fee plus a tax called a stamp duty. You can find out how much a specific car will cost to register at **CarsGuide** (http://carsguide.com.au).

TAXI SERVICES

Taxis are plentiful and reliable in the major cities, with one Australia-wide company, 13Cabs, and countless state-governed local companies. Taxis are either yellow or white, easily identified by the lettering on the sides and the "for hire" sign on the roof. Most taxis can be hailed from the side of the road, and there are taxi stands outside major venues such as airports, stations, the CBDs, and ferry terminals. While all taxis are registered, have driver registration, meters, and satellite tracking systems, it can be daunting to wait at a taxi stand late at night. Melbourne has Safe City taxi stands located around the inner city that are staffed with a security officer late at night, on the weekend, on holidays, and during special events. Many larger cities, such as Sydney, Perth, and Brisbane, have similar schemes in place to ensure the safety of taxi passengers.

Taxi fares vary with the hour and the company, but you can get an estimate of costs and travel times at **TaxiFare** (www.taxifare.com.au).

Taxi fares and travel times to and from the airport and the CBD:

- Melbourne to Tullamarine Airport: 25 minutes, $60
- Sydney to Kingsford Smith Airport: 17 minutes, $40
- Perth to Perth International Airport: 20 minutes, $45
- Adelaide to Adelaide Airport: 15 minutes, $25
- Canberra to Canberra Airport: 45 minutes, $35
- Brisbane to Brisbane Airport: 20 minutes, $45
- Hobart to Hobart Airport: 17 minutes, $41

PRIME LIVING LOCATIONS

OVERVIEW

When tourists visit Australia, they tend to head for Sydney or the Great Barrier Reef, maybe to the Outback for a taste of Australian country culture and the opal mines, Uluru (Ayers Rock), or even Kakadu. But visiting a country for leisure and moving to a country to lead your life are completely different. You can explore the continent as much as your free time allows once you're living here, but first you need to figure out where to settle.

This section covers six regions where expats and immigrants typically live: the main cities of Sydney and Melbourne, the political capital of Canberra, the leisure capital of Brisbane and the nearby Gold Coast, the southwestern cities of Adelaide and Perth, and Hobart, capital of Tasmania, which offers some of the best landscapes and outdoor pursuits and is the most atmospheric major city. Many expats choose to live in one of these six locations because of the employment opportunities as well as the amenities the cities offer. Also, more than 85 percent of Australians live within 50 kilometers of the coast, which is where all the major cities lie. There are expats who choose to make a living in the Outback, but the most popular expat destinations in Australia are all among these six.

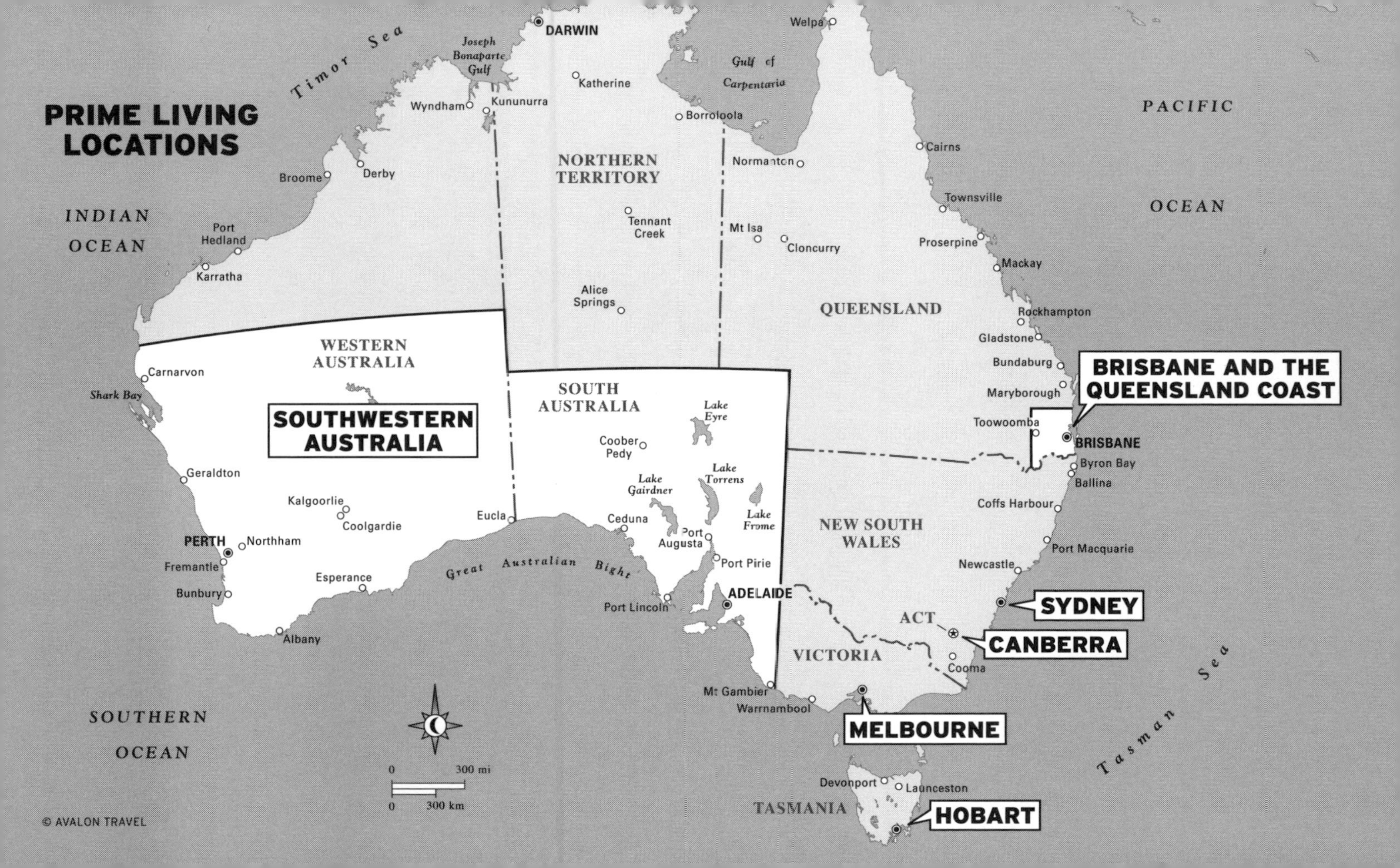
PRIME LIVING LOCATIONS
SOUTHWESTERN AUSTRALIA
BRISBANE AND THE QUEENSLAND COAST
SYDNEY
CANBERRA
MELBOURNE
HOBART
INDIAN OCEAN
PACIFIC OCEAN
SOUTHERN OCEAN
Timor Sea
Tasman Sea
Great Australian Bight
Joseph Bonaparte Gulf
Gulf of Carpentaria
WESTERN AUSTRALIA
NORTHERN TERRITORY
SOUTH AUSTRALIA
QUEENSLAND
NEW SOUTH WALES
ACT
VICTORIA
TASMANIA
DARWIN
Katherine
Wyndham
Kununurra
Broome
Derby
Port Hedland
Karratha
Carnarvon
Shark Bay
Geraldton
Kalgoorlie
Coolgardie
PERTH
Northham
Fremantle
Bunbury
Esperance
Albany
Eucla
Tennant Creek
Alice Springs
Coober Pedy
Lake Eyre
Lake Torrens
Lake Gairdner
Lake Frome
Ceduna
Port Augusta
Port Pirie
Port Lincoln
ADELAIDE
Mt Gambier
Warrnambool
Welpa
Borroloola
Normanton
Mt Isa
Cloncurry
Cairns
Townsville
Proserpine
Mackay
Rockhampton
Gladstone
Bundaburg
Maryborough
Toowoomba
BRISBANE
Byron Bay
Ballina
Coffs Harbour
Port Macquarie
Newcastle
Cooma
Devonport
Launceston
0 300 mi
0 300 km

the Sydney Opera House

SYDNEY

The vast majority of immigrants, especially from the United States, end up in Sydney, which has the biggest economy, the most jobs, and the diversity of needs that often require foreign talent. Sydney is the most international city in Australia and takes distinct pride in its diversity as well as in the energy and pace that ethnic diversity brings to city life. Many newcomers come to work in the finance industry and its many related businesses, such as law firms, many of which are based here.

Sydney is the New York of Australia in many respects. It is the financial capital, the population center, the oldest city, and like New York has a famous harbor and architectural landmarks like the Harbour Bridge and the famed opera house. It is the most cosmopolitan of Australian cities and sees itself as a "world city," a status confirmed by the incredible economic and prestige-gaining success of the 2000 Olympic Games.

Sydney has its critics, especially in other Australian cities, though rarely for its splendid weather and never for its spectacular setting. Residents in other cities feel that their own regions are more typical or authentically Australian, and like New Yorkers, Sydneysiders are thought by people from other parts of Australia to be brash and domineering. It is the most Americanized of Australian cities, and perhaps the most Americanized city outside North America.

Earlier criticisms of Sydney living, which focused on its wretched traffic and the high cost of living, are typical of any bustling major city, but Sydney has gone to considerable lengths to improve its automobile traffic with extensive expressway building. Its public transportation system is also extensive, and many Sydneysiders live without cars, even though Australia has high per-capita car ownership.

Besides its idyllic setting and great weather, the fast-growing and dynamic economy and proximity to the U.S. West Coast are a recipe for strong immigrant interest. It's overwhelmingly the top choice among immigrants, and roughly one-third of Sydney's inhabitants were born overseas, far more than in other Australian cities. In fact, more overseas immigrants live in Sydney than the population of cities such as Brisbane, Adelaide,

Melbourne's Central Business District

Canberra, and Hobart. No matter how popular Sydney is for tourists, for immigrants it is even more so.

MELBOURNE

Second only to Sydney is the large metropolis of Melbourne, famously home to a vast population of southern Europeans. It attracts flocks of students and academics who attend some of the country's most revered learning and research institutions, such as the University of Melbourne and Monash University.

While Melbourne might not quite rival Sydney for the pace of life or financial importance, it is widely considered to be the cultural capital of the country, and academics that can manage a posting to Melbourne University will be happy with the experience. The unique Australian sports culture has also found a home in Melbourne, which is the heartland of Australia's own Australian Rules football, played in front of huge crowds at venues around the city. There is also the popular Melbourne Cricket Ground, the Formula 1 Grand Prix car race, horse racing, tennis, and more. The city is filled with galleries, museums, music-filled nightclubs, extensive Victorian parks, and well-protected Victorian architecture, especially in the inner-city suburbs.

Interestingly, for all the attention that Sydney receives, Melbourne has been growing faster than Sydney in population and income since 2000, and Melbourne's population is nearing that of its larger rival. While Sydney wows visitors with its stunning locale and setting, Melbourne is generally acknowledged to be a better place to live; people are generous, easygoing, and comfortable, drawing newcomers in more slowly but with a tighter grip.

BRISBANE AND THE QUEENSLAND COAST

Tourism professionals and retirees tend to focus their immigration search on the tiny strip of land comprising Brisbane and the Gold Coast of Queensland. Tropical weather and massive government investment have produced a swath of resorts, golf courses, and condo complexes that complement the extensive collection of white-sand tropical beaches. The city is also famed as the gateway to the Great

Barrier Reef. It is absolutely the number-one destination for retirement relocations and by those seeking a warmer climate or a more laid-back culture.

The region comprises three areas. The attractive city of Brisbane itself has urban dwellers occupying towers along the Brisbane River. To the south is the Gold Coast, the more established beach center but far more commercial, with glistening beachside condo towers that would not be out of place in Florida or Hawaii. The weather is good year-round, and it has better affordability than established markets in the United States, making it a compelling alternative to similar locations in the Northern Hemisphere. To the north is the comparable but lesser known Sunshine Coast, which tends to attract price-takers plus those who want a quieter beachside lifestyle than the bustling Gold Coast provides.

CANBERRA

Next to Melbourne, the national capital, Canberra, is home base for many newcomers—typically expats more than permanent immigrants—serving in diplomatic posts, attending or teaching at the Australian National University, or working for nongovernmental organizations or lobbying firms based in the capital.

Canberra has a population of only 386,000 and is by far the newest of the major Australian urban centers, dating to 1913 with most of its development since World War II.

An old Australian political cartoon features a stern judge pronouncing, "I sentence you to live in Canberra." But times have changed. Its central planning, lakeside setting, and extensive preservation of bushland and greenbelts have made it one of the greenest and most pastoral of cities. It is the largest Australian city in the bush, rather than on the coast, which gives it distinctive scenery and weather. It also has the best traffic-congestion conditions of any city in Australia.

HOBART

Tasmania is a bit like a forgotten cousin when it comes to Australia. Some think it is another country altogether; others just forget to mention that it is indeed an Australian state, and one of its prettiest. A mere one-hour flight or 14-hour overnight

Hobart's fishing harbor

ferry ride from Melbourne, Tasmania is a wild isle full of stunning scenery and smaller towns and villages. The capital, Hobart, is the smallest Australian capital city, with a tiny population of just over 200,000. Atmospheric, bustling, and full of restaurants and arts venues, Hobart is popular with visitors, although it must be said, less popular with the permanent population. The island as a whole suffers from an exodus of young and middle-age career-minded residents, who leave to seek employment elsewhere in Australia due to the lack of local opportunities, only to return later to settle or retire.

For expats, unless you will be building your career around outdoor pursuits, relocation is likely to come through industry-specific jobs or academic and scientific work, as Hobart is the outpost for Antarctic research. It is a small island population-wise, and a fair percentage of the residents are either related to one another or at least know each other's business. If you are accepted into the group, though, and you are not a dedicated city dweller, Hobart and its surroundings can offer some of the best Australian living.

SOUTHWESTERN AUSTRALIA

Unlike the other prime living locations, which focus on small and distinct sections of the country, southwestern Australia refers to an enormous section of the country about the size of Texas. In a practical sense, it's divided between the metropolitan areas of Adelaide and environs in South Australia and Perth, the capital of Western Australia.

As beautiful as the southwest is, and popular with tourists, relocations typically tend to these two cities because of industry-specific job hires or transfers; Adelaide is a major center for the auto industry and the primary center for Australia's famed wine industry. Perth is home to the mining industry and is a major center for oil and gas exploration.

Adelaide is situated in the south-central region of the country, about 1,000 kilometers northwest of Melbourne, and it is the gateway to the famed Barossa Valley, Australia's primary wine center. The park-like city has long ago outgrown its original greenbelts, which once served as the city border and now are an inner-city ring, but

Perth Bridge

view of Adelaide

it remains one of the prettiest urban designs in the country.

Perth, which is popular with UK expats as well as the mining industry, is in the big leagues when it comes to iron, bauxite, and other primary mineral recovery companies. Oil and gas exploration continues to take place offshore, and overall Perth has ridden a resources boom that has made it Australia's third largest and fastest-growing city, where execs can commute from beachside suburbs to jobs in buildings along the majestic Swan River without the commuting hassle that haunts those who choose Sydney and Melbourne.

Both Adelaide and Perth are highly urbanized cities. More than 70 percent of the population of Western Australia lives in the Perth metropolitan area, and the same ratio holds for Adelaide and the state of South Australia. By contrast, 60 percent of the population of New South Wales lives in Sydney.

SYDNEY

Arriving in Sydney, stepping out near Circular Quay and taking in the view with myriad ferries bustling past, the sunshine reflecting off the water, and the gorgeous surroundings, it is surprising that anyone makes it past the city to see the rest of Australia. Sydney is simply stunning and can be likened to other iconic metropolises such as Dubai, New York, or Rio de Janeiro, which outshine their countries' capital cities. With its natural beauty, the Sydney Opera House, and the Sydney Harbour Bridge, Sydney is all about the harbor. One of the largest and most beautiful natural harbors in the world, the setting could not be more glorious.

Australia's largest city, with more than four million inhabitants, Sydney is spread along a sunken river valley with some of the world's most expensive real estate and most famous surfing beaches. As the financial capital of the country, the first stop for most visitors and immigrants, the media hub and entrepreneurial engine of the entire continent, Sydney not only attracts money, it demands it; it was recently named one of the most expensive cities in the world.

Pricey or not, people have flocked here since the early 1800s, and it feels like a cosmopolitan metropolis, with access to an array of world cuisines, international companies, and multicultural business

SYDNEY
Ku-Ring-Gai Chase National Park
MONA VALE
Berowra Valley Bushland Park
HORNSBY
Garigal National Park
NARRABEEN
BAULKHAM HILLS
THORNLEIGH
Garigal National Park
COLLAROY
Pennant Hills Park
WEST PENNANT HILLS
DEE WHY
BROOKVALE
CURL CURL
Lane Cove National Park
CHATSWOOD
MANLY
Middle Harbour
North Harbour
PARRAMATTA
Parramatta River
RYDE
BALMORAL
To the Blue Mountains
NORTH SYDNEY
MOSMAN
KIRRIBILLI
Port Jackson
CIRCULAR QUAY
BALMAIN
PYRMONT
CBD
DARLING POINT
SOUTH HEAD RD
BURWOOD
HAYMARKET
PADDINGTON
ANNANDALE
OXFORD ST
BONDI BEACH
JOSEPH ST
NEWTON
BRONTE
KENSINGTON
CLOVELLY
BANKSTOWN
RANDWICK
CANTERBURY RD
TEMPE
SYDNEY AIRPORT
GEORGES RD
CREEK RD
BEVERLY HILLS
STONEY
HURSTVILLE
MALABAR
Georges River NP
Botany Bay
Georges River
Tasman Sea
Towra Point Nature Res
Botany Bay National Park
SUTHERLAND
Woolooware Bay
0 2 mi
0 2 km
Bate Bay
Royal National Park
CRONULLA
© AVALON TRAVEL

owners and employees. People have a sense of optimism here that comes from the pleasant environment and also from the chance to reinvent.

THE BRIEF STORY OF SYDNEY

Anthropologists believe the Aboriginal people reached Sydney's natural harbor some 50,000 years ago, but its modern history starts in 1770, when Captain James Cook sailed into Botany Bay, just south of Sydney, and took his tale of the long-sought Great Southern Land back to Britain. A few years later, the American Revolution was hampering the transportation of convicts from Britain to the Americas, and it was decided that the land around Botany Bay was suitable for convict deportations. When the first fleet of 11 ships landed on the southern coast, Captain Arthur Phillip deemed Botany Bay unsuitable due to its lack of fresh water, but they found a nearly perfect natural harbor a little farther up the coast and eventually decided to settle at Sydney Cove, now called Circular Bay.

Sydney Cove was named after Captain Phillip's superior, Lord Sydney, and the day the first fleet arrived, January 26, 1788, is now celebrated annually as Australia Day. The first settlers were not well chosen to establish a colony on a new continent; there were no carpenters, smiths, or even farmers among the officers or the convicts. But inroads were made through teamwork, the need to survive, and sheer determination, and soon buildings made from mud, untreated wood, reeds, and basic mortar were established, together with a basic farming community and fledgling infrastructure.

Convict transportation ceased in 1850 when more and more voluntary settlers arrived with regular supply ships from the motherland. Trade routes were established with the Americas and Asia, and the wealth of the new continent began to show in imposing buildings commissioned by Governor Lachlan Macquarie, governor of New South Wales from 1810 to 1821.

The discovery of gold in the mid-1800s drew more settlers and established the wealth and grandeur of Sydney, with many tall buildings erected during this period. In the late 1800s the country moved toward federation, which was eventually established in 1901, when Sydney briefly became the capital of the new Commonwealth of Australia. History has established Sydney as a world city, with the 2000 Olympic Games a recent proud achievement.

The Lay of the Land

Sydney is all about the harbor, which effectively splits the city in two. It is located in a coastal basin bordered by the Pacific Ocean and its lovely Manly and Bondi Beaches on either side of the harbor entrance on the east, and the formerly separate settlement of Parramatta, which is slowly being swallowed up, on the west side where the broad harbor narrows into the mangrove-lined Parramatta River. On the north side the city's sprawl continues through increasingly green suburbs up to the Hawkesbury River, while Botany Bay provides a natural border on the south. The city's center, the Central Business District (CBD), with its towering skyscrapers and large colonial buildings, sits on the south side of the harbor. It stretches from the busy ferry port of Circular Quay down to the railway hub

Average Temperatures and Rainfall in Sydney

Month	Mean maximum temperature (°C)	Mean minimum temperature (°C)	Mean rainfall (mm)
January	28	19	84
February	28	19	110
March	27	18	66
April	24	14	89
May	21	11	88
June	18	9	76
July	18	8	64
August	20	9	57
September	23	12	53
October	24	14	65
November	25	16	76
December	27	18	58

Source: Australian Bureau of Meteorology

of Central Station, bordering the chic residential areas of Woolloomooloo and Darlinghurst on the east and Darling Harbour on the west.

Sydney is quite hilly, increasingly so in the west toward the Blue Mountains; some hills reach up to 1,215 meters elevation and allow tantalizing glimpses of water in the distance, even from the inner-city suburbs, which adds to the attractiveness of Sydney's residential areas.

CLIMATE

One of the best indications of Sydney's affable climate is that a lot of homes don't have heating or air-conditioning. In the winter, temperatures barely fall below 10°C, and in the summer a steady light ocean breeze allows even temperatures of around 30°C to be perceived as comfortable. Sunshine is standard, with only few damp gray days. The temperate climate and surrounding water and mountains mean temperatures are buffered and rarely extreme. Snow is practically unheard of, although the Blue Mountains are not far away and allow access to snow and skiing in the winter.

While some regions in Australia have more distinct seasons, or even tropical rainy seasons, it is often said that Sydney has the best weather on the continent, as it is beautiful year-round with only slight peaks and troughs.

Where to Live

Sydney covers some 12,000 square kilometers, with 658 officially designated suburbs and 40 local government areas, so your choice of places to live is vast. Sydney's harbor and Pacific coast are expensive and gorgeous, but unless you have a budget to match, head away from the shore for more realistic housings costs. Chances are that your work will be somewhere in the CBD, and for a reasonable daily commute the innermost northern suburbs, just across the bridge in North Sydney, and southeastern suburbs, such as Darlinghurst or Paddington, are popular. The farther out you go, the more you get for your money, but it all depends on what you want. Inner-city living in Sydney does not necessarily mean cramped apartments, and the lush parks everywhere make it feel much less urban than inner cities of this size elsewhere in the world. Apart from the few high-rises in the CBD, even inner suburbs are mostly low-rise detached houses with gardens. Often the front gardens are so green that it is difficult to get a glimpse of the houses hiding behind them. Remember that you are in the Southern Hemisphere, so look for north-facing windows for optimal light conditions. An excellent website to gauge rental and sale prices is **Domain** (www.domain.com.au).

CENTRAL BUSINESS DISTRICT AND INNER SUBURBS

Young professionals, singles, and couples like to live in the CBD or its closest neighboring suburbs such as **Pyrmont,** on the west of Darling Harbour; **Woolloomooloo** (the name was derived either from *wallamullah,* "place of plenty," or *wallabahmullah,* "young black kangaroo" in an indigenous language) to the east; and **Haymarket** to the south. There are parks and plenty of restaurants and nightclubs open late and through the weekend, with major highways running by, so noise can be a factor. Life here is fast, young, and louder than in most other parts of the city.

If you want to be close to the CBD and enjoy apartment living but don't want to be too close to the all-night weekend hubbub and noise, try **Pyrmont,** where many new developments offer city living but are quiet and secluded. Small supermarkets and specialty shops dot the area, and Darling Harbour, with its mall, restaurants, and Saturday-night fireworks, is a mere five minutes' walk away.

Apartment living in the center is common, with new developments and renovated warehouses among the available options. High-rises offer views over the stunning city center, and connections to other parts of Sydney are easy, with ferries and trains departing from Circular Quay. The other major rail hub, Central Station, is also nearby. The airport is only 25 minutes away.

There are very few schools in or near the CBD, but the choice gets wider in the suburbs bordering the innermost suburbs, so commuting is an option.

A modern three-bed, two-bath apartment with building amenities in Sydney's CBD generally sell for a minimum of one million dollars. Renting is a little cheaper at around $2,000 per week.

One-bedroom apartments in Pyrmont generally sell for a minimum of $500,000, and $700,000 for a two-bedroom apartment. Rental for a one-bedroom apartment averages $500 per week, increasing to around $700 per week for a two-bedroom.

a terrace home in Paddington

EASTERN SUBURBS

The eastern suburbs encompass some of the best real estate in Australia. Stretching from the CBD high-rises all the way to the villas overlooking the surfers' paradise of Bondi Beach, there are plenty of chic, eclectic, and very luxurious suburbs along the way. Along the harbor coast to the Pacific Ocean are suburbs such as Point Piper, Double Bay, and Vaucluse, which have apartments and mansions overlooking the harbor. You may find a long-term rental property here, but buying is extremely pricey.

More realistic are the lovely suburbs such as **Paddington,** with its excellent schools, delicate Victorian town houses, glimpses from the hill across parks to the water, and lovely shops and cafés nestling alongside residential buildings. Young families settle here, you'll get to know the woman behind the counter of the little fruit and veg shop, and you can stop for a chat and a coffee when you walk the dog.

Following the main thoroughfare of Oxford Street leads to the desirable Pacific coast suburbs of **Bondi Beach** and **Bronte,** which allow you to mix residential living with easy access to lovely beaches, fish-and-chips shops, and all the necessary amenities. Living here, away from the main beach parade, is quiet, but around the corner is one of the world's most famous beaches, full of surfers, bathers, and the lifestyle many envision when they think of Australia, and it's still only 10 minutes into town.

In the southeast, the suburbs of **Randwick** and **Kensington** still allow for quick access to the CBD and the beaches, but both have slightly more affordable accommodations. Kensington is home to the University of New South Wales and the Institute of Dramatic Art, and it's popular with students, families with students, and professors. Life is more relaxed, a little more affordable, and alternative. The boutiques are more quirky than classy, and the cafés more likely to offer vegetarian options than à la carte fine dining.

A two-bedroom, two-bath house in Paddington will average $1 to 1.5 million, and a rental will cost $800 to $1,000 per week. In Bondi Junction a two-bedroom, two-bath apartment with sea views will cost around $800 per week to rent, and at least $950,000 to buy. In Kensington a two-bedroom, one-bath apartment will cost around $450 per week to rent and $575,000 to buy.

LOWER NORTH SHORE

The hillier shore of North Sydney offers some spectacular views over the bridge, opera house, and CBD, and with the hills being a little steeper than on the south shore, there are plenty of apartment buildings with stunning views. While North Sydney may look like a version of the CBD with its high-rises, it is a lot quieter. The North Sydney CBD is a business district with shopping, but it closes down in the evenings and on the weekend, summing up north shore living: It is a lot more subdued and quiet than the central area, making it popular with professional families.

The suburbs of **Kirribilli,** meaning "good fishing spot" in an indigenous language and home to the prime minister's official Sydney residence, along with **Mosman** and **Balmoral,** are along the coast and have little beaches in bays. Kirribilli and Mosman having excellent commuter ferry service to Circular Quay on the south side. If your budget allows, opt for Mosman. It has a wonderful village feel to it, all the amenities you need, some chic boutiques and cafés, the views are great, and you hardly ever need to go into Sydney unless it's for work. The suburb combines stylish family living with beaches, great schools, views, and facilities—with a price tag—and it is very popular with expatriates.

A two-bedroom, one-bath apartment in North Sydney will cost an average of $500,000 to buy, $600 per week to rent. In Mosman, a three-bedroom, two-bath house will set you back $850 per week to rent, or $1 million to buy.

UPPER NORTH SHORE

Farther inland, away from the harbor, the surroundings are greener, the plots larger, the houses newer, and the prices cheaper. The suburbs stretching north alongside the Lane Cove Tunnel and M2 Motorway are all popular with expats for exactly those reasons. If you are not that keen on urban living, or simply want more bang for your buck, try the **West Pennant Hills** suburb, which has a lovely family feel akin to a gated community, with all the needed facilities and neighbors who know each other. Proximity to the countryside allows for sports such as horseback riding, and there are plenty of horse clubs around. Commuting into the CBD takes about an hour, depending on how far out you are, via a straight rail connection or bus. The residential areas are quiet and family oriented and have access to good public and private schools, extensive leisure facilities, and new housing in safe neighborhoods. You might not feel like you are living in a major city, but that is not necessarily a bad thing; life can be very good and a lot more affordable up north.

Neighboring **Thornleigh** is another family-friendly leafy pocket, with good-size houses, access to decent schools and train services into the city.

A spacious three-bedroom, two-bath house with extensive gardens in West Pennant Hills will cost an average of $695,000 to buy, or $550 per week to rent.

MANLY AND THE NORTHERN BEACHES

The northern beaches are the incarnation of leisurely living, surfing, and barbecues in the garden. Sydney's fashionable restaurants, expensive boutiques, and hectic lifestyle seem far away, although the CBD is only 20 minutes by fast ferry from **Manly.**

Expat Experience: Living in Sydney

Linda Marie O'Connell Norman, 54, from Chicago, is married with two grown-up children. She works as an art director and graphic designer and has been living in North Balgowlah, north of Sydney, since 1989.

Why did you come to Australia?
I married an Australian man and we decided to live here.

Did you get your job before you came to Australia, or did you look while here?
I found employment once I arrived. I sorted out my residency in Chicago before I arrived in Australia. It took about three months for the process to be completed with the Australian Embassy in Chicago. I found employment fairly easily, as I had immigrated to the UK and was working in London as a graphic designer prior to living in Sydney.

What do you love most about living in Sydney?
I love the breathtaking seaside, which is never far away, and the weather!

What's your least favorite aspect of living in Sydney?
It has been a great challenge to afford housing in Sydney. It has taken all of our married life to pay off our mortgage.

What do you miss most about the United States?
I miss my family. I'm from a large family of six children: three boys and three girls. My mother remarried and now our extended family is 10. So we are now five brothers and five sisters! We have a great time together.

Which goodies do you miss from home?
My son is coming back from overseas, and he is bringing a box of Frango Mints. We've learned to make Chicago deep-dish pizza! Yum! And I miss clothes shopping in the USA. Most things here are overpriced. When I go home, I stock up and bring what I need back here, especially jeans!

Which suburbs do you recommend for new expats moving to Sydney?
I love the Manly area. I make an effort at least one day a week to get to Manly even if it's for a quick walk along the beachside. Perfect for meeting a friend for a coffee, lunch, or drink. It's so convenient. If I could afford it, I would probably move to Freshwater, where there is a village atmosphere and a bit more vibrancy than North Balgowlah.

How did you find acceptance into the Australian community?
I have many Australian friends. I find them to be extremely friendly and natural people. Australians love sports and the outdoors, so it's a perfect fit for me. I don't have many Americans friends here. Many that I have met and become friends with have returned home once their jobs have finished here.

What piece of information would you liked to have known when you first arrived?
Had I known that I was going to have children, I would have liked to have understood the

Linda Norman and family

education system here better. It's a bit geared toward the privileged, and the Higher School Certificate still makes my head reel. The marking system is mind-boggling. My children went to local Catholic high schools; we couldn't afford the college prep private schools. My children have done fairly well, both graduating from Macquarie University. I prefer the US university system, where students go away and live on college campuses while studying. My children are still living at home with us trying to put enough savings away to move out of home. So, if you can, start saving now so your children can study in the USA—I think they will benefit in the long run, especially if they want to work back in the USA.

What's your best tip for newcomers? First thing they ought to do?
Make sure you find a job that pays well. Sydney is like New York—it's expensive. Also, join a gym or sporting club. You will get to meet "real" Australians doing what they love, no pretenses.

How do you like working here? How does it differ from the United States?
I think the wage to housing cost is way out of balance. I enjoy working here from a creative point of view. People are open-minded about new and interesting designs but the economy is so much smaller that it's harder to get things done properly on time and within budget. Budgets for all projects are pretty meager. I'm not keen on the GST as a small-business owner either. Too much paperwork for a business with five or fewer employees and we are already taxed to the gills.

If you leave again, what will you miss most about Australia or Sydney in particular?
If I leave, I will miss my friends and my children. I'm not sure my children would come with us if we decide to travel back. Although they are dual citizens, they've spent their entire lives here, except for the holidays overseas. I would miss the lovely environment: the beaches, the birdlife, the easy outdoor lifestyle. I would also miss the good food and having so many things to do.

The harbor views are replaced here by the Pacific Ocean stretches along the rugged coastline famed for its ideal surfing conditions. The area is perfect for downtime; weekends can be spent utterly relaxing and enjoying one of the best coastlines in the country. The daily commute to Sydney may be time-consuming if you are not directly in Manly and have to drive to the ferry terminal, but the quality downtime that is possible in the neighborhood make it worthwhile for many expats.

Properties tend to be large and secluded, with an emphasis on outdoor entertainment. There are some good schools, public and private, but many have a predetermined catchment area, so be diligent in checking that before you decide on a property.

A three-bedroom, two-bath house in Manly will cost around $1,300 per week to rent and $3 million to buy.

THE INNER WESTERN SUBURBS

The suburbs adjoining the CBD to the immediate west are popular with expats and families. Traditional housing, Victorian row houses, and a mix of architecture from classic to art deco make up the mostly residential areas of **Annandale** and **Balmain.** These city suburbs are quiet and leafy with plenty of restaurants, coffee shops, and bookstores. Historic buildings are common, the bridge can be viewed from the other side, and life is a mix of hard work and lots of play, although play is more urban-oriented than beachy or sporty. There are plenty of public and private schools, plus the University of Sydney and the School of the Arts nearby. Streets in these suburbs vary from arty to trendy, alternative to middle-class, but each suburb is generally set up as a village within the city, with most amenities close by, and commuting into CBD is easy via public transportation. It takes around 20 minutes to get to Sydney's CBD by ferry or bus.

A two-bedroom, one-bath house in Balmain will cost an average $900,000 to buy and $600 per week to rent, with similar prices in Annandale.

THE GREATER WESTERN SUBURBS

The greater western suburbs are a more recent addition to Sydney's sprawl. They have expanded past the Olympic Park and several large industrial complexes, such as large oil refineries, along the Parramatta River, with its idyllic mangroves lining the water. In the past those living in the west were called "Westies," an epithet that implied lower-class, uneducated, and unsophisticated stereotypes, but more recently new luxury developments are drawing increasingly sophisticated Sydneysiders who want to live a little farther out of the city and save some cash. It pays to have a look at the area first, as there are still some pockets where family living might not be as safe as in others. **Parramatta** still has a lower socioeconomic demographic than suburbs closer to Sydney, and a closer inspection is worthwhile. Parramatta is now well within the greater western suburbs and has great infrastructure since the 2000 Olympics, making the daily commute easy. From Sydney's CBD, Parramatta is around 55 minutes by train and about one hour by ferry. By car, it takes around 30 minutes if the traffic is good.

A two-bed, two-bath house in Parramatta will cost around $500 per week to rent and $450,000-500,000 to buy.

SOUTH SYDNEY

South Sydney, with its St. George and Sutherland governments comprising nearly 100 suburbs, is marked by the presence of the large and busy airport, various inner-city light-industry zones, but also proximity to Botany Bay, which allows coastal living and views.

The general South Sydney area is close to the airport and a little run-down. Despite these factors there are plenty of lovely quiet and safe roads that would appeal to either young professionals and even families who do not have the budget to move into the wealthier eastern suburbs, yet like the proximity to the city center. The commute into the CBD from here is around 30 minutes by train or bus.

Newtown has recently become trendy, full of restaurants and quirky shops, and Tempe, next door, is, according to local property developers, also an up-and-coming area. Although next to the airport, it is progressing, but with still some good entry-level properties available.

Traditionally the enclave of Italian and Greek immigrants in the 1950s and 1960s, these suburbs have recently seen a lot of redevelopment by people taking advantage of the easy commuting distance to the CBD. Good properties are available within secluded residential corners. A good look around is certainly worthwhile, as there is a real mix of quiet and secure housing and more eclectic living to be found in this area.

A two-bed, two-bath house in **Tempe** will cost around $600,000 to buy and $600 per week to rent.

Daily Life

MEDIA RESOURCES

Sydney has three daily papers: the *Sydney Morning Herald,* a comprehensive broadsheet; the *Daily Telegraph,* a daily tabloid; and the all-Australian broadsheet *The Australian.* There is also the *Australian Financial Review.* Several TV channels serve the city, including the Australian Broadcasting Corporation (ABC), which has several channels, including news and a kids channel; Special Broadcasting Services (SBS), which, among other programming, airs news in a variety of languages, acknowledging Australia's multicultural nature; and the commercial channels Seven, Nine, and Ten, plus a handful of smaller channels.

Internet connectivity is comprehensive, with wireless connections available throughout the city. A score of radio stations play everything from the latest dubstep to golden oldies, jazz, classical, news, and foreign broadcasts.

EXPAT RESOURCES

The American Society of Sydney (www.facebook.com/TheAmericanSocietyOfSydney) is a good resource for expats looking to build community. **The American Australian Association** (www.americanaustralian.org.au) is another great expat resource; or try the Meetup group Sydney Americans at www.meetup.com/sydney-expat-americans.

HEALTH CARE

As is befitting for Australia's largest city, Sydney has some of the country's best hospitals. Most of the best-known hospitals are near the CBD, including Sydney Hospital, Royal North Shore, and Royal Prince Alfred, with more than a dozen major public and teaching hospitals throughout the city. Among the finest are those affiliated with the two major universities: the Prince of Wales, affiliated with the University of New South Wales, and Royal North Shore, affiliated with the University of Sydney. Within

Welcoming the New Year in Sydney

New Year's Eve fireworks in Sydney

There is no doubt that Sydney is naturally one of the most stunning cities on this earth, but when it wants to, it can even improve on its natural beauty. As one of the first cities to welcome the New Year, its firework spectacular has been watched by millions around the world on television. But if you are in Australia, even if Sydney is not your home, a visit to Sydney at New Year's is an absolute must—there simply is no better celebration to watch live.

One of the first things to remember is that New Year's Down Under falls in the middle of the summer holidays, so there is no need to wrap up warm; just put on your summery glad rags. Then, whatever you are planning to do, book early. For organized venues and events, places are limited and sought after.

The main focus of the celebration is the Sydney Harbour Bridge, or the "old coat hanger" as it is affectionately known. A view of the opera house and the bridge is preferable, but fireworks are set off throughout the harbor, and a star-spangled flotilla of boats parades the length of the harbor between the two main fireworks events. There are two occasions to see the magic in the sky: Traditionally, Sydney sends off the first volley of fireworks at 9pm for the younger generation before bedtime, and then the proper full fireworks go off at midnight. The 9pm version is a smaller teaser of the fireworks to follow later.

The best place to enjoy the night is on a boat in the harbor, and it is amazing that by midnight the water seems to have pretty much disappeared beneath the sea of boats. All types and sizes are puttering around on the water, full of revelers and merrymakers. Many are private vessels, but plenty are ferries and cruise ships on which tickets for the night can be secured. Tickets usually include dinner, dancing, and a glass of bubbly at midnight, and prices range from $200 to several hundred dollars.

The cheapest way to enjoy the night is by coming early, and I mean early: surprisingly many camp overnight, and by 10am the really good spots are already taken, especially those by the opera house, at Mrs. Macquarie's Chair in the Botanical Gardens, or on any of the north shore beaches overlooking the bridge. This obviously takes planning and dedication, especially as numbers admitted and items taken are limited and scrutinized by security, ensuring that people don't get too crowded.

If you have the budget, being crowded need not be an issue; you can enjoy dinner and drinks in one of the many hotels and bars overlooking the harbor, but you will need to book early and be prepared to part with several hundred dollars per person for the privilege. Some of the best and priciest hot spots for the night are the Shangri La, the bar at the top of the Sydney Tower, or indeed the Opera Bar below the Opera House, where an entrance fee of $300 is charged, excluding drinks.

Either way, it is a night not to be missed, and whatever your budget, Sydney does its best not to disappoint; you will certainly welcome the New Year in a spectacular fashion.

the public-hospital sector are the large general hospitals, which cover all health needs. There are also hospitals or clinics that specialize in pediatrics, oncology, eye problems, and the like.

Sydney is at the center of New South Wales's extensive health system, which comprises four basic health regions: Northern Sydney-Central Coast; Southeastern Sydney-Illawarra; Sydney Southwest, and Sydney West. Whether you qualify for the government health care scheme, Medicare, or if you opt for private insurance, all of the doctors' "surgeries" (offices), clinics, and hospitals are open to you. Because public hospitals have been known to experience severe patient backlogs and emergency care is subject to delays, even if you qualify for Medicare you'll get better service and have better peace of mind if you go with a private health insurance supplement to Medicare.

SCHOOLS

In Sydney there are public schools, faith-based schools, and private and independent schools, with both coed and single-sex schools. A very good government website, **My School** (www.myschool.edu.au), can help you choose among schools in your given area. It provides a history of National Assessment Program—Literacy and Numeracy (NAPLAN) test results, allowing you to check the performance of each school.

Most schools have websites that take you through their enrollment process, and more often than not allow you to register your child online, attaching relevant documents such as copies of passports and immunization records.

Expats often opt for private schools because they arrive in the middle of the school year, get help from their company with paying the fees, or want to stream their children toward the International Baccalaureate (IB). There are plenty of excellent private schools in Sydney, including St. Francis of Assisi Primary School in Paddington, Sacred Heart Primary School in Mosman, the Montessori East Preschool and Primary School in Bondi, Sydney Grammar School in Darlinghurst, and Abbotsleigh in North Sydney. There is no longer an American school in Sydney, but there are the Lycée Condorcet (International French School of Sydney) and the German International School of Sydney.

SHOPPING

It is worth coming to Sydney just for the shopping, with everything from small-town strip malls to luxurious designer stores, large suburban malls, and individually quirky boutiques. The CBD is also the central shopping district, where you can find major retailers such as American Apparel, Billabong, GAP as well as Australian retailers such as Witchery, Country Road, and Sussan mixing with high-end designer shops such as Hermès, Chanel, and Cartier. Many of the shops have taken over old Georgian and Victorian buildings; Burberry, for example, now sells its checked wares on George Street in a vast old bank building complete with tall marble columns. The CBD brims with department stores such as Myers and David Jones, pretty arcades such as The Strand, and a beautiful old market building, the Queen Victoria Building, now given over to a mix of major retail and high-end shops.

Each suburb has its own little high street (shopping street) or strip mall, giving it a village flair and its own identity. Two of the best are Oxford Street in Paddington, full of quirky designers and interior decorating shops, and Military Road in Mosman, brimming with a mix of eclectic cafés and individual boutiques. For flavors from back home, there is a Costco Wholesale store in Sydney, and the website **USA Foods** (www.usafoods.com.au), which sells and delivers American goodies such as Twinkies, Reese's, and Cheerios that you might struggle to find in local supermarkets.

Shops are generally open 9am to 6pm, and Thursday is late shopping day, when stores stay open until 8 or 9pm. More and more shops stay open later on Saturday, when stores traditionally closed at lunchtime, and some are even open on Sunday. Supermarkets and convenience stores are open around the clock. Depending on the area you live in, it can take some getting used to that everything is closed by 6pm and on the weekend.

Getting Around

PUBLIC TRANSPORTATION

Trains, light-rail, trams, buses, ferries—Sydney uses them all. The public transportation system is so extensive and reliable that unless you live more than 20 kilometers out of the CBD, have free parking, or have hobbies that require carrying surfboards, horse tackle, or lots of children, it makes a car pretty much unnecessary. The main hubs are Central Station, south of the CBD, and Circular Quay to the north. From either one you can connect to anywhere in the CBD and surrounding suburbs. Buses have the widest range into the depths of the suburbs.

To ride the entire NSW transport system, including trains, buses, most ferries, and light-rail in Sydney, the Blue Mountains, Central Coast, Hunter, Illawarra, and Southern Highlands, your best option is to get an Opal Card. For one-off trips there are also Opal Single Tickets or Opal Single Bus Tickets.

The Opal Card is a rechargeable smartcard which you can buy and recharge at most corner shops. The card itself costs a onetime fee of $10 per adult and $5 for children, and you can determine the charge you will be loading the card with, depending on your commuting needs. If you will only use public transport sporadically, then you can get single bus tickets, which depending to distance and zones traveled cost from $2.60 to $5.40 per adult, and $1.30 to 2.70 per child. With an Opal Card you'll get reduced fares, which would bring the above tickets down to $2.10 to $4.50 per adult, and $1.05 to $2.25 per child, so well worth getting if you will commute to work.

To find your way around the city's extensive public transportation options, load the TripGo app onto your smartphone. This app allows you to input your current location and your destination, and it gives you details of all the modes of transportation available; it even gives you directions if there is some walking involved. Alternately, log on to the **New South Wales Transport website** (www.transportnsw.info), which provides all the information you will need to find the best way from your home to work or school.

HIGHWAYS

Since the updating of the infrastructure for the 2000 Olympic Games, Sydney's roads are safe, comfortable, and get you where you want to go without too much chance of getting lost. Commuter traffic is a major pain, morning and evening, with delays exactly where you don't want them. If you have a choice, opt for public transportation to and from work; it might also be crowded, but it will be less stressful. About 160,000 vehicles per day use the Sydney Harbour Bridge; in 1950 there were 32,000 vehicles per day.

Sydney has easy connections with major highways stretching out into the various suburbs. The Pacific Highway connects the CBD across Sydney Harbour Bridge with the north, all the way to Brisbane and beyond. There is a toll charged when crossing Sydney Harbour Bridge southbound only, as well as for the Sydney Harbour Tunnel; tolls are max $4.00. On the north side, Military Road gets you to most suburbs along the way to Manly.

Southbound, Southern Cross Drive connects to the airport, while Parramatta Road is a fast westward commute to Parramatta past the docks and Sydney Olympic Park. To the east, Oxford Street winds through the suburbs. It's not fast, but it hits all the main suburbs along the way to Bondi Beach; it's the route the buses use as well.

Once you head out of the sprawling city limits, you may encounter toll roads, including the Eastern Distributor, with a toll charged only northbound, and the M5 East Freeway and the M5 Southwest Motorway, the Westlink M7, the Hills M2 Motorway, and both the Lane Cove and the Cross City tunnels, all of which charge a toll in both directions.

Parking is a continuous bugbear with Sydneysiders, as it is limited and expensive. Rates vary with location and the time of day, but in the CBD parking meters cost $7 per hour 8am to 6pm, and $3 per hour on weekends. Secure parking can be even pricier. Residents can apply for parking permits that allow them to park outside or near their homes for a reduced cost, which can be reduced even more if you drive a low-emission vehicle. Prices for permits start at around $100 per car per year, depending on the local government area, the neighborhood, and the type of house and car.

SYDNEY AIRPORT

Sydney's Kingsford Smith Airport, named after a local aviation pioneer, is roughly a 20-minute taxi or airport express train or bus ride from the CBD. On the south edge of Sydney's sprawl, the runway extends into Botany Bay, and the approach over Sydney is beautiful, giving you views over the harbor, the opera house, and the bridge if the weather is favorable.

Security checks are the same as in other countries on departure, but on arrival, inspections are intensive due to Australia's strict import laws. No food, plants, or animal items, dead or alive, not even an apple left over from the journey, are allowed into the country, and getting caught inadvertently smuggling something in can lead to serious delays and inconvenience after a long journey. Make sure there is nothing in your checked luggage, and double-check your carry-on before leaving the plane.

There are three terminals for international (Terminal 1), domestic (Terminal 2), and Qantas domestic (Terminal 3) flights, and the airport is spacious, comfortable, and has plenty of shops and cafés. There is also a duty-free shop in arrivals for last-minute gifts.

Australia is served by airlines such as Qantas, Jetstar, Virgin Australia, Tigerair, and Skywest, plus some smaller local airlines. International flights are pricey, but domestic airlines often have special deals allowing internal flights at reasonable prices. Flights to other capitals in Australia are relatively short: Perth is under five hours, Brisbane and Melbourne just over an hour, Adelaide just over two hours, and Hobart about 90 minutes.

MELBOURNE

Melbourne, pronounced "MEL-ben," was ranked in 2016 as the most livable city in the world by *The Economist.* It really does seem to have it all: It is a lovely bustling metropolis with a CBD full of shops, cafés, and meeting places. The laneways, full of award-winning restaurants, are favorite hangouts of locals and visitors alike, and the bayside suburbs boast lovely sandy beaches, while the parks all around make you forget that you are in Australia's second largest city. The surrounding Victoria countryside is varied and gorgeous, with undulating hills, rugged mountains, coastal drives, perfect surfing conditions, natural beauty and history, and stunning hikes all within a couple of hours' drive from the city center. Add to that a calendar full of events that ensures there's always something to look forward to, and you have a city that is extremely livable.

The four million odd Melbournians' love of coffee and eating out, preferably three times a day, sitting outside in any weather is probably only rivaled by their love for Australian Rules football and the Melbourne Cup, for which residents even get a day off work. The sport madness does not stop there but adds, among others, cricket, Formula One, and tennis to amuse its fans.

Once Australia's most powerful and richest city, Melbourne is certainly not in Sydney's shadow. The lighthearted

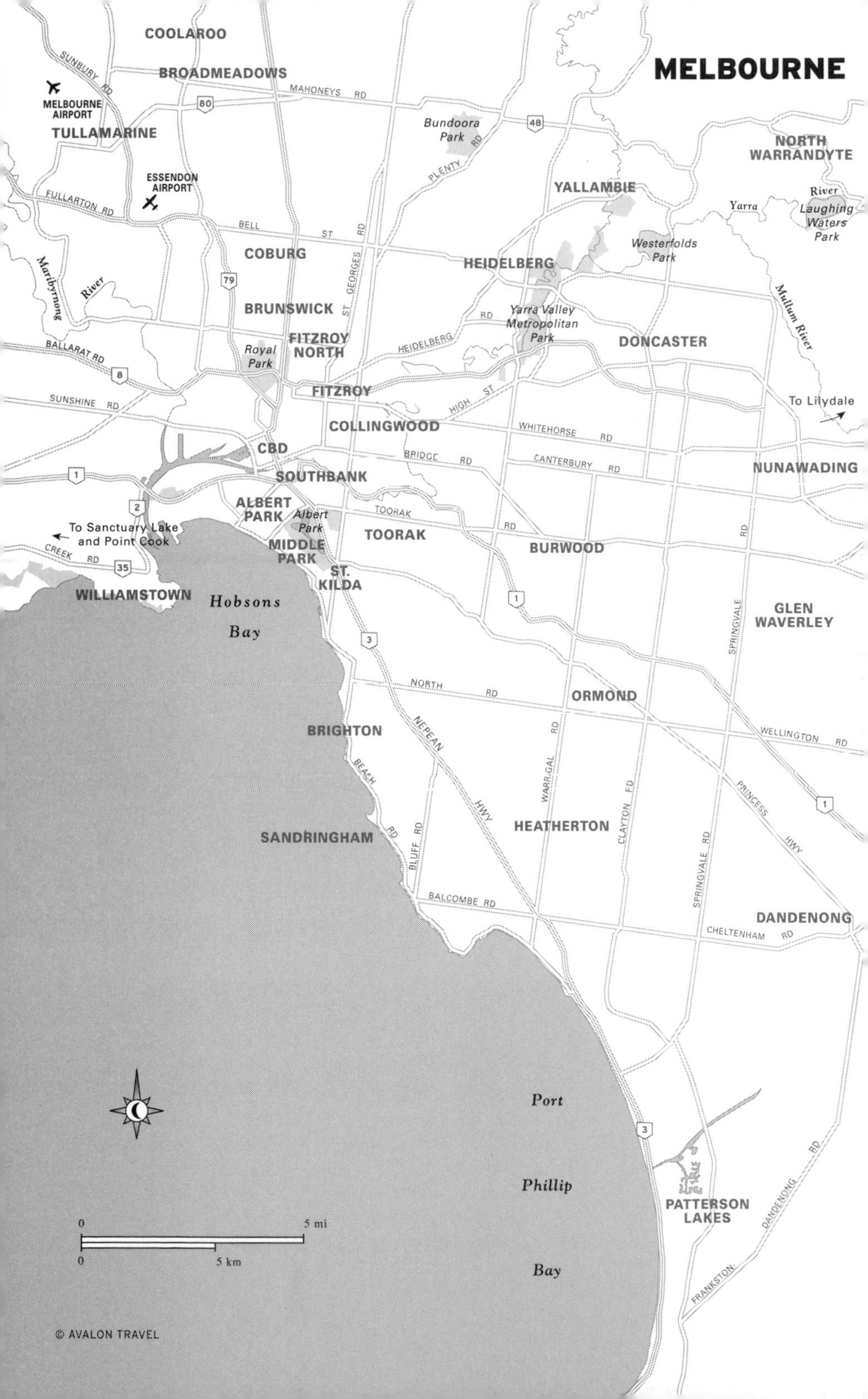
MELBOURNE
COOLAROO
BROADMEADOWS
MELBOURNE AIRPORT
TULLAMARINE
ESSENDON AIRPORT
SUNBURY RD
MAHONEYS RD
FULLARTON RD
BELL ST
Bundoora Park
PLENTY RD
NORTH WARRANDYTE
YALLAMBIE
River
Yarra
Laughing Waters Park
Westerfolds Park
COBURG
HEIDELBERG
Maribyrnong River
BRUNSWICK
ST GEORGES RD
Yarra Valley Metropolitan Park
Mullum River
FITZROY NORTH
Royal Park
HEIDELBERG RD
DONCASTER
BALLARAT RD
FITZROY
SUNSHINE RD
HIGH ST
To Lilydale
COLLINGWOOD
WHITEHORSE RD
CBD
BRIDGE RD
CANTERBURY RD
NUNAWADING
SOUTHBANK
ALBERT PARK
Albert Park
TOORAK RD
To Sanctuary Lake and Point Cook
TOORAK
MIDDLE PARK
BURWOOD
CREEK RD
ST. KILDA
WILLIAMSTOWN
Hobsons Bay
GLEN WAVERLEY
SPRINGVALE RD
NORTH RD
ORMOND
BRIGHTON
NEPEAN HWY
WELLINGTON RD
BEACH RD
WARRIGAL RD
CLAYTON RD
PRINCESS HWY
SANDRINGHAM
BLUFF RD
HEATHERTON
BALCOMBE RD
DANDENONG
CHELTENHAM RD
Port Phillip Bay
PATTERSON LAKES
DANDENONG RD
FRANKSTON
0
5 mi
5 km
© AVALON TRAVEL

Average Temperatures and Rainfall in Melbourne

Month	Mean maximum temperature (°C)	Mean minimum temperature (°C)	Mean rainfall (mm)
January	26	14	48
February	26	15	48
March	24	13	50
April	20	11	57
May	17	9	56
June	14	7	49
July	14	6	48
August	15	7	50
September	17	8	58
October	20	10	66
November	22	11	60
December	24	13	60

Source: Australian Bureau of Meteorology

rivalry between the two cities is still ongoing. The 1850s Victoria gold rush gave Melbourne its magnificent legacy of Victorian-era construction, city landscaping, and development as well as its unrivaled collection of universities such as Monash and the University of Melbourne that have kept Melbourne at the top of the list for academics.

It has been said that where Sydney is full of flash, Melbourne is full of substance; for Sydney's harbor there are Melbourne's gardens; for Sydney's ferries there are Melbourne's trams; for Sydney's rugby there is Melbourne's Aussie Rules; for Sydney's mercurial economy built on world finance, trade, and stock flotation, there are Melbourne's rock-solid, large-scale, traditional corporations operating in agriculture and natural resources. And Melbourne did come first in that livability survey while Sydney wasn't even in the Top 10.

THE BRIEF STORY OF MELBOURNE

The city of Melbourne sits at the point where the Yarra River empties into Port Phillip Bay and has been occupied for nearly 40,000 years. When Europeans arrived in the 1830s, the Wurundjeri people occupied the Yarra Valley, and they transferred the land of modern-day Melbourne in exchange for an annual rent of "40 blankets, 30 axes, 100 knives, 50 scissors, 30 mirrors, 200 handkerchiefs, 100 pounds of flour, and 6 shirts" in what was known as Batman's Treaty, as it was negotiated by Tasmanian farmer John Batman. Subsequently the British government nullified the treaty and a swarm of squatters descended on the area. The resulting confusion over land titles led to the formation of British administration at Melbourne in 1837, and ultimately the colony of Victoria was separated from New South Wales in 1851. The city itself was named for the British prime minister, Lord Melbourne.

Just after the establishment of Victoria, gold was discovered just north of Melbourne, in Ballarat, and the biggest gold rush in history was on. The population of Victoria swelled from 76,000 to 540,000 by 1861, and more importantly, a miner's movement for reduced fees and political representation led to an uprising at the Eureka Stockade in 1854 that is credited as the birthplace of representative democracy. Ten thousand miners massed in meetings that ultimately led in the short run to the doomed Eureka Rebellion but in the long run to universal male suffrage in elections for the lower house of the Victorian parliament.

The miners who participated in the Eureka Stockade uprising were known as "Diggers," and soldiers in the Australian Army are still known by that name. The Diggers took an oath of allegiance, "We swear by the Southern Cross to stand truly by each other and fight to defend our rights and liberties," and raised a flag featuring the Southern Cross constellation against a blue field. The Southern Cross today is part of the Australian national flag.

As the port of entry to the goldfields, and the banking center for the mining industry and ultimately the financing center for Australia's agricultural industries, Melbourne became one of the largest and richest cities in the British Empire. The term "Marvelous Melbourne" was coined by journalist George Sala to reflect the gorgeous Victorian architecture, town houses, and gardens of the city. The worldwide recession of the 1890s hit the city hard, and although Melbourne served as the national capital of Australia from 1901 to 1927, Sydney caught up with Melbourne in population during this time.

Melbourne served as Allied Headquarters for the Pacific Theater in World War II, and after the war a resources boom and the 1956 Olympic Games reestablished the city's prosperity. Melbourne continued to serve as the banking and corporate center of the country until the 1970s, when Sydney's ties to the United States became more important than Melbourne's ties to London.

A dedicated effort since a tough recession in the early 1990s has resulted in prosperous times for Melbourne in recent years, and since 2000 the city has been growing in population and economics faster than any major city in the country.

An overview of Melbourne would be woefully incomplete without a mention of sports. Where Sydney disappears to the beach on weekends, Melbourne heads for cricket, footy parks, or racecourses. Melbourne Cricket Ground is the most prestigious venue for international matches, and the Etihad Stadium packs in more than 50,000 for Aussie Rules football. Aussie Rules draws the biggest crowds of any type of sports in the country, and its great champions are remembered in song and story. In racing, the Melbourne Cup horse race is run at Flemington Racecourse in November, and it is such a big deal that it is a public holiday in Melbourne, while across the country business shuts down for a few minutes while the race is run. It seems like the whole country has a wager down on race day.

Melbourne's Yarra River

The Lay of the Land

Melbourne sits on the Yarra River and stretches along horseshoe-shaped Port Phillip Bay with its suburbs reaching far along the coast. Farther inland, the CBD is situated on the north bank of the Yarra as it makes its final turn toward the bay. The Hoddle Grid, laid out in 1837 and subsequently expanded, demarcates the 48-block traditional city area, hemmed by Southern Cross Station in the west, the Queen Victoria Market in the north, Parliament House to the east, and the Yarra River on the south, making the CBD very easy to navigate.

The city includes numerous major landmarks within walking distance, including Parliament House, the Town Hall, Flinders Street Station, Federation Square, the Royal Exhibition Building, and the Melbourne Cricket Ground.

Outside the CBD, the metropolitan area is of the low-density sprawl type typical of cities that expanded after the development of railroads and automobiles. The suburbs radiate to the north of the city toward the Yarra Valley and maximize waterfront living by wrapping around the shores of Port Phillip Bay to the southeast and, to a more limited extent, the southwest.

There are five recognized areas of Melbourne, each with a number of independent shires and cities, and numerous suburbs within each city or shire: the city, the northern suburbs, the southeastern suburbs, the southwest suburbs, and the western suburbs. In all, there are more than 500 recognized suburbs in the metropolitan area.

CLIMATE

One thing everyone says about Melbourne is "four seasons in one day," and it's true. Melbourne officially has a mild temperate climate and four distinct seasons each year, but the weather changes fast and Melbournians are used to dressing in layers and always carrying both sunglasses and umbrellas. The city experiences frosts and fogs in winter but has not had a snowfall since 1951, although a sleet storm struck in 1986 and hail can occur suddenly at any time of year. While quite cool in winter, the city is notoriously hot and dry in summer, with temperatures sometimes exceeding 40°C. Clouds and rain are frequent, but so is the sunshine. It really is quite unpredictable, but nothing that stops people from sitting outside any time of year.

Where to Live

Melbourne is a sprawling city, spreading its tentacles far into the adjoining countryside. Officially there are hundreds of suburbs. Many are small and run into each other, making it overwhelming to figure out where to start looking. As a very general guideline, stick to the south and east of the CBD. The north, although there are some lovely pockets, has more lower socioeconomic enclaves than anywhere else, and although it is cheaper, it's better to look elsewhere. The west and inner west used to be workers' neighborhoods for the docklands, and although the area is up and coming, with some neighborhoods becoming quite fashionable, the general rule is to look elsewhere if you have family and want a safe environment. Farther out, across the bridges, you can find leafy suburbs with more affordable accommodations than close to the city.

CITY OF MELBOURNE

Melbourne's CBD offers plenty of apartments, in imposing Victorian buildings or shiny new apartment blocks with modern amenities, in the middle of bustling city life and a stone's throw from the offices in the CBD or along St. Kilda Road. Just five tram stops away from the CBD are mostly detached single-family homes nestled next to parks and offering the chance to entertain in your own garden, with shops and restaurants nearby.

The inner-city suburbs offer an eclectic mix of architecture: Victorian terraces

Melbourne has a thriving coffee culture.

(row houses) with intricate ironwork, called Victorian lace, on porches and balconies; sleek art deco villas; traditional 1950s homes; and hypermodern residences with glass fronts and decking in the gardens. The vast majority of homes are detached, with front and back gardens, generally fenced or walled in for privacy. The size of the properties varies from mansions overlooking the sea to houses that may appear to be small garden sheds from the front but seem to expand on the inside due to lots that are much longer than they are wide.

The suburbs of **Albert Park** and **Middle Park** are known for excellent examples of Victorian town houses with easy access to the CBD, Albert Park with its Formula One track following the outline of the lake and the horseshoe bay. Affluent family lifestyle includes sitting outside for breakfast on the weekend in one of the many cafés, popping into South Melbourne Market for fresh produce, and playing with the kids in Albert Park.

A three-bedroom, two-bath house in Middle Park will cost around $1.2 million to buy and $1,000 per week to rent.

St. Kilda is famed for its nightlife and alternative lifestyle but nevertheless has plenty of decent family residences just around the corner from St. Kilda Botanical Gardens, where flocks of cockatoos descend every night at sunset. While you get the odd strange person walking past, most roads are leafy and quiet, and access to the beach and shops is fantastic. It is a lot of fun to live here and not too stuffy or serious.

Just north of the CBD lies trendy **Fitzroy,** an up-and-coming suburb in close proximity to the university and abuzz with life, quirky boutiques, and cafés, becoming slightly quieter toward **Fitzroy North,** near the park and its antiques shops. A two-bed, one-bath apartment in Fitzroy would cost around $500,000 to buy and an average of $500 per week to rent.

SOUTHEASTERN SUBURBS

Along the bay due southeast, past St. Kilda, which is the last inner-city suburb, is fancy **Brighton,** with its old and newer-money mansions close to the beaches and yachting marinas. Life here is quiet and family-oriented but far from the city, its amenities, and its fun. Train connections and the Nepean Highway lead straight into the CBD, but the trams do not run this far, and the school run and commute may take a little planning. That said, the beach and locality make up for any of those inconveniences.

A little farther inland, the suburb of **Ormond** is ever popular with families, offering quiet suburban living with housing prices at a reasonable level. It is popular with locals and expats alike because of its quiet living, community-oriented neighborhood, and proximity to trains and shops. You will get to know your neighbors well, and the kids can play in the quiet streets.

Farther southeast, suburbs such as **Dandenong** still count as reasonable commuter suburbs, with housing prices much more affordable, plenty of amenities around, and a connection into town via train or highway. The good thing about living farther down in the southeast is that you are within easy reach of the hilly countryside and the beautiful Mornington Peninsula, both of which are bursting with things to do on the weekend.

In Ormond you can rent a three-bedroom, two-bath house for around $550 per week; to buy would cost $900,000. In Dandenong, you can rent a three-bedroom, two-bath house for around $380 per week; to buy would cost around $420,000.

Expat Experience: Living in Melbourne

Burr Henly, 61, originally from Seattle, has been living and working as an attorney in Melbourne for 19 years.

Why Australia?
My wife and I had three small daughters in a tiny apartment in Manhattan and were increasingly frustrated with the New York housing options. A headhunter called me about a job for a U.S. lawyer in Melbourne. My wife is Australian, from Brisbane, and we decided to pursue the job opportunity as we both were attracted to spending some time living in Australia.

What do you love most about living in Melbourne?
I love it when Melbourne embodies the best of all its influences, such as Italian coffee, English gardens and town planning, Vietnamese food, and American music.

What do you miss most about the United States?
My family and black American culture.

Which suburbs do you recommend for new expats moving to Melbourne?
Anything in the inner city. The outer suburbs are too car-dependent and miss out on the best Melbourne has to offer.

How did you find acceptance into the Australian community?
Australians are open and friendly people. There can be an anti-American undercurrent, though, and new arrivals from the United States should pay attention to the fact that beneath superficial similarities to the States are many fundamental differences.

What piece of information do you wish you had known when you first arrived?
When people say you need to pick a footy team in Melbourne, they are not kidding.

What's your best tip for newcomers?
Buy a Melways map book, but try to walk as much as possible. Melbourne is great to explore on foot.

What's your least favorite aspect of living in Melbourne?
When Melbourne reflects the worst of its influences, such as Italian accounting, English sports hooliganism, Vietnamese gangs, and American town planning.

How does working here differ from the United States?
Work here is generally more relaxed than in New York, and people try to strike a better work-life balance.

If you were to leave again, what would you miss most about Melbourne?
If I went back to Seattle, I would miss the weather here. People love to complain about it, but the climate is wonderful.

NORTHERN SUBURBS

The north of Melbourne has nice neighborhoods and unpleasant ones; looking for a property here is not something to be done from afar, as hands-on research of the individual suburbs is advisable. **Brunswick** offers proximity to the city, but the northwest is close to the airports, which may be an advantage for regular travelers. Avoid Coburg, as it is not

The Melbourne Cup

"The race that stops a nation" goes the slogan for the Melbourne Cup, and for once the promotion department isn't kidding. Eighty percent of Australian adults put a bet down on this horse race, run the first Tuesday in November at Flemington Racecourse. The date puts it in competition with the American presidential elections, but there isn't really any competition at all, except on the racecourse, where horses from Australia, New Zealand, and Japan compete for $5 million in prize money in the most prestigious two-miler in the world.

The Cup is a public holiday in Melbourne and the Australian Capital Territory. But don't try to accomplish anything anywhere during the half hour around the race, because the whole country stops to watch. Before the race, the closest equivalent to the red carpet at the Oscars is the Spring Carnival, which just about keeps Australian couture milliners in business. As many as 120,000 spectators crowd the racecourse on the day, but viewing it with friends, family, coworkers, or fellow students is just as fun. Office "sweeps" (bets) are conducted for small stakes, and winning the "pool" is cause for a bit of a celebration, and perhaps a few drinks at the pub thereafter.

safe. Farther northeast, suburbs such as **Heidelberg** offer homes on quiet roads with easy access to the city center. A small town center gives a village feeling, and while the city is easily accessible, the closeness to the lush green Yarra Valley is a distinct positive point; the farther out you go, the more land you get for your money.

In Heidelberg, a three-bedroom, two-bath house will set you back $650,000 to buy, and $450 per week to rent.

EASTERN SUBURBS

Toward the east, suburbs become greener with increasing distance. There are spacious suburbs like **Toorak,** with easy tram connections into the city and plenty of desirable family homes and gardens close to small village-like centers that have the necessary amenities, plus lovely boutiques, stores, cafés, and restaurants. It is an old residential suburb, with some families in place for generations, and it has a lovely settled feel. Families know each other, shops are small and personal, and there is easy access to good schools and plenty of tennis courts and other leisure facilities. Alas, the prices reflect that.

Farther out, suburbs such as **Lilydale** allow you to live practically in the Victoria countryside but with suitable connections to Melbourne via highway or train. The advantage of the outer suburbs is not only the proximity to the Yarra Valley countryside but also that lots get bigger and more affordable farther away from Melbourne. What is somewhat missing is the community feeling, as there are a fair number of small industrial parks and industry around, but mostly along the main roads. But if you want a sizable house and your budget won't cover villa living in the inner city, it is worth looking in the eastern suburbs.

In Toorak a three-bedroom, two-bath house can cost you $800 per week to rent and over $1 million to buy; in Lilydale the same size house will cost $450,000 to buy and $350 to rent.

WESTERN SUBURBS

Melbourne's inner western suburbs are separated from the city by the Yarra River, the docklands, and industrial parks. They are some 15 to 20 kilometers from the CBD among lush countryside and often stunning views of Melbourne across Port Phillip Bay. Once beyond the city limits, prices are much more reasonable and lots significantly larger. Life is quieter but still only 20 minutes' drive from the bustle of Melbourne. Train stops and easy access to the highway leading into Melbourne's CBD make this area popular with families who want a little more space and a little less noise.

Farther out is **Sanctuary Lake,** part of **Point Cook** suburb, a new development akin to a gated community complete with a golf course, a gym, and pool access for residents. Situated around a lake and wetlands, there is plenty of space for outdoor living, and Melbourne can even be reached via a safe bicycle path. Although it is still new, a community is starting to form, with kids meeting at the pool and people joining the golf club. A mere 25 kilometers out of Melbourne, the neighborhood offers suburban life near the countryside and the city, with plenty of affordable brand-new housing.

In Point Cook, a modern three-bedroom, two-bath house will cost $340 per week to rent or $500,000 to buy.

Daily Life

MEDIA RESOURCES

Melbourne has two daily newspapers, the relatively conservative *The Age* and the popular *Herald Sun,* plus the national newspaper *The Australian* and the daily *Australian Financial Review.* The *Herald Sun,* along with *The Australian,* are owned by Rupert Murdoch's News Corp. The rival Fairfax company publishes *The Age* and the *Financial Review.* The best resource for buying and selling real estate as well as finding a job is the Saturday newspapers, when they run their main classifieds for homes, flats, and cars. Numerous free community newspapers will be put through your letter box weekly, giving you insights into what's going on in your area plus details about houses to rent or buy.

Melbourne receives all five major over-the-air television networks—the commercial Seven, Nine, and Ten Networks, and the government-run SBS and ABC—as well as major cable and satellite services from Optus, Foxtel, and Austar.

An excellent online guide to Melbourne is the official city guide **What's On** (www.thatsmelbourne.com.au). It has everything from nightlife, dining, and shopping to some excellent material on sports, parks, and other recreation. To check out the numerous restaurants and cafés Melbourne is famous for, get an up-to-date *Good Food Guide,* published annually by *The Age.*

EXPAT RESOURCES

In Melbourne, the Australian American Association, Victoria is a great expat resource. Contact Sam at samcjm@bigpond.com, or find them on Facebook.

HEALTH CARE

The Victorian health system is similar to others in Australia and includes a network of hospitals, community health centers, home and disability care, a health screening system, and a dental system. If you qualify for Medicare, the majority of your medical care is paid for, although nearly half of Australians take out supplementary health insurance so that they have more choice of doctors and more options to speed up appointments. If you have private health insurance, you can visit any medical center or hospital.

The teaching hospitals in Melbourne are the Royal Melbourne in Parkville and the Austin and Mercy complex in the

Australian Rules Football

Also known as "Aussie Rules" or "footy," Australian Rules football is the most popular form of footy played in sports-mad Australia. Rugby Union, Rugby League, and soccer all have a following, but the biggest crowds come for Aussie Rules. Based in Melbourne, where for years the only major Aussie Rules professional competition was the Victorian Football League (VFL), today the competition features 16 national teams. Even the heart of Australian rugby, Sydney, is devoted to the Sydney Swans. Perth and Adelaide have two teams, Brisbane and Sydney one each, and the remaining 10 come from the Melbourne area.

Aussie Rules is played on a massive ground, up to 180 meters long and 155 meters wide. The game is divided into four quarters of 25 minutes with 18 players on each side. The ball is advanced by running, or kicking, but runners must bounce the ball every 10 meters, and kicking is the preferred medium. A player who cleanly catches the ball is awarded a "mark" and may take a free kick, used to tactically advance the ball up the field. Scores are made by kicking the ball through the goalposts, six points for a goal and one point for a "behind," a near miss through a secondary goal post on the right or left.

Professional teams often score more than 100 points in a game, and the competition is known for high speed, grueling fitness requirements, and the athletic skill in kicking long distances for goals, or for soaring leaps to grab a clean "mark."

northern suburbs, while the other majors are the Royal Children's, Royal Women's, St. Vincent's, the Queen Elizabeth, and the Flinders Medical Center, associated with Flinders University, all in the 300- to 700-bed range. The state's **Department of Health** (http://health.vic.gov.au) is the major online portal that covers the services provided across the state.

SCHOOLS

Melbourne has excellent schools and offers a wide choice of public (state-run) schools, faith-based schools, and private and independent schools in both coed and single-sex formats. There is a bias toward same-sex schools and the belief that they are better educators than coed schools, but Melbourne offers plenty of excellent coed schools as well.

A very useful government website called **My School** (www.myschool.edu.au) and one called **Better Education** (http://bettereducation.com.au) can help you select schools in your neighborhood, as both provide a history of National Assessment Program—Literacy and Numeracy (NAPLAN) test results, post codes, and marks, allowing you to check the performance and location of each school.

There are a number of private schools in Melbourne, all charging fees according to the entry level, with higher years incurring more expensive fees. Although schooling is free in Australia for citizens and permanent residents, if you are in Australia on a 457 temporary resident visa, you will have to pay fees even for public schools. Perhaps for that reason, expats often opt for private schools, which also offer more flexibility when you arrive in the middle of the school year. Private schools will also take your children as long as they fit their criteria, whereas public schools take students who live in their catchment districts, and if you don't, they are not be obliged to offer you a space.

One of the best private schools in Melbourne is Wesley College, a coed school offering both primary and secondary education with the option of the International Baccalaureate (IB). The school has various campuses around the city. Other good schools include Melbourne Girls Grammar School, which also has a school for boys, both offering primary and secondary education at various campuses; Scotch College, a boys primary and secondary in Hawthorn; and Mentone Grammar School, a coed school for primary and secondary education in the southern suburb of Mentone, to name but a few.

SHOPPING

Melbourne is a shopper's dream. The CBD offers all the usual mass retailers and high-end stores plus the popular department stores Myers and David Jones. Shops line Swanston Street, Collins and Bourke Streets, and Elizabeth Street, but don't just stick to the main drags, as the laneways are what makes Melbourne unique. Peep into each little alley as you walk past as there are plenty of individual boutiques and arcades to discover. Don't miss the beautiful Block and Royal Arcades. The Melbourne Central Mall in the CBD is a more modern mall and railway station with cinemas, shops, restaurants, and even a museum and a small free library.

For fresh produce, Melbourne's many markets offer local, seasonal, and artisanal products in lovely surroundings. The best markets are Queen Victoria Market, reportedly the largest open-air market in the Southern Hemisphere, in the north of the CBD; South Melbourne Market; and Prahran Market, just off Chapel Street. In addition, there are regular farmers markets, which are advertised in the local newspapers.

For an eclectic mix of boutiques offering anything from chic clothing to interior decor items and even bric-a-brac and antiques, visit Chapel Street, which stretches for miles across several suburbs. Each corner has its own individual taste; start off at the intersection of Toorak Road and work your way up.

Chatsworth Shopping Centre is a great mall just outside the inner city limits but well worth a visit. A great range of anything from day-to-day stuff at Kmart to luxury designer clothes, the mall fills every shopping need under one roof, something you will appreciate if you are new in town and need to buy several unrelated items.

Getting Around

PUBLIC TRANSPORTATION

With traffic at peak times at a standstill and parking in the CBD very expensive to use on a daily basis, Melbourne's extensive public transportation system brings relief to stressed commuters. With more than 200 stations, the metropolitan train network connects extensively from the CBD outward to the northern, eastern, and southeastern suburbs, although with slightly fewer connections in the west. Metropolitan buses and Melbourne's iconic trams fill in the gaps to take you through the city center and into most inner suburbs. All Victoria's trains, trams, and buses are administered by Public Transport Victoria (PTV), which offers an easy journey planner and smartphone app to find the best connections.

For your first visit and to get an overview of Melbourne's city center or to connect throughout the CBD, travel on the iconic City Circle tram, a free service running every 12 minutes in both clockwise and counterclockwise directions. Also

Flinders Street Station in Melbourne

note that, within the CBD grid, all trams are free. Just look at the sign at the tram stop, it will tell you if it is within the free zone.

Outside the CBD, fares on public transportation have to be paid with Myki smartcards, which are rechargeable at most stations and newsagents and offer discounts for students, seniors, veterans, and disabled people; there are also special visitors' fares. Fares range from $3.90 for a single trip in Zone 1 up to $4.96 for travel in Zone 2, but tickets are capped at $7.16 for Zone 1 and $12.12 for Zones 1 and 2 per day. Find the right pass at **Myki** (www.myki.com.au), where you can also track tram times. The initial purchase price for a new smartcard is $6 for adults, and $3 for children, and you can pick up a visitors' card at the Melbourne Visitors Center on Federation Square to tide you over.

HIGHWAYS

Melbourne's highways and expressways weave a web through the city and its suburbs, making connections easy if not necessarily fast during peak times. The main thoroughfares are the Princes Highway, a road that leads from Sydney through Melbourne along the coast past Adelaide, stretching nearly 2,000 kilometers and across three states. In Melbourne the highway connects the southeastern suburbs from Dandenong diagonally across the city center to the northwest.

The Nepean Highway starts in the center with St. Kilda Road and follows the curve of the bay southeast along the Mornington Peninsula, and the Monash Freeway (M1) connects the southeast with the north through the center. The City Link, a toll road for which you can purchase 24-hour, weekend, 30-day, or continuous passes, starts in the CBD and heads north to the airport.

Speed limits are strictly enforced and are generally 110 km/h on the highways and expressways, 60 to 70 km/h on faster inner city roads, and 50 km/h on residential streets unless otherwise marked.

Parking is a mix of expensive secure multistory parking lots and street parking, which can be free for up to four hours, depending on the area. Even in the center of town there are usually street parking spots that allow you to park for an hour for free, but there is no leeway, and staying even a minute extra can cost you a severe fine. For residents, parking permits for your street can be bought from individual local councils for around $50 per year, depending on the area, and you can even purchase a guest parking permit when you have visitors.

MELBOURNE AIRPORT

Tullamarine Airport is a busy international and domestic hub with 7.5 million international and nearly 22 million domestic passengers annually. The airport hosts more than 30 airlines and connects with main hubs in the United States, Europe, the Middle East, and Asia. Local budget airline Jetstar has recently reinstated its direct route to Honolulu.

Getting into the CBD from the airport is easy with the Sky Bus, connecting the airport with the Southern Cross railway station in the CBD every 10 to 15 minutes during the day and every 30 minutes through the night for $19 one-way, $38 round-trip. Taxis take around 25 minutes, and all major car rental companies have kiosks in the arrivals area. Note that if you're driving, the City Link road is a toll road. Check that your rental car is equipped with an automatic payment transponder; if not, avoid the City Link and use the Western Ring Road instead.

BRISBANE AND THE QUEENSLAND COAST

Everybody in Australia has an opinion on Brisbane and the Gold Coast: "Brisbane is too lazy for its own good"; "It's on a river, not the coast, so obviously something's missing." And the Gold Coast? "It's the Florida of Australia, full of retirees and partying students"; "Too many high-rises mar the view." These are the opinions of people who often haven't even visited these places. Brisbane is in fact a lovely city, set on a meandering river that offers great waterfront living with a relaxed attitude. It's the sunshine, you see. And the Gold Coast? The apartment buildings really aren't that overwhelming when there are miles of soft sand beach facing the Pacific Ocean, with its rolling waves and spectacular views. If you live in one of the apartments, you can enjoy the vistas, and if you live farther inland, you won't even see the high-rises. As for the retirees and students, yes, they're here, but what better climate and setting to retire in, and the schoolies only come for a brief period once a year.

Brisbane, Australia's third largest city, is the gateway to the tropical beaches of the Queensland coast and the Great Barrier Reef. The Brisbane River runs past the CBD and the eastern suburbs toward

BRISBANE AND THE QUEENSLAND COAST
Maroochydore
Mooloolaba
Sunshine Coast
Blackbutt
Caloundra
Kilcoy
Beerburrum East State Forest
Bribie Island
Bribie Island NP
Caboolture
Moreton Island NP
Crows Nest
Esk
Lake Wivenhoe
Lake Samsonvale
Deception Bay
Redcliffe
Moreton Island
Moreton Bay
Brisbane Forest Park
Strathpine
BRISBANE AIRPORT
Toowoomba
Gatton
Bardon
Indooroopilly
Toowong
BRISBANE
Brisbane River
Mt Gravatt
Blue Lake National Park
Cleveland
Ipswich
Tingalpa Res
North Stradbroke Island
Beenleigh
Southern Moreton Bay Islands NP
Glen Rock State Forest
Tamborine National Park
South Stradbroke Island
Main Range National Park
Boonah
Arundel
Beaudesert
Nerang
Benowa
Gold Coast
Warwick
Gambubal State Forest
Coolangatta
Lamington National Park
Koreelah National Park
Mt Barney National Park
Tweed Heads
Woodenbong
Murwillumbah
Beaury State Forest
Border Ranges National Park
Toonumbar National Park
Brunswick Heads
Nightcap National Park
Kyogle
Yabbra National Park
0
20 mi
0
20 km
Byron Bay
Lismore
© AVALON TRAVEL
Ballina

Brisbane's iconic Story Bridge

Moreton Bay, and along the Pacific Coast there are almost 200 kilometers of attractive destinations in both directions. Besides the proven sources of wealth in tourism and real estate, Brisbane is also home to a growing cadre of entrepreneurs in information technology and financial services. Old-line industries such as mining, paper, oil refining, shipbuilding, and railcar construction also exist here. The metropolitan area is home to more than two million people who enjoy the famously warm subtropical climate; the population has nearly doubled since 1980 as more people discover the outstanding arts, cultural, and sporting venues and events. Like most Australian cities, Brisbane has a sophisticated public transportation and highway infrastructure that features unique ferries and jet catamarans cruising along the Brisbane River.

THE BRIEF STORY OF BRISBANE

The area surrounding Brisbane was occupied for centuries by the Turrubal people. The first Europeans in the area were on the 1770 expedition of Captain Cook, who named the bay after the president of the Royal Society, Lord Morton. A geographer misspelled the name as Moreton Bay, and gave no name at all to the freshwater river that would eventually be named the Brisbane River; Queenslanders have been feeling misunderstood ever since.

Brisbane was founded in 1825 as a penal colony for repeat offenders and was named for Thomas Brisbane, governor of New South Wales, who sponsored an expedition by John Oxley to the area in 1823.

The location was chosen for the Brisbane River's abundance of freshwater after an attempt the previous year to establish a penal colony slightly north at Redcliffe foundered because of the inconsistent water supply. The new colony was located on a floodplain area surrounded by hills, and it flourished as a penal colony until free settlers began arriving in 1838. The Brisbane government had been instrumental in exploring the agricultural potential of the vast continent, and in Queensland the original focus of

Schoolies and Toolies

The Australian phenomenon of "schoolies" is a three-week-long period of celebrations between mid-November and early December, following the end of final exams and graduation from school. School graduates, called schoolies, descend on coastal resorts for a weeklong vacation with thousands of other schoolies. Seen as a rite of passage, throwing off the shackles of school and enjoying what is often their first trip without their parents, the teenagers often indulge heavily in everything they shouldn't. The tradition, similar to spring break in the United States, started back in the 1970s on the Gold Coast.

Head down to the beach promenade of Surfers Paradise after 10am during schoolies week and you'll see queues of students nursing sore heads at the kebab shops, along with groups of young people just being together, having fun, and enjoying the onset of a new chapter in their lives as adults.

Opening with the traditional first run into the sea, the week is filled with parties, music, and plenty of fun. Decried by the media as a week of overindulgence in alcohol, drugs, and sex, violence and accidents have also marred the supposedly simple fun event.

Queensland's government has tightened supervision for the safety of the young revelers by registering each official schoolie, giving them a photo ID and wristbands for entry to organized alcohol-free music and party events in safe venues as well as calling in extra police and security guards and raising awareness of "toolies." Toolies are often older than the real schoolies who join the youth with unsavory ideas in mind, causing problems along the way; most violence and arrests have been blamed on the gate-crashing toolies.

The most popular destination for schoolies week is still Surfers Paradise on the Gold Coast, with tens of thousands of students boosting the Queensland economy each year. Other popular destinations are Bali, for those who can afford it, and even Fiji, where reportedly entire islands have been designated schoolie resorts for three exciting weeks per year.

the colony was agriculture. The city of Brisbane became a regional center serving the interests of plantation owners who were opening vast tracts of Queensland to sugar and pineapple cultivation, among other crops.

In 1859 population growth and the distance from Sydney led to the formation of Queensland, named for Queen Victoria. Its borders were drawn to demarcate Brisbane and everything north, although the southern border partly follows the course of the Darling River. Brisbane was made the capital, and the ensuing years saw growing prosperity, especially after the rise of sugar cultivation in the mid- and late 19th century.

Even after federation in 1901, Queensland continued to be beset by the problems of isolation, and the state embraced aviation early in its history; in 1920 Queensland became the original home of the Queensland and Northern Territory Aerial Services, now known around the world as Qantas.

Increasingly, important mineral discoveries made Brisbane a center for industrial and mining corporations as well as an agricultural hub. Today, the state remains the center of the Australian aluminum industry, and as the closest major port to Southeast Asia, the city is home to several major electronics firms that use Brisbane as the point of entry for imports. The port is the major export point for sugar as well as significant volumes of coal and container cargo.

Following World War I, Brisbane benefited from increasing attention to Queensland's abundant sunshine, spectacular beaches, and proximity to the Great Barrier Reef. The tourism industry began a major buildup with construction of the Surfers Paradise Hotel in 1925. The name Gold Coast dates from the 1940s and was coined by real estate developers referring to lucrative financial opportunities rather than abundant sunshine. Today, tourism ranks with mining as the most important industry in the state, and the Gold Coast is an urbanized stretch of hotels, golf courses, and residential high-rises that continue from Beenleigh, just south of Brisbane, for 65 kilometers toward the New South Wales border.

Queensland has always gone its own way in managing its affairs, which has resulted in American observers comparing the state to the independent streak seen in Texas. For example, in 1922 the state Labor government appointed a "suicide squad" of politicians to the state's unelected upper house, the Legislative Council, and they voted themselves out of existence. Queensland remains the only state in Australia without an upper house.

Brisbane grew past one million in population back in the 1970s, and the Gold Coast is now the most important tourism and second-home mecca in the country, rivaled only by Cairns along the northeast coast. The city continues to play host not only to spectacular events such as the Commonwealth Games, the Goodwill Games, and the 1988 World's Fair but also, as the state's capital, to an independent style of brash politics that often pits the urban strength of the Labor Party against the rural strength of the conservative National Party. Numerous maverick politicians such as John Bjelke-Petersen, Pauline Hanson, and Senator Barnaby Joyce hail from the Sunshine State, as does former prime minister Kevin Rudd. Perhaps the most famous Queenslanders globally are golfer Greg Norman and the late naturalist Steve Irwin, who popularized the state through his daredevil animal documentaries.

The Lay of the Land

Brisbane is several kilometers inland from the mouth of the Brisbane River, and the CBD is in an S-shaped bend in the river. Set on a floodplain, the city center is subject to periodic flooding, although surrounding urban areas and local countryside are safe on a series of low mountains and hills.

The CBD is compact and easily covered on foot. It has the most thoughtfully named street grid in the country, with the streets running parallel to the river named after the male members of the royal family and the cross streets named after female members. It's practically impossible to get lost; the southern bend in the river is dominated by the Botanic Gardens and the main government building. Overall the city is beautifully presented, and even though it's a busy commercial center, it feels more relaxed than other cities.

Numerous bridges of myriad designs cross the river and connect the north and south parts of the city. The most significant is the William Jolly Bridge, southwest of the CBD, which connects the CBD with the artsy South Bank area. The iconic Story Bridge, northeast of the CBD, connects Kangaroo Point with Fortitude Valley, known as "The Valley." The Valley is a shopping and restaurant hub and home to Chinatown with its bargain-filled mall.

While Brisbane has reached a population of more than two million, the city is not as sprawling as some other Australian

Average Temperatures and Rainfall in Brisbane

Month	Mean maximum temperature (°C)	Mean minimum temperature (°C)	Mean rainfall (mm)
January	30	21	132
February	30	21	133
March	29	20	96
April	27	17	67
May	24	13	62
June	22	12	61
July	22	10	24
August	23	11	41
September	26	14	32
October	27	16	86
November	28	19	103
December	29	20	156

Source: Australian Bureau of Meteorology

capitals. Rather than forming a vast urban area, the inner suburbs quickly give way to bushland that leads to larger suburbs and small individual towns.

CLIMATE

Brisbane has a warm, sultry, but not suffocating subtropical climate with almost daily sunshine interrupted by rainfall. Like most of the continent, rainfall is not regular but rather alternates between periods of drought and years of deluge and flooding. For the past few years Brisbane has been affected by a severe drought, which has resulted in Stage 6 water restrictions, the highest ever imposed on a major Australian city. In Stage 6, all outdoor water use is banned except by special permit, sprinklers can't be used, and swimming pools can't be refilled. The target consumption is 98 liters of water per person per day. Generally, though, restrictions are lifted as quickly as they are put on when conditions change, and forecasts vary seasonally, with Brisbane typically receiving abundant rainfall, especially in the summer, with an average of more than 15 centimeters per month.

Where to Live

The outlying areas of Brisbane can be stunningly beautiful but quite decentralized. You won't see the Victorian row houses so typical of Melbourne or Sydney; virtually all homes are detached and have some breathing space. Brisbane's waterfront real estate is fairly affordable, especially compared with the skyrocketing land prices of Sydney's waterfront.

Many expats coming to the area are looking for second or retirement homes on the Gold Coast south of Brisbane or the Sunshine Coast to the north. The Gold Coast is far more established but far more commercial. The glistening beachside condo towers are reminiscent of Florida or Hawaii, and year-round good weather—and better affordability compared to some established markets in the United States—make it a compelling alternative to comparable locations in the Northern Hemisphere.

Taking everything into consideration, Brisbane and the Queensland coast are great places to land and settle in Australia. The weather is near perfect, and Sydney is "only" 1,000 kilometers away on the Pacific Motorway, a leisurely drive in Australian terms.

BRISBANE CBD AND INNER CITY

Brisbane's CBD nestles in a bend on the north side of the meandering Brisbane River and is a mix of lovely historic buildings and modern skyscrapers with a number of apartment buildings overlooking the many bridges. The CBD spreads along the river into Fortitude Valley, toward the northwest, a formerly sleazy but recently newly discovered area, although it's still not necessarily appropriate for family living, with lots of nightlife and noise. Gorgeous hilly **Paddington** is northeast and has plenty of trendy cafés and single-family houses in typical Brisbane tongue-and-groove design. Although the neighborhood is geared toward families, it is becoming popular with affluent, young professionals that are drawn to its eclectic restaurants and boutiques. **Kangaroo Point** is a lovely area due south with more

riverside living

apartment living. Property along the river's edge is the most sought-after and the priciest. The demographic here is mixed, but tends more toward young professional couples rather than family living.

A three-bedroom, two-bath apartment in Kangaroo Point will set you back around $500,000 to buy and $800 per week to rent; a three-bedroom, two-bath detached house in Paddington will cost around $700,000 to buy and $600 per week to rent.

NORTHERN SUBURBS

The northern suburbs begin with the areas around the inner city and the river such as **Springhill,** with its brilliant views across the city and access to parks and the popular Brisbane Grammar School. It is among the most expensive places to live in the city but offers the ideal location for commuting ease and for access to the CBD. It's popular with affluent professionals and empty nesters. Farther north, along the Doomben rail line, the land gets hillier and provides some views of the CBD. The more affluent areas are east of the rail line, with middle- and working-class families on the west side. Farther north along the line, family-friendly **Albion** is a quiet and safe neighborhood that features a lot of big expensive suburban homes in increasingly green settings. There is a popular beach community at **Sandgate,** also a popular weekend getaway in the summer. This neighborhood offers affluent beachside living, which is quite rare near Brisbane due to the wetlands, yet it is a 30-minute commute to the city center.

A three-bedroom, two-bath house in Springhill will set you back around $650 per week to rent and $850,000 to buy; in Albion a similar property costs around $700,000 to buy and $550 per week to rent. A four-bed, two-bath house in Sandgate will set you back around $750,000 to buy and $450 per week to rent.

EASTERN AND SOUTHERN SUBURBS

Past the inner suburbs of South Bank and Kangaroo Point, with their trendy apartment living and access to cafés and restaurants, are suburbs such as the wonderfully named **Woolloongabba, Greenslopes,** and **Sunnybank.** These areas are still within easy commuting distance to the city but surrounded by wild bushland. Step away from the main roads, such as the M3, which runs south through the southern suburbs all the way to Sydney, and you may forget you are within a few miles of Australia's third city. The lots are larger and more affordable. These suburbs are on the city outskirts of Brisbane, within easy reach of the city's amenities, have their own community centers, schools, doctors, and shops. The mostly single-family houses here range from small bungalows to vast colonial-style villas. The Pacific Highway and the easy train connections take you into the city within 10 minutes maximum. A two-bed, one-bath apartment in Woolloongabba costs around $400 per month to rent.

East from the central part of the city, closer to the coast through the wetlands, are **Manly** and **Thornlands.** Both are within reach of the ocean and have views over the wetlands and their profusion of wildlife. Keep in mind that this it is not beachfront living the way it is near Sydney or Perth with sandy beaches—for those you'll have to go farther up or down the coast. The vast majority of housing offerings here are single-family detached houses. Both suburbs attract families, although Thornlands tends to be very popular with retired couples. Manly has excellent facilities and the coed Manly State School, dating back to 1910, which is highly recommended by local residents.

Expat Experience: Living in Brisbane

Audrey Ciccone, 52, from Vancouver, Canada, is a freelance HR consultant who has lived in both Perth and Brisbane.

Audrey Ciccone

Why did you come to Australia? And why Brisbane?
I came with my husband, an engineer who works for an American company that bought an engineering firm in Perth. He went to set it up in Perth, then we moved to Brisbane with the same company.

What do you love most about living in Brisbane?
Lovely walks along the river. It's so easy to get around in. And it's summer all year around, which is great news for Canadians.

What's your least favorite aspect of living in Brisbane or Australia?
I must admit that Perth is still my favorite place; it has a huge expat community and is very welcoming. In Brisbane, it is difficult to find people like yourself.

Sunshine Coast or Gold Coast?
Gold Coast because you can walk on the beach forever and ever. It is hard sand, so you can walk easily, and it goes on for miles. I find the Sunshine Coast has no center and is a little disjointed.

What do you miss most about Canada?
Funnily enough, pierogies, the Polish dumplings. They are very difficult to get here, only on occasion in the Polish Club. And other treats from home, such as Frosted Mini Wheats, although it's better that they're far away . . .

Which suburbs do you recommend for new expats moving to Brisbane?
All depends on your budget. I'd recommend suburbs such as Thorneside, Grange, Wavell Heights, and my own, Kalinga (Wooloowin), but these are more expensive than young people could maybe afford. Coorparoo and Manly are better for young families. Avoid Logan, though, as it can be a bit rougher around the edges. And be aware of which way the water flows; Brisbane is very hilly and you can easily get flooded.

What piece of information do you wish you had known when you first arrived?
How important it is to be near the rail system, which connects you to the city. And how difficult the utilities are to hook up. Be prepared to be without the Internet for 21 days, even if you're moving within Australia. The system is set up for people staying put, not moving.

What's your best tip for newcomers, and the first thing they ought to do?
Accept any invitation you get. Anytime you meet up with somebody, you begin to build a network, and you can sort out whom to keep on later.

What's the best way to meet other expats?
Social media. I have found 85 percent of my work contacts through Twitter.

Both suburbs offer typical suburban living, with a community atmosphere, away from the anonymity of the inner city.

A three-bedroom, two-bath house in Sunnybank will cost approximately $400 per week to rent, and $350,000 to $600,000 to buy. Toward the coast, a three-bedroom, two-bath house in Manly will set you back around $520,000 to buy and $450 per week to rent.

WESTERN SUBURBS

To the west, hilly Brisbane becomes even hillier with plenty of leafy suburbs perfect for families, such as **Bardon** and **Toowong.** The countryside is full of outdoor activities such as horseback riding and access to the nearby forested parks. Houses are large, detached, and a mix of slightly older and modern. Each neighborhood has its "village center" that offers shops, medical centers, schools, and all the amenities you'll need without having to make the trip into town. Still, access into central Brisbane is easy via Milton Road, a fleet of regular buses, and a ferry terminal just off Toowong.

A three-bedroom, two-bath house in Bardon or Toowong will cost around $730 per week to rent and $730,000 to buy.

GOLD COAST

Yes, there are quite a few high-rise towers lining the stunning beach, and it does bustle with tourists pretty much year-round, but the endless beach really is stunning, and a mere few hundred meters inland, the tourists thin out and lovely residential areas offer green hilly living with easy beach access. The stretch between the busy coast and the M3 Pacific Motorway is pure idyllic countryside; rivers and lakes decorate residential suburbs, and small towns nestling in the surrounding bush feel far away from tourist hot spots. **Benowa** and **Sorrento** are set among canals fed by the Nerang River, just inland from Surfers Paradise, offering plenty of large houses with access to the water. Brisbane is about an hour away on the Pacific Motorway, and a direct bus link as well as the Airtrain connect to Brisbane Airport with stops along the way, including the CBD, making commuting possible if not necessarily ideal.

A two-bedroom, one-bath house in Benowa will cost around $300,000 to buy and $300 per week to rent, and a two-bedroom, one-bath apartment with parking in Surfers Paradise will cost $300,000 to buy and $300 per week to rent. A two-bed, one-bath apartment in Sorrento costs around $250,000 to buy and $490 per week to rent.

SUNSHINE COAST

Called the northern echo of the Gold Coast, the Sunshine Coast, about an hour's drive north of Brisbane along the M1 Bruce Highway, is also a great tourist destination but not to the same extent as the Gold Coast. The area is known for its beaches as well as for the hinterland's fantastic Glass House Mountains, prehistoric volcanic plugs rising from the lush green bush, also famous as the setting for Steve Irwin's Australia Zoo. Wetlands and bushland stretch to the coast, and the high-rise development is much less extreme than south of Brisbane. Towns such as **Maroochydore** and neighboring **Mooloolaba** combine touristy seaside promenades with quiet residential backstreets, offering the best of both worlds.

A three-bedroom, two-bath house in Maroochydore or Mooloolaba costs $420,000 to buy and around $400 per week to rent.

NORTHERN NEW SOUTH WALES AND BYRON BAY

One hour south of the Gold Coast is the New South Wales border, a growing area of interest for those who are seeking the same lifestyle benefits of the Gold Coast and Sunshine Coast but with less noise and bustle and a little better affordability—although the word is out and more people are flocking here, sending housing prices up. **Byron Bay** has been a beach mecca for years, and the extensive recent development has a far more natural look and less congestion than points north. It's certainly worth a look for those considering the Gold Coast area who want to avoid the excesses of Surfers Paradise. The M3 expressway leads right through the area, and while it is not exceedingly convenient to Brisbane—under two hours' drive—that city is still accessible for a day or weekend shopping trip.

A three-bedroom, two-bath house in Byron Bay costs around $700 per week to rent and around $600,000 to buy—although lovely oceanfront houses can go for several million dollars.

Daily Life

MEDIA RESOURCES

Brisbane has one newspaper, the tabloid *Courier-Mail,* which has a Sunday edition known simply as *The Mail,* but residents can also get the national newspaper, *The Australian,* as well as the daily *Australian Financial Review.* The *Courier-Mail* is owned, along with *The Australian,* by Rupert Murdoch's News Corp. The rival Fairfax company produces the online-only *Brisbane Times,* which competes with the *Courier-Mail*'s website. There are several free community newspapers, including the *Brisbane News,* along with the monthly *Brisbane Circle* and the fashion-conscious *Style* magazine. The Gold Coast and Sunshine Coast also have free local community newspapers in addition to the Brisbane media.

Brisbane receives all five major free-to-air television networks—the commercial Seven, Nine, and Ten Networks and the government-owned SBS and ABC—as well as major cable and satellite services from Optus, Foxtel, and Austar, and a good choice of radio stations. An excellent online guide to Brisbane is **Weekend Notes** (www.weekendnotes.com/brisbane).

EXPAT RESOURCES

A good expat resources is the Australian American Association, Brisbane Chapter. They can be contacted by phone (61/07-3278-6366) or via www.americancommunityaustralia.com.

HEALTH CARE

Brisbane has dozens of private and public hospitals in the city and the surrounding suburbs. Some notable institutions are Mater Private Hospitals, which operate private adult, children's, and maternity hospitals, and although officially a private institution, services are also available to uninsured individuals. Mater is a large research and training group with hospitals all around the area. There are also the renowned Royal Brisbane and Women's Hospital, the Queensland Institute for Medical Research, and many other private clinics and medical facilities, making Brisbane one of the major centers for medical care and a city popular with up-and-coming doctors and nurses.

SCHOOLS

In Queensland, children are required to attend school between ages 6 and 17, although children are encouraged to

Brisbane's bustling markets

complete year 12. Primary school is years 1 to 7, and high school is years 8 to 12.

There are more than 50 private schools in Brisbane. The premier boys' secondary schools include Brisbane Grammar. Although it is one of the highest fee-paying schools in the state, is also one of the best. It consistently tops academic performance charts and takes pride in its balanced approach to teaching.

Premier girls' schools include Brisbane Girls Grammar, and notably Somerville House (Brisbane High School for Girls), which is a day and boarding school that boasts similar results as Brisbane Grammar for Boys. Somerville House has a diverse student population and offers musical and academic scholarships.

Brisbane is home to the University of Queensland, one of the eight elite Australian universities and ranked among the top 50 universities in the world. Griffith University has five campuses and around 33,000 students in the Brisbane and Gold Coast area; Queensland University of Technology is the city's other major institution of higher learning. The University of the Sunshine Coast is located on the Sunshine Coast.

The other postsecondary option in Queensland is the Technical and Further Education (TAFE) path, which offers technical and vocational education, often in conjunction with apprenticeship programs or other employer-sponsored education in areas such as tourism, computers, construction, and visual arts. More than 250,000 Queenslanders take TAFE courses each year. TAFE courses can lead to a diploma but not a bachelor's degree.

SHOPPING

Brisbane's CBD is a little jewel of easily maneuvered streets packed full of major retailers and designer shops. In the streets around Elizabeth Street, together with malls and department stores such as Myers and Queen Street Mall, you'll find everything you need and want for the entire family. Connected to the CBD are Chinatown and Fortitude Valley, which come to life every weekend with the Valley Markets. For trendy boutiques interspersed with cafés and restaurants, don't miss lovely James Street, toward the river.

A little northeast of the CBD is fashionable Paddington, where you can shop along a stretch of road that starts at the historical Barracks, a convenient daily shopping and dining destination with supermarkets and grocery shops, and continues down Given Terrace and into Latrobe Terrace. Individual boutiques, cafés, and restaurants line the streets, ending with tempting antiques shops set in unique little houses with residential roads falling off to the sides down the rather steep hills.

Getting Around

PUBLIC TRANSPORTATION

The myriad of buses on Brisbane's roads, run by at least a dozen different operators, are at first confusing, but they certainly reflect the fact that Brisbane has one of the largest bus fleets in Australia, connecting along the coast of Queensland, making commuting—and visiting the beach—an easy undertaking. The public transportation system also includes an excellent rail system based at Central Station and Roma Street station, plus a fast ferry service via CityCat across the undulating river.

The Go Card, an electronic pass that works on buses and trains, including the excellent Airtrain, as well as the ferries, can be purchased at most stations, online, and at retailers displaying the Go Card sign in the window; the value on the card can be replenished at the same places. Fares start at $3.35 for an adult one-way ticket within one zone, and the Airtrain costs $17.50 for a transfer from the CBD to the airport. There are discounts for students, disabled people, seniors, and others, and the card is cheaper than buying tickets as you go, even if you don't use public transport often.

Brisbane has many different bus companies.

HIGHWAYS

As in England, Queensland has an M and A naming convention for its highways. Major highways are named with M and a number (M1, M2), while secondary highways are named with an A (A1, A2). The main highways are the Pacific Motorway (M3), which heads south to the Gold Coast, and the Bruce Highway, which heads north toward Cairns. The Gateway Motorway is a toll road that connects the Sunshine Coast and Gold Coast via a Brisbane bypass. Tolls are around $4.50 per journey, and fines for nonpayment are steep. A small transponder that is stuck in your windshield can be purchased online from **GoVia** (www.govia.com.au). Request one if you rent a car to make toll payment automatic and stress-free. The system works nationwide.

The Ipswich Motorway heads into the southern suburbs, and the Western and Centenary Freeways connect Brisbane with its western suburbs. Traffic congestion is a problem, especially at the Brisbane River bottlenecks. A tunnel is being constructed under the river to relieve some of the pressure.

Brisbane's speed limits are expressed in kilometers per hour (km/h) and are typically 50 km/h in congested suburban areas, 60 km/h for major suburban roads, 80 km/h for highways, and 100 or 110 km/h for expressways.

BRISBANE AIRPORT

At the sprawling airport northeast of the CBD, the domestic and international terminals are several kilometers apart but connected by regular transit buses and the Airtrain rail system, which connects to the CBD and as far south as the Gold Coast, and as far north as the Sunshine Coast.

The airport is one of the busiest in Australia, with some 50,000 domestic and 13,000 international passengers passing through the airport daily. Operating with just a single runway, delays are common, with about 72 percent of arrivals on time.

Direct international connections to Brisbane include Abu Dhabi and Dubai in the Middle East; Dallas and Los Angeles; many Asian hubs, including Singapore, Hong Kong, and Kuala Lumpur; New Zealand; and other nearby countries. The domestic hub is the busier of the two, with hundreds of weekly flights connecting Australia's capitals and smaller airports around the continent.

CANBERRA

Canberra (pronounced CAN-bra) is an odd capital city. Not only is it one of the smallest of Australian capitals, with 382,000 inhabitants, it is also the one that feels least like a city. When you approach any other Australian city, you spot the high-rises of the central business district in the distance, giving you that sense of "city" and arrival and a vague idea where you are in relation to the center. When you approach Canberra by road, you don't know that you are actually there until you either see the Telstra Tower on the summit of Black Mountain overlooking the capital or hit one of the two bridges crossing Lake Burley Griffin, or indeed stand in front of Capital Hill. Landmarks are rare and difficult to spot due to the sprawling nature of the city and the forest it's built into.

It is admirable that development is not allowed even on the surrounding forested hilltops, even though they would be prime real estate with stunning views across the lush countryside that covers the Australian Capital Territory (ACT). Despite the temptation, it has been decided that the hills are to be kept accessible to all, so green they will stay. When people talk about the green Australian cities, they tend to mean parks and nature reserves; when they talk about Canberra, they mean nature as it always has been in the area, with a few square kilometers

CANBERRA
To Gungahlin and Mitchell
DUNSMORE ST
FEDERAL HWY
GINNINDERRA DR
DOWNER
23
Canberra Nature Park
Majura Pine Plantation
ST
ANTILL
LYNEHAM
DICKSON
WATTLE ST
MAJURA AVE
ALT 23
To Belconnen
O'CONNOR
BELCONNEN WAY
MACARTHUR AVE
AINSLIE
Canberra Nature Park
BARRY DR
DAVID ST
LIMESTONE AVE
TURNER
NORTHBOURNE AVE
BRADDON
CLUNIES ROSS ST
To Tuggeranong Pkwy
CIVIC
FAIRBAIRN
Lake Burley Griffin
West Basin
AVE
PARKES WAY
CAMPBELL
Central Basin
AVE
MAJURA RD
COMMONWEALTH
RUSSEL
Stirling Park
CANBERRA AIRPORT
YARRALUMLA
East Basin
CAPITAL HILL
BRISBANE AVE
Jerrabomberra Wetlands
AVE
ADELAIDE
Jerrabomberra
MELBOURNE AVE
KINGSTON
DEAKIN
MANUKA
Molonglo
23
CAPTAIN
CANBERRA
River
KENT ST
FLINDERS WAY
Canberra Nature Park
GRIFFITH
Creek
COOK
AVE
HUGHES
RED HILL
52
NARRABUNDAH
WODEN
HINDMARSH DR
To Weston Creek
O'MALLEY
YAMBA AVE
0
500 yds
0
500 m
23
To Tuggeranong
© AVALON TRAVEL

taken for building the various circles that accommodate the government offices and the city center, plus the lake—but that is it. The suburbs are set in bushland with tall old trees dominating the scene, plots for houses nestled underneath, and many areas given over to nature reserves rather than manicured parks. You'll find kangaroos hopping down your lane if you live in the southern suburbs, just a few hundred meters from Parliament House. You won't find a greener city.

Canberra is all about work and play, with an emphasis on play. The agenda of local events is brimming with high-profile shows, plays, exhibitions, and festivals, and the unspoiled natural environment around the city offers a multitude of outdoor options—hills and mountains for hiking, climbing, skiing, and camping. For those who heed the call of the big city on occasion, Sydney is a mere three hours' drive along the Hume Freeway, and the beaches are roughly the same distance. The atmosphere is nothing if not cosmopolitan, with most countries' embassies here and a welcoming local culture. Even though Canberra often gets a bad rap for being boring, it really is quite difficult to get bored with all the variety. Maybe, as one American expat said, "Boredom is a state of mind. Canberra has so much to offer that you'd need a very small and dispassionate mind to ever get bored here."

THE BRIEF STORY OF CANBERRA

The area that forms the ACT was historically home to two indigenous groups who had been here thousands of years; European contact occurred in 1824 when employees of grazer Joshua John Moore built a small homestead in the area. Moore purchased the land in 1826 and named his property Canberry. Appropriately for a capital city, the name means "meeting place." Other families soon established the Yarralumla and Duntroon properties, which gave their names to the modern-day governor-general's residence and the national military college.

The region seemed destined for complete, happy obscurity until a controversy over the location of the national capital erupted between Sydney and Melbourne after federation in 1901. Originally the town of Dalgety in the Snowy Mountains was selected, but Sydneysiders protested that it was too close to Melbourne, and everyone agreed it was too far from the Sydney-Melbourne train line.

Lake Burley Griffin, with the Telstra Tower in the background

Incidentally, Dalgety has fewer than 100 residents today. Canberra was selected as a compromise site, because it was less than 300 kilometers from Sydney, close to the rail line, had been thoroughly surveyed, and had access to freshwater. At the time Canberra was selected, the Australian Capital Territory was home to 1,714 people and 224,764 sheep. The state of New South Wales ceded 2,330 square kilometers for the new Australian Capital Territory, which continues today to be underpopulated bushland except for the capital city itself. Canberra is home to more than 95 percent of the territory's population on about 30 percent of the ACT's land.

The federal government took its time moving to Canberra. Architect Burley Griffin submitted his plan in 1911, and groundbreaking took place in 1913, but the provisional Parliament House was not completed until 1927, and the first embassy did not appear in Canberra until 1940. Several government departments did not make the transition to Canberra until after World War II, and Lake Burley Griffin was not completed until 1963.

After the war, development of Canberra accelerated, and the government created housing projects to provide homes in North Canberra and South Canberra for the growing population. Several new towns, such as Belconnen and Woden, were developed, and further development included three satellite tracking stations operated for the U.S. space program. Neil Armstrong's first step on the moon was transmitted via the Honeysuckle Creek tracking station. The city grew in population from less than 200,000 to more than 300,000 people between the 1960s and the 1990s.

Canberra received a significant facelift in 1988 at the time of the Australian Bicentenary, and a permanent federal parliament building finally replaced the provisional building, which had been used for 70 years. Also in 1988, the Australian Capital Territory was given full self-governing powers and elected its first Territorial Legislature.

The Lay of the Land

Canberra is set among low hills on an elevated plateau beside the Molonglo River, about 145 kilometers inland from the east coast, 290 kilometers from Sydney, and just over 700 kilometers from Melbourne. The small territory is filled with rolling low hills, typical of Australian bushland, and a bowl of slightly larger hills that surround the city. The Molonglo River was dammed to form Lake Burley Griffin. The lake divides the city into the traditional areas of North Canberra and South Canberra. Two scenic bridges traverse the lake and unite the city, although there are now multiple alternate routes that connect the northern and southern suburbs.

The central city was originally designed by Walter Burley Griffin as a series of circles with broad avenues connecting them, so the streets are not platted in a typical grid pattern but tend to meander and get newcomers lost.

One of the most appealing things about the city is its location just two hours from the ski slopes of the Snowy Mountains, Australia's only ski resort area. Canberrans also often spend weekends on the southern New South Wales coast, usually

an aerial view of Canberra

somewhere around Bateman's Bay, which is two hours from the city by car.

According to locals, there is a distinct difference between the north and south sides of Canberra, with residents from the north not liking to go south of Lake Burley Griffin and folks from the south avoiding the north. It could have to do with the city-country orientation, with the north side having a more metropolitan feel to it and the south side closer to the mountains with a feeling more like country living.

CLIMATE

Owing to its bush location, away from sea breezes and climate-impacting currents, Canberra is cooler and drier than most major Australian cities. The rainy season is in the spring and early summer (Oct.-Jan.), while the driest part of the year is the late fall and early winter (Apr.-May). The city enjoys distinctive seasons with warm summers, changeable but pleasant spring and fall seasons, and quite regularly snowy winters, although there are no extremes in either season.

Where to Live

CIVIC AREA

The Civic area is not densely populated, but it well worth considering as the most urban and liveliest place to be in the city. Canberra's building codes used to limit buildings to just two or three stories, but it now allows up to 13 stories, still low compared to other cities. Due to these restrictions, there are no urban canyons to contend with, but rather a great collection of shops and restaurants along Northbourne Avenue, the main road in Civic.

Civic is also home to Canberra Centre, Canberra's primary shopping mall, a three-story sunlit but indoor shopping mecca with 300-plus retailers. It includes a multiplex movie theater.

Average Temperatures and Rainfall in Canberra

Month	Mean maximum temperature (°C)	Mean minimum temperature (°C)	Mean rainfall (mm)
January	29	14	60
February	28	14	51
March	25	12	56
April	20	7	49
May	16	4	48
June	12	1	38
July	12	0	52
August	14	1	48
September	16	4	65
October	20	7	62
November	24	10	59
December	26	12	46

Source: Australian Bureau of Meteorology

Canberra's City Walk is a pedestrian mall that features an attractive and fun collection of shops and restaurants; the picturesque Garema Place has extensive outdoor dining adjacent to City Walk. Living in Civic gets quieter at night, with shops closing, but plenty of restaurants make it popular with young professionals who seek the city's entertainment after work.

A two-bed, one-bath apartment in the city will cost you around $500,000 to buy and $500 per week to rent.

INNER NORTH CANBERRA

Immediately north of the Civic area is North Canberra, which includes slightly older, more commercial suburbs such as **Braddon.** This area tends to cater to working-class families and young urban professionals who like the convenience of being close to Civic. There are small shopping centers that offer all necessary amenities, and while the overall look may be a little more lower-income, there are some nice quiet roads, and the proximity to Civic cannot be underestimated.

A two-bed, one-bath apartment in Braddon will cost you around $450,000 to buy and $450 per week to rent.

BELCONNEN

In the northwest district, Belconnen is home to Canberra Stadium, which features the Canberra Raiders rugby team, as well as the University of Canberra. The district dates back to the 1970s, and most buildings were constructed in

Expat Experience: Living in Canberra

Patrick "Pat" McNeil, 52, originally from Dickinson, North Dakota, claiming Arizona as home after his military service, has been living in Canberra for 8 years.

Why did you come to Australia?
I am retired U.S. Navy and was stationed at the U.S. Embassy in the Defense Attaché Office in Canberra from 1985 to 1989. I met and married my Aussie wife and continued my military career outside Australia for another 15 years, but returned to provide our son with some stability through his final three years of high school.

Why Canberra?
We looked at all the major metropolitan areas, like Sydney and Melbourne, as well as some urban growth areas such as Newcastle and the central coast. After months of research, we wound up looking back at Canberra: First, we were not financially sound, so with family in Canberra, we had some place to establish a base while settling into the new lifestyle, but the most important factor was the family-friendly atmosphere and the quality of education. Compared to the other capital cities, crime, drugs, and other bad influences on young people are minimal in Canberra. Not to mention the fact that the quality of education, both secondary and postsecondary, are high in comparison.

What do you love most about living in Canberra?
Canberra is a city of over 300,000 residents, yet it still retains the small country-town atmosphere. In our 15-year absence, the city has grown, not only in area but culturally as well. The hospital where our son was born is now the site of the National Museum and is only one of a number of cultural venues hosting world-class exhibitions. The sports atmosphere and variety here is incredible, which not only allows for great spectating but participation as well. Canberra is the home of a multitude of diplomatic missions, which brings with it the need to satisfy their culinary needs, and Canberra does it in style. And finally, location, location, location: Canberra is two hours from the big city, two hours

the 1980s. The residential streets offer reasonable green and pleasant living in modern estate-type houses and some low-rise apartment blocks. The center of activity is the Belconnen Town Center, which features a large Westfield shopping mall and several blocks of residential apartments around parkland and the shores of Lake Ginninderra. The combination of already shabby-looking facilities and distance from Civic and the diplomatic sections of town make this an area that is more visited (for the stadium) than lived in.

A two-bed, one-bath apartment will cost around $390,000 to buy and $375 per week to rent.

GUNGAHLIN

Gungahlin is the far northern district of the city and home to several excellent golf courses, primarily The Lakes. The district is brand-spanking-new, and there are a number of homesites available for longer-term residency plans; houses for resale are usually less than 10 years old and tend to be larger than in the older parts of the city. There is a good mix of apartment and single-house living, and a main shopping district offers all the necessities, but the suburbs lack a feeling of community and can be somewhat soulless, without much atmosphere, even though there are plenty of young families around. There are rumors that the building quality is also somewhat lacking. It from the coast, and two hours from the mountains, placing it in the perfect location to appreciate all facets of Australian life.

What's your least favorite aspect of living in Canberra or Australia?
Primarily, the cost of living. Value for money is rare. The cost of clothing versus the quality of the clothing is off the charts, not to mention the sizing standards are inconsistent across the board. Whether it is produce or restaurants, housing or utilities, the quality of the product or service is seldom worth the cost.

What do you say to people who find Canberra boring?
If anyone thinks Canberra is boring, they are not looking very hard to pique their interests. Canberra is filled with many clubs and hobby enthusiast organizations. I find it difficult to believe anyone could be bored unless they want to be bored.

What piece of information do you wish you had known when you first arrived?
More, much more information regarding U.S. and Australian tax laws, particularly with respect to military retirees, especially regarding U.S. citizens living abroad. Not many expats realize the IRS still requires you to file (not necessarily pay, but file) taxes every year regardless of your country of residence or citizenship.

What's your best tip for newcomers, the first thing they ought to do?
Ask yourself where you see yourself in retirement, and research how you are going to get there. Then research it thoroughly to make sure you will be able to reach your goals based on your contributions to the Australian superannuation system. Again, this probably does not apply to the majority of newcomers, but more to the retired veterans. When you come into a workforce from one retirement system to another and only have half the time or less to contribute to the nest egg, it really adds to the stress of acclimating to the new environment.

could well be though, that the district will improve with age once the community is more established.

One main point to be aware of when considering moving to northern Canberra: The suburb of **Mitchell,** which lies at the border of the North Canberra and Gungahlin districts, is one of only two suburbs—the other is Fyshwick—where brothels are allowed to operate legally. Mitchell is also home to a number of other adult-entertainment options, and accordingly the district has tended to provide a higher degree of expat shock than others. But for some it offers a distinctive experience not typical of the countries that new arrivals come from.

A three-bed, two-bath house in Gungahlin will cost around $500 per week to rent, and $500,000 to buy.

INNER SOUTH CANBERRA

Just around the Capital Hill circles are a handful of leafy stylish suburbs, such as **Kingston** and **Manuka,** both with small centers full of shops, cafés, medical centers, and everything needed for daily life. Gorgeous villas are set in plush gardens very close to the native bush. There are plenty of parks and nature reserves in the neighborhood, making living here a lovely mix of suburb and countryside. Both Kingston and Manuka have a buzz and atmosphere of people knowing each other; people stop and greet each other in the cafés, and family living is pleasant.

These are wealthy suburbs where families and young professionals tend to settle.

A little farther south lies one of the most affluent suburbs in Canberra, **Red Hill,** which is home to, not surprisingly, a pretty hill for walking on the west edge of the suburb, as well as the prestigious Canberra Grammar School. The views from the hills are utterly stunning, finally allowing a glance at the whole of Canberra, something that is nearly impossible from ground level. Personally, I recommend Manuka and Red Hill as my favorite suburbs of Canberra; both offer family living, a lovely choice of homes, and a community atmosphere.

To buy a three-bed, two-bath house in Manuka or Kingston will cost above $850,000; to rent it would be around $900 per week. Red Hill prices are very similar, depending on the size of the lot.

WODEN VALLEY

A little farther south of the city and to the west of the Tuggeranong Parkway, alongside Yarra Glen, with excellent connections straight to the city center, is the Woden district, which is home to Canberra Hospital and to **O'Malley,** one of the embassy districts of Canberra. Woden Town Centre is in **Philip,** which adjoins O'Malley and is home to a Westfield shopping center as well as the Lovett Tower, Canberra's tallest building, although that's a little like calling the 2,228-meter Mount Kosciuszko one of the world's great summits. Aside from the diplomatic delights of O'Malley, Woden is a pleasant, middle-class area that is home to a number of town houses. This area is mostly popular with families due to its proximity to the countryside and nature reserves.

A three-bed, two-bath house in Woden, O'Malley, or Philip will cost around $500,000 to buy and $480 per week to rent.

WESTON CREEK

The only suburb west of the city is the small enclave of Weston Creek. The district dates back to the 1960s, and many of the buildings were built in the 1970s and 1980s. It's a younger, slightly less affluent area that features primarily houses and town houses. Weston is home to one of the few bilingual schools in Australia, Lyons Primary School, which features Italian and English instruction. It primarily caters to English-speaking students and is a distinctive option for parents with younger children. Weston Creek is on the edge of Mount Stromlo, which has excellent views of the city. Owing to the distance from commercial areas, Weston Creek is not a typical choice for new arrivals, but adjoining the bush, it offers a more rural version of Canberra living. Weston Creek lies to the west of the Tuggeranong Parkway. It takes about 10 minutes to drive into the center of the city.

A three-bed, two-bath house in Weston is $500,000 to buy and an average $550 per week to rent.

TUGGERANONG

A 20-minute drive from the city center, the Tuggeranong Valley to the south of Canberra is an easy commute with countryside living. The snowy region of Mount Thredbo is nearby, and serious hiking trails start at Tidbinbilla National Park just on the doorstep. All of Tuggeranong is relatively low density, yet the center of activity at Tuggeranong Town Center offers a more urban experience, with eateries and shops alongside the small, pretty Lake Tuggeranong. There is a large shopping mall, the Tuggeranong Hyperdome, for daily conveniences. Lots tend to be larger and more affordable. Not dissimilar to the northern suburb of Gungahlin, this is a new development, but one that has already grown into its setting and offers a much better family atmosphere than its northern counterpart, with plenty of activity centering around the artificial lake.

A three-bed, two-bath house in Tuggeranong will cost approximately $450,000 to buy and $430 per week to rent.

Daily Life

MEDIA RESOURCES

For Canberra news, the *Canberra Times* is the main daily newspaper, although *The Australian* offers fairly good coverage of Canberra because of its national political coverage.

CityNews is a free glossy weekly newspaper-cum-magazine complete with real estate listings. The websites **OutInCanberra** (http://outincanberra.com.au) and **Canberra Guide** (http://canberraeguide.com) provide a great online start for things to do, see, and eat in the city. Another popular online destination is **CitySearch** (http://canberra.citysearch.com.au).

For television, the three main networks (Seven, Nine, and Ten) are available in the form of Prime, WIN, and Southern Cross Ten in addition to the two government channels, ABC and SBS. Foxtel provides the satellite service, and cable comes from TransACT. Several radios stations offer programming in most formats, catering to all tastes.

EXPAT RESOURCES

Canberra has a very active Australian American Association, which is very welcoming to newcomers. Visit: www.australianamericanact.com.

HEALTH CARE

For residents of the ACT there is a single point of entry that streamlines the local health service, making getting help very easy. Either use the website or call to speak to a representative of the **ACT Government Health services** (www.health.act.gov.au, tel. 13 2281), who will explain the services, make appointments for you, or transfer you to a nurse or doctor to help you further.

The two major public hospitals in Canberra are the 500-bed Canberra Hospital in Garran and the Calvary John James Hospital, which is in the Deakin district, and there are several specialist medical centers around town. There are also several **Walk-In Centres** (www.walkincentre.act.gov.au), open seven days a week, which offer anyone free one-off treatments for minor injuries or illnesses.

SCHOOLS

It is widely recognized that Canberra's school system is the best in Australia, with the highest percentage of students completing their secondary education and continuing on to university and other higher education.

The ACT government offers some 87 public (state-run) schools, and there are also nearly 50 independent private and Roman Catholic schools. Some of the best schools are Canberra Girls Grammar (in Deakin) and Canberra Grammar (in Red Hill), both south of the city and generally at the top of the scoring system. Canberra schools operate with Priority Placement Areas, which basically means that if you want your child to attend a certain public school, you have to live in its catchment area. If you live within the area, the school has to take your child, and if you live outside the area, you may have a chance of getting a place through a waiting list.

Canberra is also home to the Australian

National University (ANU), one of the group of eight elite Australian universities. It's highly regarded as a research institution. ANU is on the northwest shore of Lake Burley Griffin and the best prospect in Australia for overseas students. The University of Canberra is located in the north of the city and home to some 13,000 students, including 3,500 international students from more than 90 countries.

The other higher-education option in the ACT is the Canberra Institute of Technology (CIT), which is the ACT's Technical and Further Education (TAFE) school. CIT offers a wide selection of programs in technical and vocational education. Due to the large government presence in ACT, all schools and higher-education institutes are multicultural and cosmopolitan places to learn.

Bear in mind that the Australian academic year runs according to the calendar year, with courses and terms starting in January-February after the summer break, and continue until December, with several shorter term breaks interspersed.

SHOPPING

While there are plenty of malls in the suburbs, such as the extensive and very good shopping center in Tuggeranong and the Westfield in Belconnen, north of Lake Burley Griffin, there is also the city center in Civic, where the primary shopping area is Bunda Street, complete with the Canberra Centre, a popular mall, plus smaller shops and restaurants along City Walk.

For more individual shops and a lower concentration of boutiques, cafés, and restaurants, go to Kingston and Manuka, which are a little more upmarket and classy. An excellent and very popular arts and crafts market is held in the Old Bus Depot in Kingston every Sunday; it's a good source for eclectic shopping and satisfying international food treats.

Getting Around

PUBLIC TRANSPORTATION

Public transportation in Canberra is easy in that it only has bus services and no streetcars and ferries to contend with. Canberra has a citywide bus service known as ACTION that runs seven days a week and connects with all major areas of the inner and immediate outer city. With Canberra running mostly along a north-south axis, the Blue Rapid bus service connects the northern suburbs from Belconnen through the city down south to Tuggeranong. It operates on a five- to eight-minute service schedule between 7am and 7pm weekdays.

Ticketing is via the prepaid MyWay smartcard, which can be purchased at main stops, stations, and some retail outlets. This system is cheaper than buying a single ticket each time you're on the bus and allows travel within a 90-minute transfer period. Remember that in Canberra, you need to swipe your card when you get on and off for each journey. Single adult fares start at $2.98 and are capped at $9 per day during the week, and $5.45 at weekends.

There is talk of a high-speed rail link between Canberra and Sydney at the moment, but as in the past, when it looks like it may go ahead, budget numbers come in and it all goes quiet again. There is a business-class bus link between Canberra and Sydney, which offers commuters free Wi-Fi, USB and AC power sockets, and it is cheaper and quicker than flying between the cities. The bus is operated by **Greyhound Australia** (www.greyhound.com.au) and costs from $37 one-way, which is one-third of the airfare between the two cities.

HIGHWAYS

Driving in Canberra can be a challenge until you know your way around town. You simply can't see the city for the trees, and there are only fleeting glimpses of guiding landmarks; that said, there are a few main roads that connect the north and south and lead to suburbs, and even better, they tend to be named after the suburbs they lead to. There is the Tuggeranong Parkway, allowing you to drive to the farthest southern suburb within 15 minutes; the Belconnen Way, leading to Belconnen; the Gungahlin Drive, heading up north; you get the idea. The inner city consists of a number of interconnected circles that can be confusing at first. But the city is small, the roads are actually well laid out and signed, and traffic is relatively easygoing.

The ACT government is very keen on drivers sticking to the speed limits, and there are plenty of speed cameras on the roads, so beware. They will photograph your license plate if you speed, and you will incur not only hefty fines but also demerit points, an accumulation of 12 of which will result in your license being suspended. Over special periods, such as the Christmas and New Year's holidays, the government can slap double demerit points on you.

The main road to Sydney is the M31, the Hume Highway. It's a three-hour journey if there's no traffic, but closer to Sydney the Hume can get busy, so allow a little extra time.

Surrounding the city are ring roads, which can be used by residents in outlying areas to cut down travel time. Canberra Airport is near the Eastern Ring Road.

CANBERRA AIRPORT

Canberra International Airport is east of the city in Pialligo, about 10 minutes by car from Civic outside of peak periods, and it's a snap to use. Only five airlines serve Canberra, offering nonstop service to Adelaide, Brisbane, Darwin, Gold Coast, Hobart, Perth, Melbourne, Sydney, Newcastle, and, internationally, Singapore and Wellington. The airlines are Qantas, Tigerair, Virgin Australia, Fly Pelican, and Singapore Airlines.

Needless to say, going through the airport is quick and straightforward. There are a couple of cafés and a bookstore, but otherwise few distractions. A new terminal opened for Canberra's centenary in 2013.

There is an Airport Express shuttle bus ($12 each way) that drops you in the city center within 10 minutes; all the main car-rental companies are represented, and taxi service is quick and affordable. There are even several ski buses that take skiers directly to the New South Wales ski resorts from the airport.

HOBART

Hobart is Australia's second-oldest city and probably the one with the nicest atmosphere. Small, remote, and surrounded by some of the most stunning countryside Australia can offer, this little gem is often forgotten when people talk about Australia. Tasmania's countryside is renowned for its outdoorsy types of activities, and little Hobart can hold its own against Melbourne and Sydney when it comes to art and food experiences.

The city is home to just 227,000 people, making it the smallest of Australia's capitals. Some 40 percent of Tasmania's population of 517,000 live in this compact city, but add to that the 800,000 tourists who flock to Tasmania every year, making it the second industry after metal processing, and you can picture Hobart's little fishing harbor and its popular Salamanca Place humming with people on beautiful summer evenings. Mainlanders consider Hobart almost a suburb of Melbourne, and weekend visitors from Melbourne take the 50-minute flight or the overnight ferry.

Compared to Melbourne and Sydney, Hobart offers expatriates a different sort of experience. In the rest of Australia nearly 70 percent of residents have one or more relatives born abroad in the last generation, but in Hobart the Europeans settled in the early 1800s and did not much add to their stock. Only 12 percent

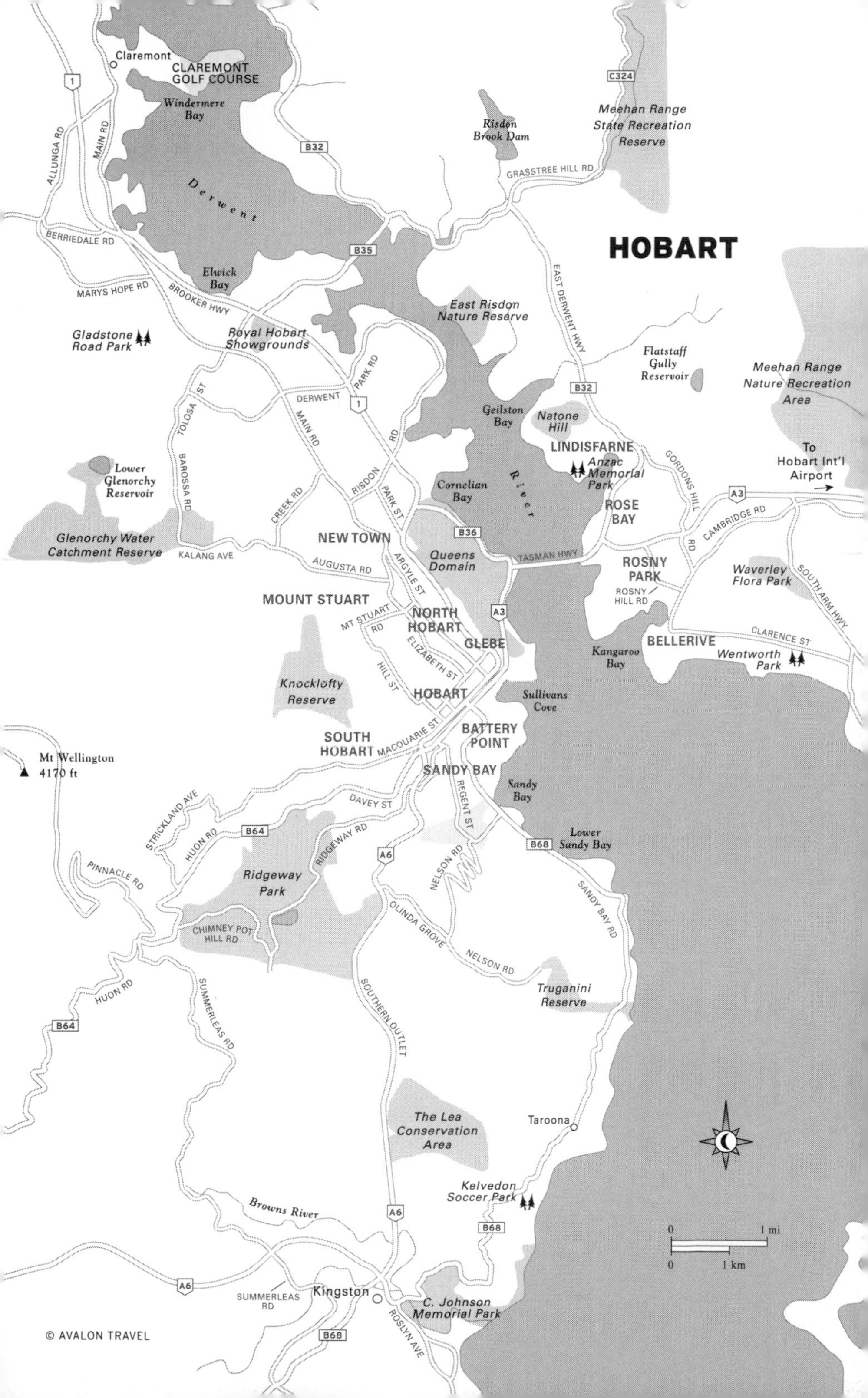
HOBART
Claremont
CLAREMONT GOLF COURSE
Windermere Bay
Derwent
Elwick Bay
Risdon Brook Dam
Meehan Range State Recreation Reserve
GRASSTREE HILL RD
C324
B32
B35
ALLUNGA RD
MAIN RD
BERRIEDALE RD
MARYS HOPE RD
BROOKER HWY
Gladstone Road Park
Royal Hobart Showgrounds
East Risdon Nature Reserve
EAST DERWENT HWY
Flatstaff Gully Reservoir
Meehan Range Nature Recreation Area
To Hobart Int'l Airport
PARK RD
DERWENT
TOLOSA ST
BAROSSA RD
MAIN RD
RISDON RD
Geilston Bay
Natone Hill
LINDISFARNE
Anzac Memorial Park
GORDONS HILL RD
A3
CAMBRIDGE RD
Lower Glenorchy Reservoir
CREEK RD
PARK ST
Cornelian Bay
River
ROSE BAY
Glenorchy Water Catchment Reserve
KALANG AVE
NEW TOWN
B36
AUGUSTA RD
ARGYLE ST
Queens Domain
TASMAN HWY
ROSNY PARK
ROSNY HILL RD
Waverley Flora Park
SOUTH ARM HWY
MOUNT STUART
MT STUART RD
NORTH HOBART
GLEBE
ELIZABETH ST
HILL ST
Knocklofty Reserve
Kangaroo Bay
BELLERIVE
CLARENCE ST
Wentworth Park
HOBART
Sullivans Cove
SOUTH HOBART
MACQUARIE ST
BATTERY POINT
Mt Wellington 4170 ft
SANDY BAY
Sandy Bay
STRICKLAND AVE
DAVEY ST
REGENT ST
HUON RD
B64
RIDGEWAY RD
A6
NELSON RD
B68
Lower Sandy Bay
PINNACLE RD
Ridgeway Park
OLINDA GROVE
SANDY BAY RD
CHIMNEY POT HILL RD
NELSON RD
HUON RD
SUMMERLEAS RD
SOUTHERN OUTLET
Truganini Reserve
The Lea Conservation Area
Taroona
Kelvedon Soccer Park
Browns River
A6
B68
0 1 mi
0 1 km
Kingston
SUMMERLEAS RD
C. Johnson Memorial Park
ROSLYN AVE
© AVALON TRAVEL

of Tasmanians were born overseas, but 73 percent have at least one convict ancestor, and being able to trace their family back to the first few ships that landed on the island is more common than not. Rather than the multicultural mix you find in other Australian capitals, here you'll find Australians that may be baffled by newcomers but are nevertheless welcoming and generally happy that you chose their remote corner in the world to settle in.

Tasmania suffers from an exodus of young people seeking careers elsewhere. The main population demographic is young families, the middle aged, and older people, while those in their late 20s to 40s leave the island due to the lack of professional opportunities; they tend to return once done with their careers.

The top three expat groups in Tasmania are British, Dutch, and German, but there are also Americans; the Australian American Association is a thriving little group of U.S. expats and locals always ready to welcome new arrivals and teach them the ropes of living in this outpost. You'll enjoy living in Hobart most if you love the water, but you'll do fine if you like art and eating out, as there are many good restaurants in town, and the famous MONA museum is just up the road from the city, within a 10-minute drive or an easy ferry ride. However small, Hobart offers plenty for those who are willing to venture this far south.

THE BRIEF STORY OF HOBART

Hobart's history is not pretty. The island of Tasmania was first spotted back in 1642 by Dutch navigator Abel Tasman, who named the island Van Diemen's Land after the Dutch East Indies governor Anthony van Diemen. Tasman's name only appeared when London-based mapmakers Laurie and Whittle's 1808 *An Elegant Imperial Sheet Atlas* included a map with both names, Van Diemen's Land and Tasmania. Usage proliferated in the 1820s, and in 1856 the name was officially changed.

After the English arrived in Sydney, the use of Tasmania as a convenient stopover began, and prolific explorer Matthew Flinders first circumnavigated the island, proving that it was indeed an island. Britain's second colony was established in 1804 in Risdon Cove, a little farther upriver from Hobart, but it was later relocated to Hobart because of its better freshwater supply. The first arrivals were not all convicts, although many accompanied the original settlers, but soon penal colonies were established on Sarah Island in Macquarie Harbor in 1822, on Maria Island in 1825, and at Port Arthur in 1830. By the 1850s half of Tasmania's population were convicts, with the name of the colonies bringing fear to potential transportees in Britain due to the harsh life and dreadful conditions. The cities of Launceston and Hobart were reportedly riddled with disease, prostitution, and utter lawlessness, and conditions did not improve until the abolition of convict transportation in the 1850s.

The original inhabitants of Tasmania, several Aboriginal groups that had walked across the landmass that once existed from the mainland some 12,000 years before, suffered enormously with the arrival of the Europeans. Diseases that they had no immunity against killed most of them; fences built by the settlers seriously disrupted their nomadic lifestyle; and the rest were slaughtered by the newcomers in the so-called Black Wars. In 1828 martial law was declared by Lieutenant-Governor Arthur, and Aboriginal people were systematically murdered, incarcerated, or forced at gunpoint from districts settled by Europeans. In the 1830s, the Black Line, a military plan to round up the Aborigines, began; George Augustus

The Tasmanian Devil

If you are of a certain age, you will think of a Tasmanian devil, *Sarcophilus harrisii,* as a snarling, whirling little cartoon pest who devours anything in sight, with enormous jaws and a bit of a temper. And you are not far wrong. Up to 65 centimeters long and weighing nine kilograms—roughly the size of a large domestic cat—these black furry carnivores with white markings eat any meat, dead or alive, small or large. And they make an enormous amount of noise while they are eating it. Devils, as they are locally and lovingly called, are known to be able to eat an astonishing 40 percent of their body weight in a mere 30 minutes. Do not try that at home.

As with most unusual creatures living in Australia, Devils are marsupials, meaning that they carry their underdeveloped young in a pouch until they can fend for themselves, which can be up to four months. Nocturnal and shy, although they don't seem that way, they were once also found on mainland Australia, but it is thought that competition for food from the introduced dingo made them extinct and only left an endangered pocket population in Tasmania. Although there is plenty of food for the creatures on the island, they are now threatened by devil facial tumor disease (DFTD), which causes growths around the mouth, face, and neck. The disease develops rapidly and is fatal: Once infected, animals die within six months of the lesions first appearing.

Many zoos in Australia are part of the Save the Tasmanian Devil program, taking in breeding pairs, hoping to release them into the wild once the disease is wiped out. At the moment, authorities are working hard to eradicate DFTD from Tasmania, and the program aims to hold up to 1,500 breeding animals in order to maintain a stable population of this iconic animal.

Robinson began his probably well-intentioned mission to protect the indigenous people and took them to a settlement on Flinders Island. The plan was not successful, and the few survivors died unhappy, ill, and isolated from their home. The last full-blooded aboriginal Tasmanian was Truganini, a woman who survived on Flinders Island and helped with the attempted settlement of others. She traveled to Melbourne, where she and her group became outlaws, ended up wounded and in court, and were sentenced to being sent back to Flinders Island. She eventually died in Hobart in 1876, about age 64.

On a less genocidal note, Jane Franklin, the governor's wife, achieved undesirable popularity among the convicts in the mid-1800s for her scheme to rid the island of snakes; her husband was mortally afraid of the animals. She offered one shilling for every dead snake brought to her. She spent a fortune, some £600 in one season, on this enterprise before being asked to abandon it in the interests of convict discipline.

When the gold rush turned the state of Victoria and Melbourne into some of the richest places on earth, people began to look for gold in Tasmania too. A convict first found gold in the 1850s in the northeast of the island. The gold rush did not set in until the 1860s and 1870s, when mines were established and personal fortunes made.

"Civilization" slowly brought prosperity and peace, with the penal colony of Port Arthur closing in 1877, and in 1901, when the Commonwealth of Australia was proclaimed, Tasmania becoming a full state.

The Lay of the Land

Hobart is located in the southeast of the island of Tasmania, on the estuary of the Derwent River, which flows into the Southern Ocean a few kilometers downstream. The skyline is dominated by Mount Wellington (1,271 meters), at certain times of the day throwing parts of the city into the shade.

Hobart's CBD and main residential areas are found on the west side of the river, with the airport and a handful of suburbs on the east side. Three bridges span the river, the most important and busiest being the Hobart Bridge, whose sleek elegance dominates the estuary and the views of the city. From nearly everywhere in the city, great views can be had of mountains, water, the skyline, the bridge, and the colorful roofs of the homes along the river. The first overall

Hobart is located on the Derwent River.

Average Temperatures and Rainfall in Hobart

Month	Mean maximum temperature (°)	Mean minimum temperature (°C)	Mean rainfall (mm)
January	23	12	41
February	22	12	36
March	21	11	36
April	18	9	43
May	15	7	36
June	13	5	33
July	13	4	42
August	14	5	47
September	15	6	42
October	17	8	47
November	19	9	45
December	21	11	54

Source: Australian Bureau of Meteorology

impression is like a small town by a fjord in Scandinavia, and the weather is similar to Scandinavia as well.

The proximity to the natural bushland and the mountains is what Hobartians cherish most about living in this city, and visitors come from all over the world to enjoy the wild and rugged countryside. Yet the closeness to the bush and forests can also have dangerous consequences, as many residents found to their detriment in the 2013 bushfires; record temperatures reached 41.8°C in January, costing lives, homes, and farms.

CLIMATE

Hobart is situated at 42 degrees south latitude, the domain of the legendary Roaring Forties, strong westerly winds in the Southern Hemisphere. The island of Tasmania has various microclimates, and the weather can be very different on the other side of the bay, the river, or the mountains. Generally speaking, it is significantly colder in this small state than elsewhere in Australia, but the city of Hobart has a mild temperate maritime climate with four distinct seasons. The warmest months, January and February, are also the driest. Hobart is exposed to the southerly winds from the Antarctic but is protected by Mount Wellington from the worst westerlies, and to some extent by Mount Nelson in the south. The weather is not quite as changeable as in Melbourne, but it is still wise to dress in layers.

Where to Live

INNER CITY

The inner city offers a mix of accommodations options, with stunning apartments overlooking the bustling harbor or nestled alongside Salamanca Place, buzzing with restaurants and the weekend market. The CBD mostly shuts down after 5:30pm and can be an eerily quiet place on the weekend, although more cafés are creeping in and offering weekend brunches, and foodie markets are attracting visitors. In both **Inner Hobart** and **Glebe** it is wise to hang around at different times of the day and the week to get a feel for the area before jumping into moving here, as there may well be safety issues with certain streets, especially after the offices and shops are closed.

A two-bedroom, one-bath apartment in Inner Hobart costs around $350,000 to buy and $400 per week to rent.

NORTHERN SUBURBS

North Hobart is quite central and a lovely, busy inner-city suburb that offers a vibrant lifestyle in period apartments and houses, surrounded by cafés and shops. Young professionals and families flock here for the buzz. Despite its name, **New Town,** just a little farther out from North Hobart, is one of the oldest suburbs of Hobart and full of lovely period homes. Close to the popular single-sex Roman Catholic schools, this is quite a genteel area that attracts families. Farther north of New Town you cross what some locals call the "latte line," meaning the end of proximity to the city's many trendy cafés and shops. There is a sprawl of suburbs along the relatively busy Brooker Highway, and as you get farther north, the lots get bigger, the homes become more affordable, but the charm of inner Hobart is lost. That said, **Claremont,** a town separate from the city and the home of a Cadbury chocolate factory, is a popular outpost of Hobart, with many families choosing it to be closer to the countryside; it's still only 15 minutes' drive into the center of Hobart.

It is a little cheaper to live in Claremont than in North Hobart or New Town. The price difference is mostly due to the commuting distance being around 10 minutes by car, as compared to 10 minutes on foot, and the proximity of the amenities in North Hobart and New Town.

In North Hobart or New Town a three-bedroom, two-bath period family house with views will cost around $500,000 to buy and $450 per week to rent. In Claremont a three-bedroom, two-bath house with gardens will cost around $350,000 to buy and $300 per week to rent.

SOUTHERN SUBURBS

South of the CBD are gorgeous city suburbs such as **South Hobart,** full of period homes; **Battery Point,** along the bustling Salamanca Place area; and lovely **Sandy Bay.** These are the loveliest and most prestigious suburbs of Hobart, full of upmarket properties, some on the edge of the river with views across the estuary and the hills across the bay, as well as offering good schools, lots of shops and restaurants, and historic elegance. Prices are unsurprisingly higher than elsewhere in Hobart, but if your budget allows, amenities are close and the community is well established.

Farther south, the road leads to the town of **Kingston,** complete with a large sandy beach, a near-holiday feeling, and full amenities to supply the population of

20,000. You can reach Kingston either via the winding Sandy Bay Road or the much faster Southern Outlet Road, getting you there from the CBD in 15 minutes.

South Hobart and Battery Point are very popular with the younger crowd due to their proximity to Salamanca and its bars and restaurants. Sandy Bay and Kingston are more family-oriented areas.

In Sandy Bay a large three-bedroom, two-bath period house will set you back around $550 per week to rent and $750,000 to buy. In Kingston, a large three-bedroom, two-bath period house costs around $500,000 to buy and $350 per week to rent. In Battery Point, a modern two-bed, one-bath apartment costs around $420,000 to buy and $320 per week to rent.

EASTERN SUBURBS

There is a distinct east-versus-west feeling in Hobart, with many residents of the west coast never considering moving across the river, as it is simply "too far away." Considering that the stunning Hobart Bridge gets you across the river in a mere two minutes, this bias is somewhat unfounded, and you can find some gorgeous suburbs on "the other side." There is, for example, beautiful **Bellerive,** on the southern side of pretty Kangaroo Bay. Of course, there are stunning views, plus a small historic town center, a marina, and easy access to the ferry and water taxis to whisk you across to the city.

But there are some lower-income suburbs here that you want to avoid, such as Rosny and Mornington, which tend toward the soulless suburb cliché of "the wrong side of the river." Just north of the bridge are **Rose Bay** and **Lindisfarne,** both lovely suburbs with a mix of lots and homes ranging from the very common tongue-and-grove wooden structures to period homes, with some apartments thrown in. Close to the water, these are leafy suburbs with small community centers where people know each other and family living is prevalent.

All these suburbs attract families rather than young professionals, because it is quieter and across the river from Hobart's center.

In Bellerive, Rose Bay, or Lindisfarne, a three-bedroom, two-bath home costs about $450 per week to rent and $550,000 to buy.

WESTERN SUBURBS

There are only a couple of suburbs to the west of the city: **West Hobart** and **Mount Stuart,** nestled in the foothills of the imposing mountains to the west. West Hobart sprawls from the city up the hills and is a lovely mix of old and new houses. It provides a nice combination of inner-city proximity and suburban house lots with easy access to the bush and the mountains. People here go out for brunch on the weekend to one of the many small restaurants, visit the local fresh produce markets, and tend to be families more than single professionals. Depending on which street you chose, the views can be spectacular. Views are even better from the lofty Mount Stuart, an extension of West Hobart closer to the mountains, allowing fantastic vistas across the river and city. Houses are alone on their lots, most are single-story structures, and it is a very quiet family-oriented area.

West Hobart and Mount Stuart are about a seven-minute drive from the immediate city center. From West Hobart it is probably around 10 minutes to walk, from Mount Stuart, if you are on the hilly outskirts, it will take around 20 minutes to walk.

In Mount Stuart and West Hobart, a large four-bedroom, two-bath house with views would cost around $550,000 to buy and $400 per week to rent.

Expat Experience: Living in Hobart

Dr. Xiufang Dai (not her real name), age 50, is originally from Washington State and has been living in Hobart for six months, although she has lived in other parts of Australia for the last 20 years. Married with three children, she works as a consultant in education and business management.

Why Australia?
I migrated to Australia because of a job I was offered, and I have stayed because I fell in love with the Australian culture, people, and lifestyle, which, in my opinion, has the correct balance of work, rest, and play compared to the puritanical work ethic of the United States. I moved to Hobart because of work and because I had never been to Tasmania.

What do you love about Tasmania?
My favorite thing about Tasmania is the natural beauty: the waterways, coastlines, mountains, waterfalls, streams, and wildlife. I am an outdoorsy person and enjoy camping, hiking and bushwalking, fishing, quad biking, snowboarding, and so on, and the fresh air here must be the cleanest I have ever smelled.

What is you least favorite thing about Tasmania?
What I dislike most is the amount of rain. It is the wettest place I have ever lived, anywhere. Since moving here it has averaged four days a week of rain, but I guess that is why it is so green all the time.

How does your work experience differ here from working in the United States?
I found Australians in New South Wales very welcoming and accepting of me when I first arrived, but found it difficult to be promoted as a woman, as the culture is very machismo, but I have managed to break through the glass ceiling with the help of some of the more progressive males of my age.

What would you have liked to have known before you signed up?
When I first arrived in Australia, I wish someone had explained the tall poppy syndrome. Americans are taught to have high self-esteem and to be confident, but here it can be perceived by others as arrogance. I could have used a few lessons on how to act humble and with humility, hiding and covering up my talents and skills and allowing others to discover them, compared to tooting one's own horn in the typical American way. I have had to "dummy down" my CV on many occasions in order to get a job because being too talented makes people feel fearful of previous accomplishments. In the United States a good boss knows how to manage people who are smarter than they are and see it as an asset to the company; in Australia people are threatened by the tall poppies. So this is the biggest difference between the two cultures.

How did you go about making friends?
I have more Australian friends than American friends; in fact, Hobart is the first place I found the Australian-American Association, which has lovely people in the club.

What do you advise any new arrival to do?
There are three things one must do before leaving Australia again: (1) visit Uluru and (2) ride the train called The Indian Pacific between Perth and Sydney, as people do not realize how big the country is from end to end and how beautiful the red center is; and (3) learn how to do the Tim Tam explosion.

Daily Life

MEDIA RESOURCES

Hobart has three daily tabloid newspapers, the popular *Mercury,* founded in 1854 and published continuously ever since; the more local community-oriented *The Advocate,* and *The Examiner,* plus the national newspapers *The Australian* and *Herald Sun* as well as many international papers.

Hobart receives all five major over-the-air television networks (the commercial Seven, Nine, and Ten Networks, and the government-run SBS and ABC), as well as major cable and satellite services from Optus, Foxtel, and Austar, with local channels of WIN TV, SCTV and TDT and a locally based ABC network.

To keep up-to-date with Hobart's many festivals, check **EventFinder** (www.eventfinda.com.au/whatson/events/Hobart) for details on events.

EXPAT RESOURCES

The Australian American Association of South Australia has a division in Hobart, and membership inquiries can be made at www.aaahobart.org.

HEALTH CARE

There is a good range of hospitals and medical care in Hobart, most notably at the government-run Royal Hobart Hospital, Australia's second-oldest, dating to 1804. It is Tasmania's largest hospital and its major referral center as well as a major clinical teaching and research center, working closely with the University of Tasmania and other institutions. The Royal Hobart Hospital provides a comprehensive range of general and specialty medical and surgical services, including statewide services such as cardiac surgery, neurosurgery, extensive burns treatment, hyperbaric medicine, neonatal and pediatric intensive care, and high-risk obstetrics. Hobart's second hospital is the Hobart Private Hospital, in the city center, where inpatient and day-patient services include general medical and surgical services, obstetrics (including a special care nursery), cardiology services, and a critical care unit. Hobart Private Hospital also has an emergency facility, a large suite of operating rooms, and day-surgery facilities.

Then there are St. Helens Private, The Calvary, and St. Johns Calvary hospitals. Most suburbs have small medical centers that can deal with minor ailments and will refer you to the larger specialist hospitals if necessary.

SCHOOLS

For its relatively small size, Hobart has a range of good schools. Some 51 schools are located in the city, the majority government schools, Roman Catholic schools, and private schools. The majority of Tasmanian and Hobart schools are coed, with a small number of single-sex schools. Government schools are nondenominational, and among nongovernment schools are many Roman Catholic schools and independent schools representing various religions; some are nonreligious. Most schools are in more densely populated West Hobart and the CBD, but most suburbs, even outlying ones, have a good range of schools. Notable schools are Fahan School for girls in Sandy Bay; the coed Friends School, based on Quaker values, which also offers the International Baccalaureate (IB), in North Hobart; and The Hutchins School for boys in Sandy Bay.

Hobart is also home to an excellent, old, and respected university, the

the bustling Salamanca Market

University of Tasmania in Sandy Bay. The large Tasman Polytechnic campus offers postsecondary studies in trades and non-university qualifications.

SHOPPING

Despite its small size, Hobart has pretty much everything you'll need or want. The CBD is a compact grid focused around Elizabeth and Murray Streets, with department stores such as Myer as well as arcades, smaller independent shops, and plenty of cafés and restaurants. Follow Elizabeth Street away from the CBD toward North Hobart for an eclectic mix of galleries, shops, and cafés on a more suburban and independent scale. One of the main shopping destinations is the weekly Salamanca Market, running along Salamanca Place every Saturday from 8:30am, offering countless stalls full of fresh local produce, quirky arts and crafts, and food from all over the world. It gets busy with tourists, so for your fresh fruit and veg, get there early. Also on Saturday is the famous MONA market on the grounds of the MONA museum just north of Hobart, a slightly eccentric market full of great food, arts and crafts stalls, and entertainment.

Getting Around

PUBLIC TRANSPORTATION

The only public transportation in Hobart are the Metro buses and some ferries. Trams and suburban railroads shut down in the late 1960s and 1970s due to economics and lack of use, but the bus routes are comprehensive and get you around Hobart and its suburbs as well as across Tasmania to other cities such as Launceston. A single inner-city bus trip costs $3.20 if you buy a ticket on the bus, reduced to $2.56 with the Metro Greencard, which can be bought and recharged at newsagents across town. Discounts apply for students, seniors, and disabled people, and the daily maximum for bus travel is capped at $9 weekdays, and $4.50 at weekends. The main bus hub is on Collins Street in Hobart, with service to most destinations.

HIGHWAYS

Driving in Hobart is a breeze, although locals will tell you differently. It has been said that Hobartians should be forced to spend a day driving on Melbourne's or Sydney's roads to gain perspective and stop complaining. You will be surprised at how short the distances are and how quick the commute into town is from anywhere around Hobart. There are four main roads connecting the suburbs with the CBD: The Brooker Highway connects the north, the East Derwent Highway connects the east, the Southern heads south, and Huon Road heads west. All these roads are free of tolls and flow smoothly with little traffic, making the commute even from distant suburbs or towns such as Claremont and Kingston a 15-minute drive; at peak hours you may have to add a couple of minutes at most.

HOBART AIRPORT

Hobart's tiny international airport, 20 minutes' drive from the city center, is efficient and easy to use. There is but one terminal, one baggage-claim belt, and two quarantine sniffer dogs. Most flights shuttle from Sydney or Melbourne. Airlines serving the airport are Jetstar, Tigerair, Qantas, Virgin Australia, and international airlines such as Singapore Airlines, Etihad, and Air New Zealand. There are also regular flights down to Wilkins Runway at Casey Station, Antarctica. Despite the range of flights taking off from here, the departure terminal is small, and although it has a newsagent, a souvenir shop, and two café-restaurants, you'd better bring something to read with you, as the selection is quite limited. All the main car rental companies are here, and their setup is almost larger than the airport terminal.

SOUTHWESTERN AUSTRALIA

According to Sydneysiders and Melbournians, beyond their metropolitan fringes is the bush; beyond the bush, they will tell you, is the Outback. Beyond the Outback is a place no one ever goes, called the Back of Beyond or the Never-Never, spoken of in hushed tones in remembrance of all the explorers who perished in search of it. Beyond that, which is to say off the edge of the world, are Adelaide and Perth, the garden-like cities of southwestern Australia with the great industries. Eastern Australians know that somewhere in the west, if you follow the setting sun, you will find the states of South Australia and Western Australia. Fans of Australian Rules football, cricket, and basketball will recall occasionally spotting teams from the far west in various national competitions. Wine aficionados are known to praise the vintages issued from the Barossa Valley in South Australia, Australia's wine region. But by and large the western states and cities are unknown to many Australians, and few people from outside the country see these states except as tourists or if the automotive, mining, or wine industries bring them here.

Adelaide and Perth are attractive cities and highly urbanized. Perth is Australia's

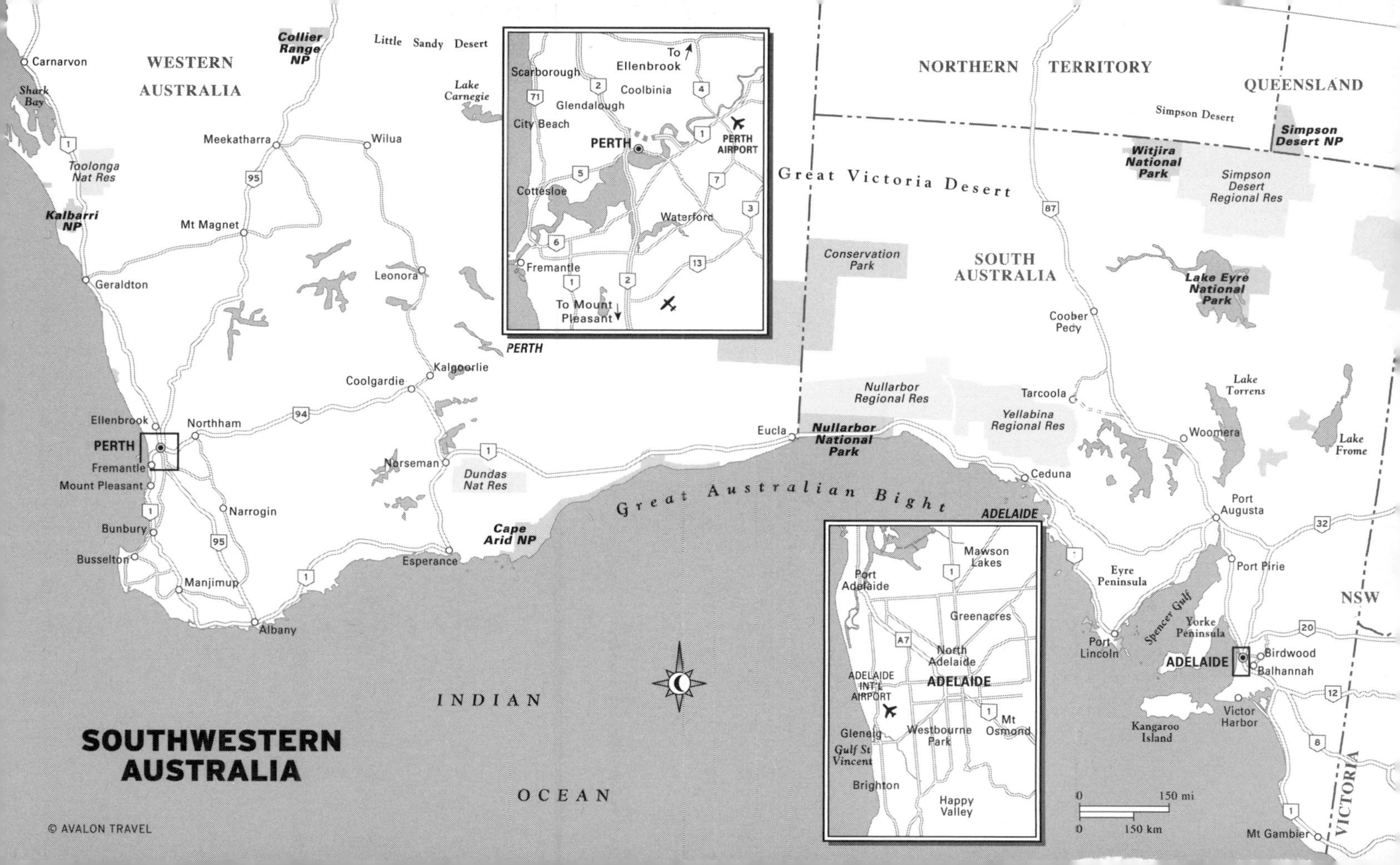
SOUTHWESTERN AUSTRALIA
© AVALON TRAVEL
WESTERN AUSTRALIA
NORTHERN TERRITORY
QUEENSLAND
SOUTH AUSTRALIA
NSW
VICTORIA
INDIAN OCEAN
Great Australian Bight
Great Victoria Desert
Little Sandy Desert
Simpson Desert
Carnarvon
Shark Bay
Toolonga Nat Res
Kalbarri NP
Collier Range NP
Meekatharra
Wilua
Mt Magnet
Geraldton
Leonora
Lake Carnegie
Kalgoorlie
Coolgardie
Ellenbrook
PERTH
Fremantle
Mount Pleasant
Northham
Narrogin
Bunbury
Busselton
Manjimup
Albany
Norseman
Dundas Nat Res
Cape Arid NP
Esperance
Eucla
Nullarbor National Park
Nullarbor Regional Res
Conservation Park
Yellabina Regional Res
Tarcoola
Coober Pedy
Witjira National Park
Simpson Desert Regional Res
Simpson Desert NP
Lake Eyre National Park
Lake Torrens
Lake Frome
Woomera
Ceduna
Port Augusta
Port Pirie
Eyre Peninsula
Port Lincoln
Spencer Gulf
Yorke Peninsula
ADELAIDE
Birdwood
Balhannah
Kangaroo Island
Victor Harbor
Mt Gambier
0 150 mi
0 150 km
Scarborough
Ellenbrook
To
Coolbinia
Glendalough
City Beach
PERTH AIRPORT
Cottesloe
Waterford
Fremantle
To Mount Pleasant
Mawson Lakes
Port Adelaide
Greenacres
North Adelaide
ADELAIDE INT'L AIRPORT
Glenelg
Gulf St Vincent
Westbourne Park
Mt Osmond
Brighton
Happy Valley

fourth largest city, and more than 80 percent of the population of Western Australia lives in the Perth metropolitan area. A similar ratio holds true for Adelaide and South Australia. By contrast, 60 percent of the population of New South Wales lives in Sydney, and around 40 percent of Queensland's population lives in Brisbane. Both cities are relatively remote, but the isolation of the southwest is rooted more in their economic self-sufficiency than in distance.

The primary reason to move to Adelaide and Perth is for the world-class wine industry in South Australia or the mining industry in Western Australia. South Australia is also the primary home of the Australian automotive industry, and expats may find themselves headed here for that reason. Teachers and students also occasionally settle in the southwest, although the universities in this region have not yet attained the international reputation of the University of Sydney or Monash.

Newcomers to either of these western capitals will find that these youngest of Australian cities have modern and well-designed city planning, along with delightful urban and suburban environments. If you hear the Outback calling, you should go and investigate; you may be pleasantly surprised.

Adelaide

Adelaide is Australia's overlooked capital. It is a little isolated, at the south side of the continent, 700 kilometers from Melbourne and 1,500 kilometers from Sydney. It is a beautiful city, historic and modern and incredibly green, with two rings of parkland surrounding the CBD and North Adelaide. These broad Park Lands, all within the inner city, are home to the Adelaide Zoo; the Oval, which is the prettiest cricket ground in the country; wild bushland; a racecourse; and more.

North Parade has an incredible assortment of impressive Victorian architecture, and the city center is bustling with shops and restaurants. Adelaide is also the first Australian city to offer free Wi-Fi to everyone within the CBD, a project that was completed in 2013. The region produces more than half of Australian wine, and Adelaide is a foodie capital where new restaurants spring up regularly with imaginative menus and incredible wine lists. It's also the second-most affordable city in Australia and attracts expats who enjoy the proximity to the sea and the countryside. The surrounding countryside has wide white beaches at Gulf St. Vincent, the Adelaide Hills offering spectacular views and living, and the Fleurieu Peninsula all the way down to Kangaroo Island, some of the prettiest countryside in the country.

THE BRIEF STORY OF ADELAIDE

The area surrounding Adelaide was originally home to the Kaurna people, who were nearly wiped out by smallpox epidemics that spread from the eastern cities even before the first British settlements here in 1836. The Kaurna cleared some the original bushland that surrounded the swampy coastal areas with their controlled bushfires that created grasslands to attract emus and kangaroos for them to hunt.

The British arrived in 1836, urged on by colonial promoter Edward Gibbon Wakefield, who later promoted the initial settlement of New Zealand. From its foundation Adelaide was intended to be a

Designing Adelaide

When it comes to the street plan, Sydney is just a jumble and a mess, relying for its beauty on its splendid setting along Sydney Harbour. Adelaide, by contrast, never had the same physical assets, but its founder based its design on Philadelphia, making it the most attractive and parklike city in the country.

Colonel William Light was given the post of surveyor-general of South Australia in the earliest days of the colony's settlement. He designed Adelaide on a grid of streets featuring wide boulevards and large public squares, and surrounding the city with a ringed system of five parklands so that Adelaide would always have fresh clean air. It was one of the last great city designs, and his placement of the city next to the Torrens River, at the point of maximum rainfall from the mountains to maximize crop yields, is generally considered a master stroke. He separated the commercial center of Adelaide from the residential center of North Adelaide so that the parklands form a figure eight around the two enclaves.

But it is the Adelaide Parklands he is most remembered for, with individual parklands numbered 1 through 29, commencing in the north near the Adelaide Golf Links and continuing clockwise around the city. The parklands are home to some of the state's most important cultural buildings, including the Adelaide Festival Centre, the Art Gallery of South Australia, the Adelaide Aquatic Centre, Government House, the South Australian Museum, and the Adelaide Zoo. Victoria Park contains a racecourse that has been proposed as a home for the Adelaide 500, a move opposed by residents.

It is ironic that, given Light's insistence on accurate surveying, his monument on Montefiore Hill is in the wrong location. Situated in North Adelaide, it is said to be on the spot where Light first envisioned Adelaide. Recent scholarship has located the scene well to the south, but Light continues to gaze southward over the city he envisioned, which remains one of the most beautiful in the world.

contrast to, and an improvement on, the convict settlements along the east coast. A free settlement, South Australia also disavowed the free land grants that pleased poor settlers but led to labor shortages in the capitals. Instead, poor migrants from Britain were given free passage financed by land sales to wealthier migrant investors, and the poor migrants formed the labor pool for the new colony. The capital city, named for Queen Adelaide, was provided from the outset with wide principal boulevards, broad surrounding parklands, and access to a steady water supply, unlike the eastern convict settlements.

Wool and silver mining were the backbone of early industry, and the colony was connected to the east in 1853 with the navigation of the Murray River. The colony became self-governing in 1856 and expanded rapidly until crop failures and a global economic depression ended a period of rapid expansion. Fortunately for Adelaide, a series of copper discoveries at Broken Hill to the north shielded the city from the heaviest impact of the recession. By the time of federation in 1901, Adelaide was firmly established as Australia's third-most populous and important city.

The boom-and-bust primary industry cycle continued to produce a boom in the 1910s and a severe depression in the 1930s, but the state capitalized on military-industrial development during World War II, which established the national auto industry. A rapid increase in job creation rates led to the introduction of subsidized immigration in the 1940s, and more than 200,000 southern and eastern Europeans immigrated to South Australia between the 1940s and the 1970s, giving

Average Temperatures and Rainfall in Adelaide

Month	Mean maximum temperature (°C)	Mean minimum temperature (°C)	Mean rainfall (mm)
January	29	17	19
February	29	17	14
March	26	15	27
April	23	12	40
May	19	10	60
June	16	8	79
July	15	8	75
August	17	8	69
September	19	8	60
October	22	12	44
November	25	14	31
December	27	16	29

Source: Australian Bureau of Meteorology

the state a much broader cultural base. Arts development dates from the 1970s and continues strongly today.

A major setback occurred in 1992 when the State Bank of South Australia, a state-owned bank that had gone on an acquisitions binge in the 1980s, suddenly collapsed as the result of a string of bad loans. This left the state mired in billions of dollars in debt. The scandal caused a financial crisis that was finally resolved near the turn of the millennium with privatization of the bank's assets. The state has finally put the bank collapse firmly in its past, but during the past 20 years Adelaide has fallen to fifth in population and in importance among the major Australian cities, losing out to fast-growing Brisbane and Perth.

THE LAY OF THE LAND

Adelaide is laid out in a series of city squares and surrounded by 730 hectares of public parks, centered on the slim but pretty Torrens River, which forms the northern border of the CBD. To the west is Gulf St. Vincent, and to the east the lush Adelaide Hills. The region around Adelaide is wine-growing country, and while there is some city sprawl, the countryside quickly takes over, allowing enjoyment of a relaxed mix of city, beach, and country living.

Climate

Adelaide enjoys a Mediterranean climate with low rainfall and humidity. The rainy season is in winter, but during the summer months the climate is pleasant and only occasionally reaches temperatures that could be considered too hot. To balance the nearly perfect climate, the water temperatures are lower than at other main beach cities due to Gulf St. Vincent being part of the Great Southern Ocean, which leads to Antarctica and is the nation's coldest.

WHERE TO LIVE

City of Adelaide

Surrounded by two rings of historic parklands, the well-organized grid of Adelaide's CBD and its residential neighbor North Adelaide offer a lovely mix of grand historic buildings and modern shopping together with a busy assortment of offices and large companies. In this area there are also both apartment buildings and single-family homes. In the **CBD,** apartments are both modern and older, including the very chic development within the old walls of the Adelaide Food Exchange, a former market that's now full of apartments, trees, and a handful of cafés. People know each other and there are lots of young families that come out to have a coffee or play with their children under the shady trees.

Toward the southern end of the CBD, stunning Victorian row houses and town houses are the norm, all within a ball-toss of a park. In the northern circle, **North Adelaide,** you can find some stunning mansions around the parklands as well as some more affordable but still stylish residences a few streets in from the parks. Residents have lived in the area for generations, everyone says hello, and the feeling is very much like a village not far from town. It's very quiet, but everything you need is just around the corner. North Adelaide is a mix of old money and trendy new developments. Families tend to like the streets lined with town houses and the close proximity to vast areas of parkland. Young professionals tend to buy or rent units in the trendier corners of the neighborhood.

A three-bedroom, two-bath house in North Adelaide will cost around $1.2 million to buy or $700 per week to rent. A compact two-bedroom, one-bath apartment in Adelaide's CBD would cost around $450,000 to buy and $450 per week to rent.

Northern Adelaide

The northern suburbs can be risky. Areas closer to the CBD, especially North Adelaide and plush Fitzroy, are safe, but farther north, Salisbury, Smithfield Plains, and Elizabeth are to be avoided. The north is industrial and has various lower-income suburbs that may not necessarily be unsafe but are not well-suited for family living. That said, **Greenacres** is a great place to live, especially if you are looking for something a little more affordable. There is a sense of community here and many young people starting out on the property ownership ladder. Very popular with expats is **Mawson Lakes,** a planned community that's a small town in its own right, full of luxurious large new homes set around lakes and canals, with schools, shops, restaurants, and a safe environment for children.

Greenacres and Mawson Lakes are around a 20-minute drive to the city center. Both suburbs are very family-oriented. Greenacres is a little more organically grown and developed, whereas the slightly more upmarket Mawson Lakes is modern and manicured, akin to a gated community with brand-new yet individual houses. These areas are perfect for families, as it is safe and convenient to get everywhere.

A new, modern three-bedroom, two-bath house in Mawson Lakes will cost $400 per week to rent and around $500,000 to buy; in Greenacres, a three-bedroom, two-bath house will cost

Truly Living Down Under

one of Coober Pedy's underground churches

Far out in the Outback, 800 kilometers north of Adelaide on the Sturt Highway, are the dugout cave homes of **Coober Pedy.** The town bills itself as the "opal capital of the world," and it has been used extensively as a set for filmmakers, usually as a stand-in for a postapocalyptic world in films such as *Mad Max Beyond Thunderdome* and *Until the End of the World,* which have given Coober international notoriety as one of the least attractive spots on earth.

In Coober's case, glory comes from holes in the desert where newcomers have been pulling opals out of the ground since 1915, when the first strikes were made, and increasingly since the Charles Sturt Highway that passes by was paved in 1987.

Owing to a shortage of wood, searing Outback heat, and the absence of electricity for air-conditioning, the residents of Coober have been digging homes straight down into the ground for generations. A typical dugout home will have as many as three bedrooms carved out of the rock, with a living room, a kitchen, and bathrooms. The houses do not require air-conditioning as they remain at a constant temperature.

Almost all of the town's residents are active in the opal trade (Australia produces nearly 97 percent of the world's opals), and more than half of them live underground in dugout houses. The residents, however, maintain one equally distinguished amenity aboveground: the Coober Pedy Golf Course, which is entirely treeless and grass-free. Golfers carry pieces of turf around the links with them to hit the ball from. The course is the only one in the world with reciprocal playing rights at the Royal & Ancient Golf Club of St. Andrews, the ancestral home of golf.

Countless Europeans have tried their luck in Coober Pedy, and most move on after a few months or years. But in a 1996 study, people of 42 different nationalities were among the residents, giving Coober Pedy the most diverse population in the country. Just not the most visible.

around $400,000 to buy and up to $400 per week to rent.

Eastern Suburbs

To the east, you are soon heading into the hills. **Adelaide Hills** is a desirable area with countryside views straight out of a romance novel, but it is true country living: Small roads wind up the steep hills past vineyards, fruit farms, and stables, the lots for houses are large, but amenities are not nearby. In slightly larger communities such as **Balhannah, Woodside,** and **Birdwood,** there are schools and some shops; other neighborhoods have only a post office and a small general store. There are school buses serving the area, but commutes into the city are long due to the narrow single-lane roads, and choices are limited. That said, if you don't need to get into the city or access city schools, the hills offer a slice of Australia that could hardly be prettier.

Commuting from Balhannah, as from anywhere in the Adelaide Hills can take a long time. Although not far from the city center on a map, the roads are rural. On a good day, without traffic, the drive takes around 30 minutes. If you do get stuck, it can take up to 45 minutes to get into town.

A three-bedroom, two-bath house with extensive gardens in Balhannah and other eastern suburbs will set you back around $450,000 to buy and $400 per week to rent. A little more money can get you a property with a vineyard attached.

Western Suburbs and Beaches

Directly west of the inner ring is Adelaide's airport and light industrial parks, but the beaches start just south of the airport. Historical **Glenelg** is the hub of the touristy beach resorts, and it bustles during the busy summer months. It offers apartment living overlooking the sea, and just a few blocks inland single-family houses have easy access to the beach. Glenelg is a little town in its own right, bustling with restaurants and shops, both the touristy and beachy and the ordinary variety. The atmosphere is relaxed and fun at the same time. The commute into town is made easy with the tram line heading from the promenade straight into the CBD.

A little farther down the coast, life is still a beach, but there are no tourists in sight. The family-oriented suburb of **Brighton,** with its pier, offers quiet living on the beachfront or near the beach,

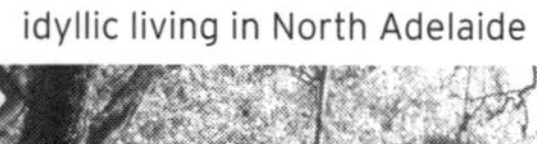
idyllic living in North Adelaide

with some gorgeous mansions but also more affordable houses, sports facilities, schools, and parks. In addition to beachside living, Brighton also has family seclusion and quiet leafy streets away from the bustle of the seafront. People exercise on the beach in the morning, and neighbors know each other.

The commute from Glenelg to the CBD by tram takes around 25 minutes. Brighton is just minutes further down south, and the train also takes about 25 minutes to get into the CBD.

In bustling Glenelg, a three-bedroom, two-bath apartment overlooking the beach will cost you $875 per week to rent and $900,000 to buy; in quieter Brighton a three-bedroom, two-bath house will cost around $450 per week to rent and $600,000 to buy.

Southern Suburbs

Just south of the inner ring of parks, suburbs such as **Westbourne Park** offer lovely quiet roads with great safe family living and plenty of green spaces, many of which turn purple in November with the flowering jacaranda trees lining the streets. You can even see them from the air when leaving or approaching the airport; it is quite stunning. There are many retirement villages and gated communities in these areas, probably because most roads are quiet, leafy, and safe.

The farther south you go in Adelaide, the greener the green city becomes. Toward the glorious Fleurieu Peninsula, suburbs such as **Happy Valley** are detached from the suburban sprawl, remote villages of their own rather than appendages of Adelaide. Hilly and green with incredible views, the sports and outdoor facilities are larger, small village centers are hubs for the community, and wineries are the local industry.

Both Westbourne and Happy Valley are great neighborhoods for families. Young professionals might find them too far away from the buzz of the CBD. Westbourne Park is a 15-minute drive from the city center, whereas Happy Valley is around 30 minutes away. The Main South Road connects Happy Valley to the CBD, which tends to get a little busy at rush hour.

A three-bedroom, two-bath house in Westbourne Park will cost around $700,000 to buy and $450 per week to rent, while in rural Happy Valley three-bedroom, two-bath house on a larger lot will set you back $$400,000 to buy and $350 per week to rent.

DAILY LIFE

To meet likeminded people, try **InterNations** (www.internations.org/Adelaide-expats/events), a website that connects expats from all nationalities in the city.

Media Resources

Adelaide is the historic home of Rupert Murdoch's News Corp. media empire, and the newspapers in town are mostly Murdoch papers. *The Advertiser* is the daily easy-to-read tabloid, while the national broadsheet *The Australian* is more conservative and intellectual in style. There is a wide selection of community newspapers, known as the *Messenger* papers, including the *City Messenger, Eastern Courier Messenger,* and the like. The weekly *Independent* has since become an online-only news source, and *The Advertiser* sports a lively website, www.adelaidenow.com.au, that serves as a popular city guide as well as a source for news and gossip.

Reflecting the importance of food and wine to Adelaide and its surroundings, many lifestyle magazines are published here that focus on life in the region. Glossies *Fleurieu Living, Sumptuous,*

Adelaide Hills Magazine, and *SA Life* are a few of these titles.

The three main television networks—Seven, Nine, and Ten—are available, along with the two government-owned channels, ABC and SBS, and satellite service from Foxtel. Big Pond sells cable and Internet service, among a number of other providers.

Health Care

Adelaide has a number of excellent public hospitals; the teaching hospital is the Royal Adelaide. Other major hospitals are the Women and Children's, the Queen Elizabeth, and the Flinders Medical Center, associated with Flinders University, all in the 300- to 700-bed range and of excellent quality. There are also a number of very good private hospitals for those with private health insurance to avoid the common delays at public clinics. St. Andrew's is a private surgical hospital, and Ashford Hospital is South Australia's largest private hospital.

Schools

School attendance in South Australia is compulsory from ages 6 to 17, and students may take a Leaving Certificate after Year 10. However, most students stay on for Years 11 and 12 to complete the SACE (South Australian Certificate of Education), which is generally a prerequisite for university studies. Adelaide has a number of schools offering the International Baccalaureate (IB) as an alternative to the SACE, with the highest concentration of IB certificate holders in the country. Adelaide also has a few specialized high schools where students concentrate their studies in the arts, music, or sports.

There are more than 100 public schools in Adelaide and dozens of private secondary schools; more than half of the private schools are religious in nature. Pembroke School, St. John's, St. Peters College, and Saint Ignatius College are among the best private schools, while Glenunga International High School, which offers the IB program, is generally considered the top public school.

The three top universities in Adelaide are the University of Adelaide, the University of South Australia (UOSA), and Flinders University. Flinders is the newest, and the University of Adelaide is the prestigious one. There are various campuses of UOSA and the University of Adelaide along the impressive North Parade on the edge of the CBD. There are also five TAFE colleges around the city, offering numerous programs for technical and vocational education, often in conjunction with work-study programs.

Shopping

Adelaide shopping is fantastic. Rundle Mall, which is the pedestrianized part of Rundle Street, is full of shopping options such as the ubiquitous Myers and David Jones department stores and a few lovely older and elegant arcades, such as Adelaide Arcade. Farther east, Rundle Mall leads into Rundle Street, a slightly more upmarket stretch of quirky and fashionable boutiques.

For fresh produce you cannot do better than Adelaide Central Market, a large indoor market with more than 100 stalls full of fruit and vegetables, meat (even fresh kangaroo), delicatessens, nuts, oils, and pretty much everything else. Next door is Chinatown, so anything you cannot find in the market will probably be available there.

In plush North Adelaide, Melbourne Street is a delight for shoppers and window-shoppers alike. Individual shops full of fashion, home decor, and arty stuff intermingle with little restaurants shaded

Central Market

under trees. A similar leisurely shopping experience is on Unley Street in the suburb of Malvern, which is perfect for a relaxed afternoon of shopping with friends.

GETTING AROUND

Public Transportation

Adelaide has a train, bus, and tram system that is not as extensive as in the larger cities, but the spread of Adelaide is not as extensive either. Trips on the tram and some buses within the CBD are free, making it perfect for those who need to connect to work within the business district or visitors who want to take in the sights within the historical district. There is a passenger information center at the corner of King William and Currie Streets where you can pick up maps, timetables, and daily or monthly passes for all modes of transportation, finding out what combination of public transport will suit your commute best. The entire transportation system is governed under **Adelaide Metro** (www.adelaidemetro.com.au), and the Metrocard is the rechargeable pass you can use on all modes of transportation. Single-trip fares start at $3.54 at peak times, and $1.94 between 9am and 3pm weekdays, with day passes priced at $10.00 for unlimited use.

At the Kenswick Rail Terminal, three kilometers from the CBD, the famous interstate trains *The Ghan, The Overland,* and *The Indian Pacific* arrive and depart on their cross-continent journeys.

Highways

Adelaide's roads spread spoke-like from the inner city and might appear to be perfect for commuting by car, but in reality all the roads leading in and out of the city are congested every morning and late afternoon. The development of the Southern Expressway and Port River Expressway has helped but not solved the congestion problem. A new expressway east into the Adelaide Hills, called the Southeastern, has also proved to be functional and popular, easing the commute in a fast-growing area.

Adelaide and North Adelaide are divided by the Torrens River, so a series of bridges—the Morphett Street Bridge, the

Adelaide tram

Adelaide, and the Torrens—are bottleneck points for commuting. The Torrens is remarkably narrow, so the bridges are short, and congestion dissolves soon after crossing.

Adelaide International Airport

Having been voted "Best Capital Airport" several times, Adelaide International Airport is a little marvel. All in one building, the airport offers convenient arrivals and departures, whether you are coming from abroad or from within the country, and the shops and cafés have been selected to ensure that waiting time is enjoyable.

International flights connect mostly to Asia and New Zealand, and there are none to the United States. Domestic flights run to most other capitals and smaller airports throughout Australia, with Qantas, Jetstar, Virgin Australia, and Tigerair the busiest airlines serving the airport.

The airport is only eight kilometers from the city center. You can get to the CBD via the Interstate Rail Terminal for around $15 per trip, a taxi ride ($20 to the CBD), or the Metro Jet Bus (from $1.94).

Perth

Just as Sydney is all about the harbor, Perth is all about the great outdoors: proximity to the Outback, the desert, and the beaches. Fine beaches, complete with undulating sand dunes, hem the Indian Ocean. The beautiful weather means staying indoors is not a viable option. The port of Fremantle, now a suburb of Perth, draws residents and visitors in droves. It harbors—forgive the pun—Western Australia's oldest building, the Roundhouse, and other attractions such as the yachting marina, cafés, the historic town center, and famous markets. Perth itself also has plenty to offer. The CBD, or city center, is full of shops, old arcades, Victorian buildings, two magnificent rivers with inviting strollable waterfronts, and one of the world's largest inner-city parks, King Park. At more than four square kilometers, the park is partly indigenous bushland and part organized botanical gardens that house many of Australia's unique flora and fauna, all accessible on treks through the park.

The city has not only the fastest rate of growth in Australia but also is home to more than 80 percent of Western Australia's population. According to the Australian Bureau of Statistics, Western Australia's population density is an average of 0.9 people per square kilometer, but considering that more than 90 percent of Western Australia has less than one person per square kilometer, Perth, in turn, has a population density of 320 people per square kilometer. But it doesn't feel crowded, perhaps due to the amazing sky, mostly blue with a few fluffy white clouds for contrast, and it seems bigger than anywhere else. No wonder everybody lives outdoors so much of the time.

THE BRIEF STORY OF PERTH

Perth was founded as the capital of a British colony of free settlers who named their settlement the Swan River Colony. The place where the Swan River meets the Indian Ocean had been inhabited by the indigenous Noongar people for approximately 5,000 years before European contact. They called it Boorloo and used the land for hunting. The first Europeans to see this land were Dutch traders in the late 17th century.

The city was named for Perth, Scotland, hometown of the British secretary of state for colonies, George Murray, who also represented Perthshire in the British parliament. Although the colony was established as a free settlement, the first permanent building was a prison, the Roundhouse, built in 1830, which still stands today in Fremantle.

A series of battles between the indigenous Australians and the European settlers resulted in the indigenous people withdrawing from the immediate area by 1843, and in 1850 the colony was opened to convicts in order to provide a cheap source of labor. The colony's importance increased steadily in the late 19th century, when it became increasingly clear that the huge Western Australia region was home to vast reserves of resources such as gold, aluminum, diamonds, coal, and oil. Perth emerged as the trading and services center for a gigantic natural resources industry and continues to grow rapidly for this reason today.

The colony, later renamed Western Australia, remained completely isolated from the rest of the country, and Western Australia was the last of the six colonies to pass a referendum in favor of federation, in 1900. The colony was promised a transcontinental railroad as an incentive. Feeling ignored by the rest of Australia during the depths of the Great Depression, in 1933 the state voted by a 2:1 margin to secede from the commonwealth, but the plan was never carried out.

After World War II, a natural resources boom was ignited in the state, and Western Australia remains one of the most important sources of aluminum, iron, and coal for the Asia-Pacific region, as well as the most important source of precious metals and diamonds in Australia. Perth has grown from the smallest capital to the fourth largest after Sydney, Melbourne, and Brisbane. At its current 10 percent annual growth rate, it will soon eclipse Brisbane to become the third-most populated city in the country. Western Australia provided its first prime minister to the nation in 1983 when Bob Hawke became the national leader.

aerial view of Perth

THE LAY OF THE LAND

Perth is far from anywhere—more than 2,000 kilometers from the nearest city with more than 100,000 people, and Singapore is closer to Perth than Sydney is. There is a three-hour time difference between Perth and Sydney, and the flight between the two cities takes around four and a half hours; still a lot faster than the three-night journey by train.

The city of Perth is relatively flat and built around the Swan and Serpentine river systems, with the Serpentine draining into the Indian Ocean south of the city near the booming city of Mandurah and Perth occupying the mouth of the Swan River where it meets the Indian Ocean. The metropolitan area stretches far north and south of the Swan, keeping most of the suburbs close to the moderating sea breezes and the attractive beaches. The historic part of Perth is quite small and covers the CBD, while the surrounding suburbs are organized into a series of municipal governments. The best-known area outside the CBD is Fremantle, which is the main port area, to the south of the CBD. The CBD itself occupies the north side of the Swan.

The CBD is oriented to the river, and the main street, St. Georges Terrace, runs parallel to the Swan. It experiences the prevailing warm westerly trade winds that create a wind tunnel effect more days than not in the canyon of tall buildings that are home to the major resources corporations. While the city is built around the water and has lush parks within the city limits, even boasting one of the world's largest inner-city parks, as soon as you drive an hour or two east, you are in the desert. Even the dirt in the suburbs is more sand than soil, but it is still very fertile if given a little help.

Climate

Described as a Californian or Mediterranean climate, Perth is the sunniest of Australian capital cities, with cooler but not cold winters and warm but not overly hot summers. In the afternoon, the Fremantle Doctor, a fresh southwesterly wind, typically brings relief to the city's streets.

Average Temperatures and Rainfall in Perth

Month	Mean maximum temperature (°C)	Mean minimum temperature (°C)	Mean rainfall (mm)
January	31	18	17
February	32	18	9
March	30	17	19
April	26	14	19
May	23	11	85
June	19	9	134
July	18	8	147
August	19	8	121
September	20	9	87
October	23	11	41
November	26	14	23
December	29	16	10

Source: Australian Bureau of Meteorology

WHERE TO LIVE

Perth is spread out along a north-south axis, and there is not really a north-south divide. Both areas have some nice suburbs, both directions become quite rural quite quickly, and both have easy train connections into the CBD. But if you can afford it, head straight west and find somewhere by the beach; this is where Perth is at its best. There are plenty of expats in the city, and one excellent starting point is the **American Women's Club Perth** (http://awcperth.com) or the **Western Division of the Australian American Association** (www.aaawa.com.au).

Central Perth

Perth's CBD, or city center, is relatively small but still offers plenty of apartment and town house living walking distance from the main business district and shopping streets. Along the main thoroughfare, St. Georges Terrace, is **Adelaide Terrace,** brimming with apartment buildings with great views across the city and the river, but it does get eerily quiet after the offices and shops have closed, and there is no atmosphere to speak of. **East Perth** is a better bet, with town houses and apartments surrounded by parks and cafés, plenty of family city living, small shops, and a distinct community feeling.

A two-bedroom, one-bath apartment in East Perth costs around $500,000 to buy and $650 per week to rent. A two-bedroom, two-bath plus garage modern apartment in Perth's CBD will cost

Fremantle Market

around $750,000 to buy and around $900 per week to rent.

North of the River

Mosman Park and **Peppermint Grove** are old-money suburbs where you need a generous budget and good luck or connections to find a place. If you can afford it, persevere, as both are beautiful suburbs, close to the beach, and within an easy commute to the CBD. More accessible is **Cottesloe,** which lines the breathtakingly beautiful Sunset Coast, with its undulating dunes and white sandy beaches for as far as the eye can see. Houses are mostly modern and neighborhoods are planned, with gated communities taking the place of organically developed villages, and "town centers" offering standard amenities such as doctors, vets, shops, schools, and plenty of restaurants and cafés. There are dog beaches, the regulars all know each other, and the atmosphere is distinctly comfortable beach living, with well-off families, kids at good schools, and mom, if she's not working, exercising with friends or walking the dog. It is a lovely place to live. Cottesloe is an easy 15- to 20-minute drive from the center. Trains from here have a direct route to the center and also take about 20 minutes.

In Mosman Park, a three-bedroom, two-bath house costs around $900,000-2 million to buy and $750 and up per week to rent. Peppermint Grove prices are similar, but can be even pricier with better beach views. In Cottesloe, a three-bedroom, two-bath house with a beach view costs $2-3 million to buy, around $2,000 per week to rent.

There is a shortage of rental property in the northern coastal suburbs, and prices are a little cheaper away from the beach.

Fremantle and South Perth

Just south of the river estuary is **Fremantle,** or "Freo," as it is affectionately known, a busy port but also a historic town, a busy leisure craft marina, and an all-round bustling place drawing tourists and day-trippers to its attractions. Property is completely different than north of the estuary, with an emphasis on

Expat Experience: Living in Perth

Pilar Adams

Pilar Adams, 32, is a lawyer from Southern California, who has lived in Perth for five years with her fiancé.

Why did you come to Australia? And why Perth?
My fiancé is from Perth and works out here in the mining industry. We met several years ago when we were both traveling in Mexico. I came out for a visit and loved it. I decided to move here on a temporary basis five years ago and have been here ever since with no plans to leave!

What do you love most about living in Perth?
The weather is great and the culture embraces a laid-back and active lifestyle. You are never far from a white-sand beach. The city is big enough that there are a lot of options for events, nightlife, and other entertainment, but not so big that you lose a sense of community.

What does Perth have that none of the other Australian cities have?
Perth and Perthites have a sense of proud independence, fostered by its isolation from the rest of the big Aussie cities.

What's your least favorite aspect of living in Perth?
Being on the other side of the continent from Sydney and Melbourne means no one from

single-story beach-type houses; it is more relaxed and much less opulent.

Closer to Perth, beautiful **Mount Pleasant** by the Canning River offers desirable waterfront property. Not far across the bridge from the CBD, it provides a chance to work in the city yet jump on the sailboat on the weekend to enjoy the serene lakes and rivers in the area.

Mount Pleasant is a perfect place to live for pretty much everybody. Young professionals commute on bicycles along the freeway into Perth's city center, and families find the parklands and proximity home ever happens to be in town or nearby for a quick visit. Perth is just far enough that it's tough to convince people from back home to come see what the fuss is about. But that isolation also has its benefits, and it's kept Perth a hidden gem and preserved that big country town feel.

Which suburbs would you recommend to other expats?
Young professionals may want to look to North Perth, Victoria Park, and Leederville, as they are very close to the CBD and have lots of cafés, restaurants, bars, and shops. Any of what are known as the western or northern suburbs are popular with families, but you will be paying a pretty penny to live in those suburbs. It all depends on what you are moving here for. If you want to be able to go to the beach for a quick dip at a moment's notice, the western suburbs will be for you.

What do you miss most about the United States?
Live broadcast events and sports from the United States being on at reasonable times. With the time difference, games will be on in the middle of the night or early morning. So I record them to watch later, but by then I usually know the outcome! Also, being from Southern California, I grew up with Mexican food, and I still haven't found a good place to get Mexican food in Perth unfortunately.

What piece of information would you liked to have known when you first arrived?
I found that when I first started looking for work (before I was a lawyer), Australian employers were more concerned that you had a particular qualification or certificate in the field, and actual experience was not given as much weight. Just be aware that if you are like many other people who got their experience on the job and don't necessarily have a formal qualification in the field, you should be prepared to explain why your actual experience overcomes any perceived deficiencies from lack of a formal degree. It can be done, but be prepared to be persuasive!

What's your best tip for newcomers?
Get a car straight away. Public transport does the job okay, but it can be very inconvenient. Being independent gives you an opportunity to explore the city and Western Australia and settle into your new life. And, if you can, try to save up money ahead of time, because Perth is *very* expensive.

What's the best way to meet other expats?
Aussies are crazy about sports. Join a social sports team. Some of my best friends are girls I met my first year living in Perth when I joined a local softball team to meet people.

to gardens and playground alongside the river perfect. It is quiet, green, and feels far away from any city hubbub, yet is only just across the river from it.

A three-bedroom, two-bath house in Fremantle costs around $600 per week to rent and $900,000 to buy; in Mount Pleasant a three-bedroom, two-bath house near the river costs around $1 million to buy and $700 per week to rent.

North and Eastern Suburbs

The "north" officially starts just a stone's throw from the CBD, and there are plenty of northern suburbs within a few minutes' commute from the city that offer a completely different lifestyle. Many suburbs line the commuter train line into town, but if you want to take advantage of living in the countryside, **Ellenbrook,** near Whiteman Park, is just 25 kilometers northeast of the city. It is a small community where people know each other and kids play together. It's like living in a different part of Australia altogether: You are likely to encounter kangaroos on the daily commute, kookaburras in the garden, and enjoy the outdoor bush living that Western Australia is famed for.

Ellenbrook is a mere 30-minute drive from Perth's CBD and has all the amenities a town of 10,000 people needs. There are schools, doctor's offices, a shopping center, and a library.

A three-bedroom, two-bath house in Ellenbrook costs around $500,000 to buy and $600 per week to rent.

DAILY LIFE

Media Resources

The daily newspaper is *The West Australian,* a tabloid covering local and some international news. There is also *The Weekend West* and community papers in the suburbs, and you can get *The Australian* and other major papers. Television coverage includes channels Seven, Nine, and Ten, plus various ABC news channels and SBS channels. Countless radio stations play mostly oldies, with some contemporary and classical music. There is also Noongar Radio (100.9 FM), an Aboriginal station with news and indigenous music mixed with contemporary fare.

Health Care

As the largest city in the west part of the continent, Perth in endowed with an excellent selection of private and public hospitals with high standards. The majority of suburbs have their own private and public medical practitioners and smaller clinics that can deal with minor complaints and which will refer you to the specialists in the city's hospitals for further treatment if necessary. Good hospitals include the Sir Charles Gairdner Hospital, the state's largest cancer treatment center and principal hospital for neurosurgery and liver transplants; or the King Edward Memorial Hospital, which comes recommended for maternity, neonatal, and gynecological needs.

Schools

In Perth there are public schools, faith-based schools, and private and independent schools, both coed and single-sex. A useful government website called **My School** (www.myschool.edu.au) helps select schools in your chosen area, as it provides a history of National Assessment Program—Literacy and Numeracy (NAPLAN) test results, allowing you to check the performance of each school.

Most schools have a website that takes you through their enrollment process and more often than not allow you to register your child online and attach relevant documents such as copies of passports and immunization records.

Expats often opt for private schools because they arrive in the middle of the school year, get help from their company with paying the fees, or want to stream their children toward the International Baccalaureate (IB). There are plenty of excellent private schools in Perth, including St. Hilda's Anglican School for Girls in Mosman Park, which has a very good reputation, as does the International School of Western Australia, a coed school, in the northern suburb of City Beach, and Wesley College for boys in South Perth. Other schools that offer the IB include Scotch College in

Swanbourne and Treetops Montessori School in Darlington.

Shopping

Perth is surrounded by wealth. The CBD offers all of the shops you'll need, from mass retailers to luxury brands and everything in between. The inner-city shops mostly stretch between Hay Street and Murray Street, with malls, arcades and department stores. For more individual shopping, head for the fantastic Claremont Quarter, where a mainstream mall is surrounded by a plethora of boutiques and cafés in a lovely setting. Beaufort Street in Mount Lawley is popular for its eclectic interior decor and accessories boutiques as well as award-winning restaurants; on the weekend, be sure to head to Fremantle for its markets, which offer fresh seasonal foods, arts and crafts, and plenty of family entertainment.

GETTING AROUND

Public Transportation

There are times, especially at rush hour, that the CBD seems to have more buses than cars on the road. Bus connections are superb, and within the inner city buses are free. There are also three Central Area Transit (CAT) bus lines, yellow, red, and blue, with a couple of others running in Fremantle and Joonalup. These services follow certain loops, are free of charge, and run every 8 to 15 minutes, except on Christmas Day, Good Friday, and ANZAC Day. To find out when your next bus is due, there is a countdown sign at each stop, and mobile apps are also available.

TransPerth also runs extensive train service from around 5:30am to midnight most days. If you live near a train stop and need to commute into the CBD with its limited parking, it is definitely the sensible choice over driving. There is also the option of a ferry commute from the Barrack Street Jetty at the foot of the CBD. TransPerth has two types of ticketing, cash tickets and SmartRider, both valid for a combination of bus, ferry, and train. Cash tickets start from $2.10 per journey, and the SmartRider smartcard gives discounts of 15 to 25 percent, with discounts for students, disabled people, and seniors.

Highways

In Perth the car is king, but the highways are struggling under rapid growth, and traffic can be tough, although rarely on the monumental scale of Sydney or Melbourne. Nearly every highway and expressway is undergoing an expansion program, causing the problem to get worse before it gets better. There are three expressways and nine highways, with the Mitchell Freeway dominating the northern corridor, the Graham Farmer taking commuters out west toward the beaches, and the Kwinana Freeway heading south toward Mandurah.

There are a handful of scenic commutes, including the Sunset Coast Tourist Drive, hugging the coast and offering great views over the beaches and the Indian Ocean. The inner-city Riverside Drive, leading into Mounts Bay Road and then into the Stirling Highway, connects the CBD with the coast and hugs the river along the way. If you live near Ellenbrook, you will drive past Whiteman Park, a protected expanse of natural bush with kangaroos and other exotic residents.

There are no toll roads in Perth, and parking is limited in the CBD, but there are secure parking lots around the city. Hourly rates start from $3.30 per hour up to $56.20 for 24-hour covered parking.

Perth Airport

Although they share runways, Perth International Airport (Terminal 1) and Perth Domestic Airport (Terminals 2 and 3) are separate entities. Around eight kilometers apart, there are regular shuttles between them, but there is continual confusion in car-rental arrangements. Make sure you give the rental company your flight number to have your car waiting at the right terminal.

Perth International Airport hosts 17 international airlines with flights to Asia, the Middle East, and Africa, but connections to the United States are made via Sydney or Melbourne. The Domestic Airport is a busy hub for fly-in workers connecting all over the country on local airlines such as Tigerair, Jetstar, Skywest, Virgin Australia, and Qantas.

You can get into Perth by taxi, rental car, and shuttle (from $15 one-way) or TransPerth bus routes 380 and 40 ($5.00 one-way) to the city center.

Even if you are traveling within Australia, on arriving in Perth you must discard all fruit, vegetables, seeds, nuts, and plants you have with you, as Western Australia has strict import laws that even apply to items grown in other states.

RESOURCES

BEST.
FitnessFirst.com.au
myki
Purchase your full fare
myki and top up here
Coins
Zoom
Collect

Embassies and Consulates

UNITED STATES

EMBASSY OF AUSTRALIA

1601 Massachusetts Ave. NW
Washington, DC 20036
tel. 202/797-3000
fax 202/797-3168
www.usa.embassy.gov.au
Office hours: 8:30am-5pm Mon.-Fri.
Passport interview hours: 9am-noon and 2pm-4pm Mon.-Fri.

AUSTRALIAN CONSULATE-GENERAL, CHICAGO

123 N. Wacker Dr., Ste. 1330
Chicago, IL 60606
tel. 312/419-1480
fax 312/419-1499
Office hours: 8.30am-4:30pm Mon.-Fri.

AUSTRALIAN CONSULATE-GENERAL, HONOLULU

1000 Bishop St., Penthouse
Honolulu, HI 96813
tel. 808/529-8100
fax 808/529-8142
Office hours: 8am-4pm Mon.-Fri.

AUSTRALIAN CONSULATE-GENERAL, LOS ANGELES

2029 Century Park E., Ste. 3150
Los Angeles, CA 90067
tel. 310/229-2300
fax 310/229-2380
Office Hours: 9am-5pm Mon.-Fri.

AUSTRALIAN CONSULATE-GENERAL, NEW YORK

150 E. 42nd St., 34th Fl.
New York, NY 10017
tel. 212/351-6500
fax 212/351-6501
Office hours: 8:30am-5pm Mon.-Fri.

AUSTRALIAN CONSULATE-GENERAL, SAN FRANCISCO

575 Market St., Ste. 1800
San Francisco, CA 94105
tel. 415/644-3620
fax 415/536-1982
Office hours: 9am-5pm Mon.-Fri.

There is no Visa Agency for travel and immigration to Australia in the consulates-general in Chicago, Honolulu, New York, or San Francisco. For queries on Australian visa, immigration, and citizenship issues, contact the Visa and Citizenship Information Service (tel. 613/216-7603, www.immi.gov.au/contacts/forms/americas).

AUSTRALIA

EMBASSY OF THE UNITED STATES

Moonah Place
Yarralumla, ACT 2600
tel. 02/6214-5600
fax 02/6214-5970
http://canberra.usembassy.gov
Office hours: 8am-5pm Mon.-Fri.

U.S. passport services, including lost and stolen passports, and visas services are not available at the embassy.

U.S. CONSULATE-GENERAL, SYDNEY

MLC Centre, Level 59
19-29 Martin Place
Sydney, NSW 2000
tel. 02/9373-9200
after hours tel. 02/4422-2201
fax 02/9373-9184
http://sydney.usconsulate.gov
Office hours: 8am-5pm Mon.-Fri.

U.S. CONSULATE-GENERAL, MELBOURNE
553 St. Kilda Rd.
Melbourne, VIC 3004
tel. 03/9526-5900
fax 03/9510-4646
http://melbourne.usconsulate.gov
Office hours: 9am-4:30pm Mon.-Fri.

U.S. CONSULATE-GENERAL, PERTH
16 St. George's Ter., 4th Fl.
Perth, WA 6000
tel. 08/6144-5100
after hours tel. 08/9476-0081
fax 08/9325-5914
http://perth.usconsulate.gov
Office hours: 8:00am-4:30pm Mon.-Fri.

CANADA

AUSTRALIAN HIGH COMMISSION, OTTAWA
50 O'Connor St., Ste. 710
Ottawa, ON, K1P 6L2
tel. 613/236-0841
fax 613/786-7621
Visas tel. 613/238-1040
www.canada.embassy.gov.au/otwa
Office hours: 9am-5pm Mon.-Fri.

AUSTRALIAN CONSULATE-GENERAL, TORONTO
175 Bloor St. E., Ste. 1100, South Tower
Toronto, ON, M4W 3R8
tel. 416/323-4280
fax 416/323-4295

AUSTRALIAN CONSULATE, VANCOUVER
1075 W. Georgia St., Ste. 2050
Vancouver, BC, V6E 3C9
tel. 604/684-1177
fax 604/684-1856

AUSTRALIA

HIGH COMMISSION OF CANADA, CANBERRA
Commonwealth Ave.
Canberra, ACT 2600
tel. 02/6270-4000
fax 02/6270-4081
Office hours: 8:30am-12:30pm and 1pm-4:30pm Mon.-Fri.

CONSULATE GENERAL OF CANADA, SYDNEY
Level 5, 111 Harrington St.
Sydney, NSW 2000
tel. 02/9364-3000
fax 02/9364-3098
Office hours: general inquiries 8:30am-4:30pm Mon.-Fri.; immigration and visa inquiries 9am-noon Mon.-Thurs.

Planning Your Fact-Finding Trip

GUIDED TOURS

AUSTRALIA WALKING TOURS
http://auswalk.com.au

INDIGENOUS GUIDED TOURS
www.ayersrockresort.com.au/experiences/aboriginal-cultural-experiences

ADVENTURE TOURS
www.adventuretours.com.au

GLOBUS
www.globusjourneys.com

INFOHUB TOUR
www.infohub.com

NATURE BOUND AUSTRALIA
www.natureboundaustralia.com

SHORT STAYS
www.stays.com.au

SHORT-TERM RENTALS

RENT AUSTRALIA
www.rentaustralia.com.au

Making the Move

VISAS AND IMMIGRATION

AUSTRALIAN DEPARTMENT OF IMMIGRATION
www.border.gov.au

AUSTRALIA MIGRATION
www.australia-migration.com

MIGRATION EXPERT
www.migrationexpert.com

AUSTRALIAN EXPATRIATE INFORMATION

AUSTRALIA EXPAT FORUM
www.expatforum.com

EXFIN: THE AUSTRALIAN EXPATRIATE GATEWAY
www.exfin.com

EXPATRIATECONNECT
www.expatsaustralia.com

AMERICAN AUSTRALIAN ASSOCIATION
www.americanaustralian.org

INTERNATIONS
www.internations.org/Australia-expats/americans

INTERNATIONAL MOVING COMPANIES

SEVEN SEAS
www.sevenseasworldwide.com

INTERNATIONAL MOVERS
www.intlmovers.com

WALKERS MOVING AND STORAGE
www.walkmove.com.au

Housing Considerations

REAL ESTATE AGENCIES

HOMEHOUND
www.homehound.com.au

DOMAIN
www.domain.com.au

LJ HOOKER
www.ljhooker.com.au

REALESTATE.COM.AU
www.realestate.com.au

CENTURY 21
www.century21.com.au

Education

UNIVERSITIES

AUSTRALIAN EDUCATION NETWORK

www.australianuniversities.com

A general guide to Australia's universities.

UNIVERSITIES AUSTRALIA

www.universitiesaustralia.edu.au

Another general guide to Australia's universities.

THE AUSTRALIAN NATIONAL UNIVERSITY

Canberra, ACT 0200
tel. 02/6125-5111
www.anu.edu.au

DEAKIN UNIVERSITY

221 Burwood Highway
Burwood, VIC 3125
tel. 03/9627-4877
www.deakin.edu.au

GRIFFITH UNIVERSITY

Southport, QLD 4222
tel. 07/3735-7111
www.griffith.edu.au

LA TROBE UNIVERSITY

Bundoora, VIC 3086
tel. 03/9627-4805
www.latrobe.edu.au

MACQUARIE UNIVERSITY

North Ryde, NSW 2109
tel. 02/9850-7111
www.mq.edu.au

MONASH UNIVERSITY

Melbourne, VIC 3800
tel. 03/9902-6000
www.monash.edu.au

UNIVERSITY OF MELBOURNE

Parkville, VIC 3010
tel. 03/9035-5511
www.unimelb.edu.au

UNIVERSITY OF NEW SOUTH WALES

Sydney, NSW 2052
tel. 02/9385-1000
www.unsw.edu.au

THE UNIVERSITY OF QUEENSLAND

Brisbane, QLD 4072
tel. 07/3365-1111
www.uq.edu.au

UNIVERSITY OF SOUTH AUSTRALIA

GPO Box 2471
Adelaide, SA 5001
tel. 03/9627-4854
www.unisa.edu.au

UNIVERSITY OF SYDNEY

Sydney, NSW 2006
tel. 02/8627-1444
www.usyd.edu.au

UNIVERSITY OF TECHNOLOGY, SYDNEY

15 Broadway
Ultimo, NSW 2007
tel. 02/9514-2000
www.uts.edu.au

ASSOCIATION OF INDEPENDENT SCHOOLS

THE ASSOCIATION OF INDEPENDENT SCHOOLS OF THE AUSTRALIAN CAPITAL TERRITORY

www.ais.act.edu.au

THE ASSOCIATION OF INDEPENDENT SCHOOLS OF NEW SOUTH WALES
www.aisnsw.edu.au

THE ASSOCIATION OF INDEPENDENT SCHOOLS OF QUEENSLAND
www.isq.qld.edu.au

THE ASSOCIATION OF INDEPENDENT SCHOOLS OF SOUTH AUSTRALIA
www.ais.sa.edu.au

THE ASSOCIATION OF INDEPENDENT SCHOOLS OF TASMANIA
www.independentschools.tas.edu.au

THE ASSOCIATION OF INDEPENDENT SCHOOLS OF VICTORIA
www.is.vic.edu.au

THE ASSOCIATION OF INDEPENDENT SCHOOLS OF WESTERN AUSTRALIA
www.ais.wa.edu.au

DEPARTMENTS OF EDUCATION

ACT DEPARTMENT OF EDUCATION
www.det.act.gov.au

NEW SOUTH WALES DEPARTMENT OF EDUCATION
www.dec.nsw.gov.au

NEW SOUTH WALES PUBLIC SCHOOLS
www.schools.nsw.edu.au

QUEENSLAND DEPARTMENT OF EDUCATION
www.education.qld.gov.au

SOUTH AUSTRALIA DEPARTMENT OF EDUCATION
www.decs.sa.gov.au

TASMANIA DEPARTMENT OF EDUCATION
www.education.tas.gov.au

VICTORIA DEPARTMENT OF EDUCATION
www.education.vic.gov.au

WESTERN AUSTRALIA DEPARTMENT OF EDUCATION
www.det.wa.edu.au

Employment

JOB HUNTING

AUSTRALIAN JOB SEARCH
http://jobsearch.gov.au

JOBS AUSTRALIA
www.ja.com.au

RECRUIT.NET
http://australia.recruit.net

SEEK.COM
www.seek.com.au

WORKING IN AUSTRALIA
www.workingin-australia.com

Finance

BANKS

ADELAIDE BANK
www.adelaidebank.com.au

ADVANCE BANK
www.advance.com.au

AUSTRALIA AND NEW ZEALAND BANKING GROUP LIMITED (ANZ)
www.anz.com.au

BANKERS TRUST AUSTRALIA
www.bt.com.au

BANK OF SOUTH AUSTRALIA
www.banksa.com.au

BANKWEST
www.bankwest.com.au

CITIBANK AUSTRALIA
www.citibank.com.au

COMMONWEALTH BANK OF AUSTRALIA
www.commbank.com.au

HERITAGE BUILDING SOCIETY
www.heritageonline.com.au

ST. GEORGE BANK
www.stgeorge.com.au

HSBC
www.hsbc.com.au

Communications

TELEPHONE AND INTERNET PROVIDERS

OPTUS
www.optus.com.au

M2
www.m2.com.au

TELSTRA
www.telstra.com

VIRGIN MOBILE
www.virginmobile.com.au

VODAFONE AUSTRALIA
www.vodafone.com.au

POSTAL AND EXPRESS MAIL SERVICES

AUSTRALIA POST
www.auspost.com.au

DHL AUSTRALIA
www.dhl.com.au

NEWSPAPERS AND ONLINE MEDIA

General

THE AUSTRALIAN
www.theaustralian.com.au

FINANCIAL REVIEW
www.afr.com

Sydney

THE TELEGRAPH
www.dailytelegraph.com.au

SYDNEY MORNING HERALD
www.smh.com.au

Melbourne
THE AGE
www.theage.com.au

HERALD SUN
www.heraldsun.com.au

Brisbane and the Queensland Coast
BRISBANE COURIER MAIL
www.couriermail.com.au

Hobart
THE MERCURY
www.themercury.com.au

Canberra
CANBERRA TIMES
www.canberratimes.com.au

Southwestern Australia
ADELAIDE ADVERTISER/ADELAIDE NOW
www.adelaidenow.com.au

SUNDAY TIMES/PERTH NOW
www.perthnow.com.au

CABLE AND SATELLITE TELEVISION
FOXTEL
www.foxtel.com.au

Travel and Transportation

COMMUTING
ADELAIDE METRO
www.adelaidemetro.com.au

BRISBANE TRANSLINK
www.translink.com.au

METLINK MELBOURNE
www.metlinkmelbourne.com.au

SYDNEY BUSES
www.sydneybuses.info

SYDNEY FERRIES
www.sydneyferries.info

SYDNEY CITY RAIL
www.cityrail.info

HOBART METRO
www.metrotas.com.au

TRANSPERTH
www.transperth.wa.gov.au

AIR TRAVEL
EXPEDIA AUSTRALIA
www.expedia.com.au

WEBJET
www.webjet.com.au

QANTAS
www.qantas.com.au

VIRGIN AUSTRALIA
www.virginaustralia.com.au

JETSTAR
www.jetstar.com.au

TIGERAIR
www.tigerair.com.au

LONG DISTANCE RAIL
RAIL AUSTRALIA
www.railaustralia.com.au

GREAT SOUTHERN RAIL COMPANY
www.greatsouthernrail.com.au

OVERLAND COACH TRAVEL

GREYHOUND AUSTRALIA
www.greyhound.com.au

Prime Living Locations

SYDNEY

State Government

NEW SOUTH WALES GOVERNMENT
www.nsw.gov.au

Health

NSW HEALTH
73 Miller St.
North Sydney, NSW 2060
tel. 02/9391-9000
www.health.nsw.gov.au

Organizations

AMERICAN AUSTRALIAN ASSOCIATION
United States Study Centre
Institute Building (H03)
The University of Sydney
Sydney, NSW 2007
tel. 02/8627-4134
www.americanaustralian.org.au

AMERICAN CHAMBER OF COMMERCE IN AUSTRALIA
Level 6, 48 Hunter Street
Sydney, NSW 2000
tel. 02/8031-9000
fax 02/9232-4988
www.amcham.com.au

AMERICAN LEGION
60 Gurney Rd.
Chester Hill, NSW 2163
tel. 02/9644-6854
austraymond@one.net.au

THE AMERICAN SOCIETY OF SYDNEY
www.americansociety.com.au
info@americansociety.com.au

MELBOURNE

State Government

VICTORIA ONLINE
www.vic.gov.au

Health

VICTORIAN GOVERNMENT HEALTH INFORMATION
tel. 03/9096-10000
www.health.vic.gov.au

Organizations

AMERICAN CHAMBER OF COMMERCE (VICTORIA)
International Chamber House
121 Exhibition Road
Melbourne, VIC 3000
tel. 03/9027-5633
www.amcham.com.au

AUSTRALIAN AMERICAN ASSOCIATION OF VICTORIA
12 Lake Boga Avenue
Deer Park, VIC 3023
tel. 03/1938-1479
www.australianamerican.org

BRISBANE AND THE QUEENSLAND COAST

State Government

QUEENSLAND GOVERNMENT
www.qld.gov.au

Health
QUEENSLAND HEALTH
Queensland Health Building
147-163 Charlotte St.
Brisbane, QLD 4000
tel. 07/3234-0111
www.health.qld.gov.au

Organizations
AUSTRALIAN AMERICAN ASSOCIATION, BRISBANE CHAPTER
GPO Box 2175
Brisbane, QLD 4001
tel. 07/3278-6366
www.americancommunityaustralia.com

AMERICAN CHAMBER OF COMMERCE IN AUSTRALIA
www.amcham.com.au

CANBERRA
State Government
ACT GOVERNMENT
www.act.gov.au

Health
ACT HEALTH
www.health.act.gov.au

Organizations
AUSTRALIAN AMERICAN ASSOCIATION
PO Box 1268
Woden, ACT 2607
www.australianamericanact.com.au

HOBART
State Government
TASMANIA ONLINE
www.tas.gov.au

Health
DEPARTMENT OF HEALTH AND HUMAN SERVICES
GPO Box 125
Hobart, TAS 7001
tel. 1300/135-513
www.dhhs.tas.gov.au

Organizations
AUSTRALIAN AMERICAN ASSOCIATION
PO Box 315
Sandy Bay, TAS 7006
tel. 03/6225-3515
www.aaahobart.org

SOUTHWESTERN AUSTRALIA
State Government
GOVERNMENT OF WESTERN AUSTRALIA
www.wa.gov.au

GOVERNMENT OF SOUTH AUSTRALIA
www.sa.gov.au

Health
GOVERNMENT OF WESTERN AUSTRALIA DEPARTMENT OF HEALTH
PO Box 8172
Perth Business Centre, WA 6849
tel. 08/9222-4222
www.health.wa.gov.au

SOUTH AUSTRALIA CENTRAL DEPARTMENT OF HEALTH
Citi Centre Building
11 Hindmarsh Square
Adelaide SA 5000
tel. 08/8226-6000
www.health.sa.gov.au

Organizations

AMERICAN CHAMBER OF COMMERCE SOUTH AUSTRALIA

GPO Box 1886
Adelaide, SA 5001
tel. 08/8212-4688
http://amchamsa.on.net

AMERICAN WOMEN'S CLUB OF PERTH

GPO Box T1669
Perth, WA 6001
http://awcperth.com

AUSTRALIAN AMERICAN ASSOCIATION, SOUTH AUSTRALIA CHAPTER

PO Box 6714
Halifax St.
Adelaide, SA 5000
tel. 04/0029-5853
www.aaasa.org.au
aaasa@chariot.net.au

Glossary

arcade: small shopping area, usually in the CBD
arvo: afternoon
Aussie: (pronounced Ozzie): Australian
avo: avocado
barbie: barbecue
barrack: to cheer
barrister: trial lawyer
battler: someone who struggles valiantly, typically financially
beaut, beauty: fantastic
bikkie/biscuit: cookie
bingle: accident
bloke: guy
bloody: very
bonnet: hood of a car
bonza: great
booze bus: police vehicle used for catching drunk drivers
bottle shop: liquor store
bub: baby
building society: savings and loan bank
bum: fanny ("fanny" is a vulgarity in Australia)
bush: anywhere beyond the city
BYO: bring your own (e.g., wine at a restaurant)
CBD: central business district; downtown
chemist: pharmacist
chips: French fries
chook: a chicken
conveyance: due diligence or inspection period
cooee: literally, within hearing distance; figuratively, far away ("he's not within cooee of Sydney")
courgette: zucchini
cozzie: swimsuit
crook: sick ("I feel crook")
cuppa: cup of tea
dag: nerd
daks: trousers
dead set: true
dear: expensive
dill: a foolish person
dinky-die: the real thing, genuine
dobber: informer
dobbing/dobbing someone in: informing, tattling
drongo: a foolish person
dunny: toilet
entrée: starter, appetizer
esky: ice chest, drinks container
fair dinkum: genuine
fair go: a fair chance
flat: apartment
Fremantle Doctor: the cooling afternoon breeze in Perth
g'day: hello
gob smacked: astonished
good on ya: well done
greengrocer: fruit and vegetable store or department
Green P: class 1 provisional driver's license
grog: liquor
gumboots: rubber boots
gum tree: eucalyptus tree
I reckon: Yes, I agree.
jersey: sweater
John Dory: local white fish

lolly/lollies: candy
L plate: learner's driving permit
Maccas: McDonald's
mateship: loyalty
mate's rate: discount for a friend
middy: small beer glass in New South Wales
milk bar: takeaway food shop
mince: ground beef
mobile: cell phone
nappy: diaper
Never Never: the Outback
no worries: no problem, you're welcome
ocker: an Australian who speaks Strine
Outback: the hot, dry interior
Oz: Australia
pav/pavlova: classic dessert made from meringue topped with cream and fruit
petrol: gasoline
pissed: drunk
plaster: Band-Aid
pom, pommy: an English person
post code: zip code
pot: small beer glass in Queensland and Victoria
pozzy: position (get a good pozzy at the football stadium)
prawn: shrimp
prezzy: present, gift
pudding: dessert
pull a sickie: call in sick for the day from work
Rack off!: Get lost!
Red P: class 2 provisional driver's license
rego: vehicle registration
return: round-trip (a return ticket)
rissole: sausage-filled pastry
rort: fraud
roundabout: traffic circle
rubbish (verb): to criticize
rubbish (noun): garbage
schooner: large beer glass
seppos: American
serviette: napkin
settlement: real estate closing
sister: registered nurse
snag: sausage
solicitor: commercial lawyer
Southerly Buster: the cooling afternoon breeze in Sydney
spill: battle, often used with respect to political leadership contests
spit the dummy: get upset
sprung: caught
sticking plaster: Band-Aid
strata: a condominium association
strides: trousers
Strine: Australian dialect
sunnies: sunglasses
surgery: doctor's office
ta: thank you
takeaway: takeout food
tall poppies: very important people (often sarcastic)
tea: dinner
tin: can
togs: bathing suit
tosser: a foolish person
tram: streetcar
Tresca: Sprite
tucker: food
uni: university (pronounced YOU-knee)
unit: apartment
ute: utility vehicle, pickup truck
veggies: vegetables
wag: skip school
wardrobe: closet
whinge: complain
wog: illness
wuss: coward
yakka: work
yewy: U-turn
yobbo: a foolish person
yonks: ages

Australian Measurements

CLOTHING AND SHOES

Dress Sizes

U.S.	AUSTRALIAN
2	4
4	6
6	8
8	10
10	12
12	14
14	16

Shoe Sizes

In Australia, shoe sizes are numbered a half size less than in the United States. To convert shoe sizes, subtract a half from the U.S. shoe size to obtain the Australian size. For example, a size 8 and a half shoe in the United States is a size 8 in Australia.

Suggested Reading

GENERAL

Bryson, Bill. *In a Sunburned Country.* Sydney: Broadway, 2001. This fact-filled, anecdote-filled cornucopia of Australiana is from perhaps the best-known travel humorist.

Horne, Donald. *The Lucky Country.* Sydney: Penguin, 1967. This brilliant exploration of Australian culture was written in the 1960s but is applicable today.

Hughes, Robert. *The Fatal Shore: The Epic of Australia's Founding.* Sydney: Penguin, 1967. An acclaimed art critic turns his eye to the convict story. His vivid writing resulted in a book considered a masterpiece on early Aussie history.

Jacobson, Howard. *In the Land of Oz.* London: Hamilton, 2011. Booker Prize winner and humorist Howard Jacobson is a Brit who is not necessarily PC about his intrepid travels through Oz in his younger years.

FICTION

Anderson, Jessica. *Tirra Lirra by the River.* Sydney: Picador Australia, 2007. An old woman looks back on an extraordinary life in Queensland and London.

Carey, Peter. *Oscar and Lucinda.* New York: Vintage, 1997. A Booker Prize winner in 1988, this is one of the most acclaimed Aussie novels ever. A love story and much more.

Franklin, Miles. *My Brilliant Career.* Sydney: Bibliobazaar, 2007. The acclaimed turn-of-the-20th-century classic, made into a landmark film in 1979 by Gillian Armstrong.

Grenville, Kate. *The Secret River.* New York: Canongate, 2005. Historical novel about a 19th-century Londoner transported to young Sydney for theft. Brilliant insight on what the first settlers had to deal with.

White, Patrick. *Voss.* New York: Viking, 1957. In the generally accepted masterpiece of Australia's only Nobel Prize winner, romance between an explorer and a young woman turns into dark obsession.

Winton, Tim. *Cloudstreet.* Sydney: Picador Australia, 2002. This is Australia's most admired work of fiction, according to Bookworm.com.au. Two rural families begin again in the big city.

LANGUAGE

Lauder, Afferback. *Let Stalk Strine.* Sydney: Australia in Print, 1989. This is a classic and hilarious study of the Australian dialect. Follow-ups include *Nose Tone Unturned, Fraffly Well Spoken,* and *Fraffly Suite.*

O'Grady, John. *They're a Weird Mob.* Sydney: Ure Smith, 1965. This 1957 classic is about an Italian journalist who takes a job as a bricklayer to learn about Australians and speaking Strine. Hilarious.

CHILDREN'S BOOKS

Lindsay, Norman. *The Magic Pudding.* Sydney: Dover, 2006. This classic children's tale features Bunyip Bluegum, an itinerant Aussie koala traveling at the turn of the 20th century in Australia.

Pedley, Ethel. *Dot and the Kangaroo.* Sydney: Echo Library, 2008. This classic children's tale was made into a film in the 1970s. A little girl becomes lost in the Outback.

Thiele, Colin. *Storm Boy.* Sydney: New Holland, 2004. Classic young adult fiction about a boy, his pelican, his father, and an indigenous Australian man.

TRAVEL GUIDES

DK Eyewitness Travel Guide Australia. New York: DK Publishing, 2012. With plenty of photographs and maps, this book gives you as much visual impact as information about Australia.

Dragicevich, Peter. *Lonely Planet Sydney.* Sydney: Lonely Planet, 2012. The definitive travel guide focused on Sydney.

Fodor's Australia 2012. New York: Fodor's, 2012. Fodor's guide is updated every year. It's packed with information and written by locals.

Lonely Planet Australia. Sydney: Lonely Planet, 2011. Everything you always wanted to know about Australia, and then some.

Suggested Films

Australia. Directed by Baz Luhrmann. 165 minutes. 20th Century Fox, 2008. Big-budget epic starring Nicole Kidman and Hugh Jackman telling the story of an English aristocrat inheriting a large cattle station, the battle with thieving cattle barons, the cattle drive through the unforgiving Outback, the bombing of Darwin in World War II, and the romance with a rather handsome drover. Great photography, showing off the Outback at its best.

The Castle. Directed by Rob Sitch. 98 minutes. Village Roadshow, 1997. A classic Aussie cult film, virtually unknown outside Oz but beloved at home, this is the story of a family whose home in the suburbs is threatened by an airport expansion. The father refuses to move, setting off a series of comic incidents in a send-up of Australian culture (or lack thereof).

Crocodile Dundee. Directed by Peter Faiman. 98 minutes. Paramount, 1986. This comedy classic introduced famed Aussie comic Paul Hogan to the world. He plays a crocodile hunter, naturally, who gets in any number of comic and romantic entanglements.

Mad Max. Directed by George Miller. 99 minutes. Village Roadshow, 1979. In this vaguely futuristic film about biker gangs and the lone policeman who takes revenge on them, Mel Gibson's voice was dubbed for the American market because producers thought his thick Aussie accent would not be understood. Amazing car chases and stunts. The sequels, *The Road Warrior* and *Mad Max Beyond Thunderdome,* were even more popular.

Muriel's Wedding. Directed by P. J. Hogan. 106 minutes. Miramax, 1995. Toni Collette's breakthrough film is a classic comedy about an ugly duckling who leaves behind a small town to explore life in the city.

My Brilliant Career. Directed by Gillian Armstrong. 100 minutes. Blue Underground, 1979. This is a coming-of-age film about a spirited young woman, expertly played by newcomer Judy Davis. It was Davis's breakthrough film, as well as Gillian Armstrong's, who went on to helm *Little Women* and *Oscar and Lucinda.*

Picnic at Hanging Rock. Directed by Peter Weir. 115 minutes. Atlantic, 1975. Weir's atmospheric mystery is about a picnic at a girls' school that results in the disappearance of three girls. It's widely considered one of the breakthrough films that propelled the renaissance of Aussie films in the 1970s.

Sunday Too Far Away. Directed by Peter Faiman. 98 minutes. South Australian Film, 1975. Jack Thompson stars in the story of an Australian sheep station in the 1950s as bonuses disappear and nonunion laborers show up. Shearers' wives used to say of their husbands, "Friday night too tired; Saturday night too drunk; Sunday too far away," which gave the movie its title.

The Year of Living Dangerously. Directed by Peter Weir. 115 minutes. MGM, 1983. This moody romantic thriller made an international star of Mel Gibson and showed that Sigourney Weaver could do more than fight off aliens. A Sydney journalist is sent to Jakarta as the 1965 coup unfolds and discovers his capacity for love and betrayal (both good and bad) through his encounters with a diminutive man named Billy Kwan (played by Linda Hunt), fellow journalists, the government, the communist conspirators, and a beautiful British intelligence agent.

Index

DE

F

G

H

I

JKL

T

UVWXYZ

Photo Credits

Title page photo: jacaranda trees in Adelaide © Ulrike Lemmin-Woolfrey; page 4 decorative details on didgeridoos © Rafael Ben Ari | Dreamstime.com; page 5 fresh flowers for sale © Ulrike Lemmin-Woolfrey; page 6 © Tktktk | Dreamstime.com; page 7 (top left) © Ulrike Lemmin-Woolfrey, (top right) © Nils Versemann | Dreamstime.com, (middle) © Danemo | Dreamstime.com, (bottom left) © David May | Dreamstime.com, (bottom right) © David May | Dreamstime.com; page 8 (top left) grape vines in Adelaide © Matthew Weinel | Dreamstime.com, (top right) a koala and her baby © Hotshotsworldwide | Dreamstime.com, (bottom) beach along the Great Ocean Road in Victoria © Ulrike Lemmin-Woolfrey; page 9 © Ulrike Lemmin-Woolfrey; page 10 © Ulrike Lemmin-Woolfrey; page 12 © Alexandramp | Dreamstime.com; page 13 © Ymgerman | Dreamstime.com; page 14 © Tktktk | Dreamstime.com; page 16 (top) © Hotshotsworldwide | Dreamstime.com, (bottom) © Uros Ravbar | Dreamstime.com; page 19 © Bjeayes | Dreamstime.com; page 20 © Rafael Ben-ari | Dreamstime.com; page 21 © Ulrike Lemmin-Woolfrey; page 22 © Ulrike Lemmin-Woolfrey; page 24 © Sam D\'cruz | Dreamstime.com; page 28 © Volodymyr Vyshnivetskyy | Dreamstime.com; page 31 © Sadequl Hussain | Dreamstime.com; page 32 courtesy Australian Made; page 33 © Filedimage | Dreamstime.com; page 34 © Ulrike Lemmin-Woolfrey; page 37 © Ulrike Lemmin-Woolfrey; page 38 © Andrew M | Dreamstime.com; page 40 © Lifeontheside | Dreamstime.com; page 41 © Ryszard Stelmachowicz | Dreamstime.com; page 44 © Dave Bredeson | Dreamstime.com; page 46 © Matthew Trapp | Dreamstime.com; page 47 © Esmehelit | Dreamstime.com; page 49 © Marco Tomasini | Dreamstime.com; page 50 © Ulrike Lemmin-Woolfrey; page 51 © Ulrike Lemmin-Woolfrey; page 59 © Bennymarty | Dreamstime.com; page 61 © Tktktk | Dreamstime.com; page 62 © Ulrike Lemmin-Woolfrey; page 63 © Ulrike Lemmin-Woolfrey; page 67 © Ulrike Lemmin-Woolfrey; page 71 © Lifeontheside | Dreamstime.com; page 77 © Redzaal | Dreamstime.com; page 78 © Ulrike Lemmin-Woolfrey; page 81 © Ulrike Lemmin-Woolfrey; page 82 © Sunflowerey | Dreamstime.com; page 85 © Ulrike Lemmin-Woolfrey; page 91 © Sunflowerey | Dreamstime.com; page 92 © Ulrike Lemmin-Woolfrey; page 94 © Tvphotos | Dreamstime.com; page 100 © Tktktk | Dreamstime.com; page 102 © Travelling-light | Dreamstime.com; page 104 © Stbernardstudio | Dreamstime.com; page 106 © Inge Hogenbijl | Dreamstime.com; page 108 © Rafael Ben-ari | Dreamstime.com; page 110 © Lee Hong Chun | Dreamstime.com; page 114 © Ulrike Lemmin-Woolfrey; page 118 © Manuel Hoo | Dreamstime.com; page 121 © Nils Versemann | Dreamstime.com; page 122 © Ulrike Lemmin-Woolfrey; page 124 © Ulrike Lemmin-Woolfrey; page 125 © Mateusz Żogała | Dreamstime.com; page 128 © Tktktk | Dreamstime.com page 129 © Ulrike Lemmin-Woolfrey; page 132 © Ulrike Lemmin-Woolfrey; page 135 © Ulrike Lemmin-Woolfrey; page 137 © Rafael Ben-ari | Dreamstime.com; page 140 © Ulrike Lemmin-Woolfrey; page 143 © Ulrike Lemmin-Woolfrey; page 145 © Mairead | Dreamstime.com; page 148 © Ulrike Lemmin-Woolfrey; page 149 © Ulrike Lemmin-Woolfrey; page 150 © Ulrike Lemmin-Woolfrey; page 151 © Jarred Seng; page 152 © Mrlloyd | Dreamstime.com; page 153 © Volodymyr Vyshnivetskyy | Dreamstime.com; page 158 © Markus Gann | Dreamstime.com; page 161 © Verve Portraits; page 164 © Volodymyr Vyshnivetskyy | Dreamstime.com; page 168 © Ulrike Lemmin-Woolfrey; page 172 © Ulrike Lemmin-Woolfrey; page 173 © Ulrike Lemmin-Woolfrey; page 180 © Ulrike Lemmin-Woolfrey; page 182 © Thomas Hansson | Dreamstime.com; page 184 © Ulrike Lemmin-Woolfrey; page 188 © Ulrike Lemmin-Woolfrey; page 190 © Katherine Balfour; page 193 © Ulrike Lemmin-Woolfrey; page 194 © Rafael Ben-ari | Dreamstime.com; page 196 © Rafael Ben-ari | Dreamstime.com; page 200 © Glenn Martin | Dreamstime.com; page 208 © Ulrike Lemmin-Woolfrey; page 211 © Redzaal | Dreamstime.com; page 212 © John White | Dreamstime.com; page 218 © Ulrike Lemmin-Woolfrey; page 220 © Andrey Moisseyev | Dreamstime.com; page 226 © zlotysu | Dreamstime.com; page 227 © Ulrike Lemmin-Woolfrey; page 230 © Ulrike Lemmin-Woolfrey; page 231 © Andrey Moisseyev | Dreamstime.com; page 233 © Experience Perth; page 235 © Lizgiv | Dreamstime.com; page 236 © Erin Guidotti; page 241 © Tktktk | Dreamstime.com

Also Available

MAP SYMBOLS

Symbol		Symbol		Symbol		Symbol
Expressway		Highlight		Airfield		Golf Course
Primary Road		City/Town		Airport		Parking Area
Secondary Road		State Capital		Mountain		Archaeological Site
Unpaved Road		National Capital		Unique Natural Feature		Church
Trail		Point of Interest		Waterfall		Gas Station
Ferry		Accommodation		Park		Glacier
Railroad		Restaurant/Bar		Trailhead		Mangrove
Pedestrian Walkway		Other Location		Skiing Area		Reef
Stairs		Campground				Swamp

CONVERSION TABLES

°C = (°F - 32) / 1.8
°F = (°C x 1.8) + 32
1 inch = 2.54 centimeters (cm)
1 foot = 0.304 meters (m)
1 yard = 0.914 meters
1 mile = 1.6093 kilometers (km)
1 km = 0.6214 miles
1 fathom = 1.8288 m
1 chain = 20.1168 m
1 furlong = 201.168 m
1 acre = 0.4047 hectares
1 sq km = 100 hectares
1 sq mile = 2.59 square km
1 ounce = 28.35 grams
1 pound = 0.4536 kilograms
1 short ton = 0.90718 metric ton
1 short ton = 2,000 pounds
1 long ton = 1.016 metric tons
1 long ton = 2,240 pounds
1 metric ton = 1,000 kilograms
1 quart = 0.94635 liters
1 US gallon = 3.7854 liters
1 Imperial gallon = 4.5459 liters
1 nautical mile = 1.852 km

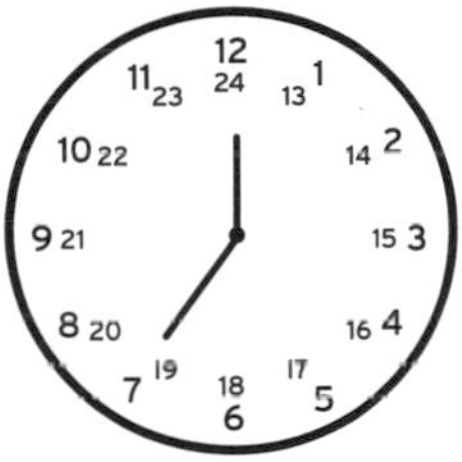

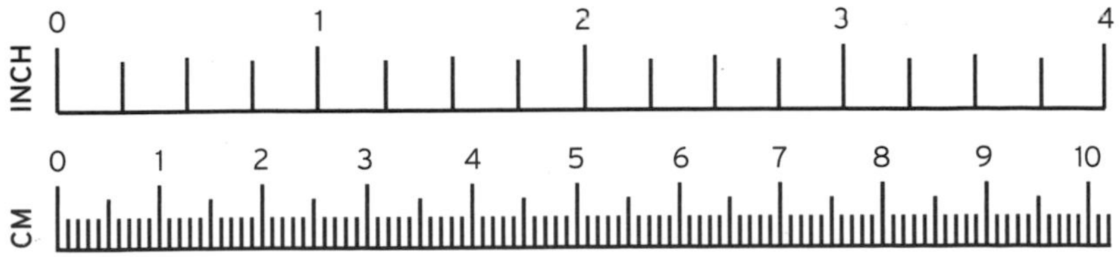

12 24 1 13 2 14 3 15 4 16 5 17 6 18 7 19 8 20 9 21 10 22 11 23

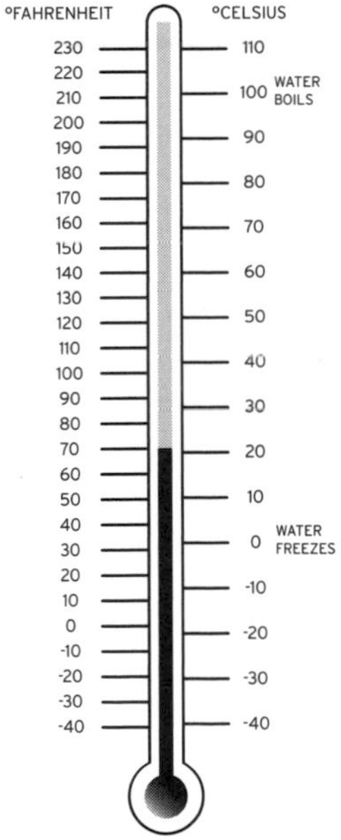

°FAHRENHEIT °CELSIUS

230 220 210 200 190 180 170 160 150 140 130 120 110 100 90 80 70 60 50 40 30 20 10 0 -10 -20 -30 -40

110 100 WATER BOILS 90 80 70 60 50 40 30 20 10 0 WATER FREEZES -10 -20 -30 -40

INCH 0 1 2 3 4

CM 0 1 2 3 4 5 6 7 8 9 10

MOON LIVING ABROAD AUSTRALIA
Avalon Travel
Hachette Book Group
1700 Fourth Street
Berkeley, CA 94710, USA
www.moon.com

Editor: Rachel Feldman
Copy Editor: Ashley Benning
Production and Graphics Coordinator: Elizabeth Jang
Cover Design: Faceout Studios, Charles Brock
Moon Logo: Tim McGrath
Map Editor and Cartographer: Kat Bennett
Indexer: Greg Jewett

ISBN-13: 978-1-63121-641-1

Printing History
1st Edition – 2008
3rd Edition – September 2017
5 4 3 2 1

Front cover photo: view of the Sydney Opera House © Richard Sharrocks / Alamy Stock

Back cover photo: kangaroo mother and joey in Queensland © Matt Murray | Dreamstime.com

Printed in Canada by Friesens